Christine Hogan is a Sydney-based write
worked as a magazine editor on publicatic
ters, *The Australian Women's Weekly*, *The Wor*
Ms. She has also worked in television as a network executive, and as a producer of news and current affairs programs and documentaries. Her first book was *Men: A User's Guide*, and she is currently writing a history of women in Australian television for the Australian Film Commission.

To contact Christine Hogan, write to her:
c/- The Harry M Miller Group
PO Box 313
Kings Cross NSW 1340
email: hmm@harrymmiller.com

The Veiled Lands

A Woman's Journey into the Heart of the Islamic World

CHRISTINE HOGAN

Pan Macmillan Australia

Every endeavour has been made to acknowledge the source of all written material used in this book.
Any person or organisation that may have been inadvertently overlooked should contact the publisher.

First published 2006 in Macmillan by Pan Macmillan Australia Pty Ltd
1 Market Street, Sydney

Copyright © Christine Hogan 2006

All rights reserved. No part of this book may be reproduced or transmitted in any form or by any means, electronic or mechanical, including photocopying, recording or by any information storage and retrieval system, without prior permission in writing from the publisher.

National Library of Australia
cataloguing-in-publication data:

Hogan, Christine (Christine Anne).
The veiled lands: a woman's journey into the heart of the Islamic world.

ISBN 978 1 40503 701 3.
ISBN 1 40503701 6.

1. Hogan, Christine (Christine Anne). 2. Women travellers – Islamic countries. 3. Women – Islamic countries – Social conditions. 4. Australians – Travel – Islamic countries. 5. Islamic countries – Description and travel. I. Title.

910.91767

Cover design by Liz Seymour, Seymour Designs
Set in 12/14 pt Bembo by Midland Typesetters, Australia
Printed in Australia by McPherson's Printing Group

Papers used by Pan Macmillan Australia Pty Ltd are natural, recyclable products made from wood grown in sustainable forests. The manufacturing processes conform to the environmental regulations of the country of origin.

For Béchir, Hakim, Nebi Bey and Salah

We are all travellers in the wilderness of this world, and the best we can find in our travels is an honest friend.

Robert Louis Stevenson

Contents

A Note on Arabic Names ix
Map of North Africa and the Middle East x

Prologue 1

Engulfed

Chapter 1 Bag Lady 11
Chapter 2 First Stop, Orientalism 15
Chapter 3 Dancing in the Desert 24
Chapter 4 Thank God, it's a Dry Day 28
Chapter 5 Sunday School 37
Chapter 6 Women of Islam 43
Chapter 7 Customs of the Country 50

Ottomania

Chapter 8 Kidnapped 57
Chapter 9 Ladies of Letters 66
Chapter 10 The Longest Day 76
Chapter 11 Sufis Unto the Day 83
Chapter 12 At Home with the Amazons 89
Chapter 13 Nebi Storms the Barracks 97

The East is Pink

Chapter 14 The Road to Petra 109
Chapter 15 A Question of Honour 118
Chapter 16 Lady and the Dame 127
Chapter 17 My First Gigolo 135
Chapter 18 Belles of the Desert 142

The Barbary Coast

Chapter 19 Night Flight from Beirut 155
Chapter 20 The Magic Kingdom 161

Chapter 21 A Brief Life 166
Chapter 22 Impossible Queens 172
Chapter 23 Industrial Tourism 178
Chapter 24 Toasts of the Coast 186

Sand, Sun and Stars

Chapter 25 Salah Redux 197
Chapter 26 A Passage to Libya 203
Chapter 27 Desert Daze 208
Chapter 28 Undercover, Under Fire 212
Chapter 29 Location, Location 218
Chapter 30 Tripoli Treats 223
Chapter 31 Taking the Veil 233

Delta Blues

Chapter 32 Lessons on Islam in the City Victorious 243
Chapter 33 Rehab in Cairo 252

Notes 259
Bibliography 269
Acknowledgements 281

A Note on Arabic Names

Transliteration of Arabic names provides some challenges. As an example, these are some of the accepted ways in which the name of Libya's first citizen are rendered: Muammar Qaddafi, Mo'ammar Gadhafi, Muammar Kaddafi, Muammar Qadhafi, Moammar El Kadhafi, Muammar Gadafi, Mu'ammar al-Qadafi, Moamer El Kazzafi, Moamar al-Gaddafi, Mu'ammar Al Qathafi, Muammar Al Qathafi, Mo'ammar el-Gadhafi, Moamar El Kadhafi, Muammar al-Qadhafi, Mu'ammar al-Qadhdhafi, Mu'ammar Qadafi, Moamar Gaddafi, Mu'ammar Qadhdhafi, Muammar Khaddafi, Muammar al-Khaddafi, Mu'amar al-Kadafi, Muammar Ghaddafy, Muammar Ghadafi, Muammar Ghaddafi, Muamar Kaddafi, Muammar Quathafi, Muammar Gheddafi, Muamar Al-Kaddafi, Moammar Khadafy, Moammar Qudhafi, Mu'ammar al-Qaddafi, or Mulazim Awwal Mu'ammar Muhammad Abu Minyar al-Qadhafi.

Throughout this book, I have tried to use commonly accepted versions of names. Sometimes, I have varied the same name, such as Tariq and Tarek, or Masoud and Massood, to indicate different people.

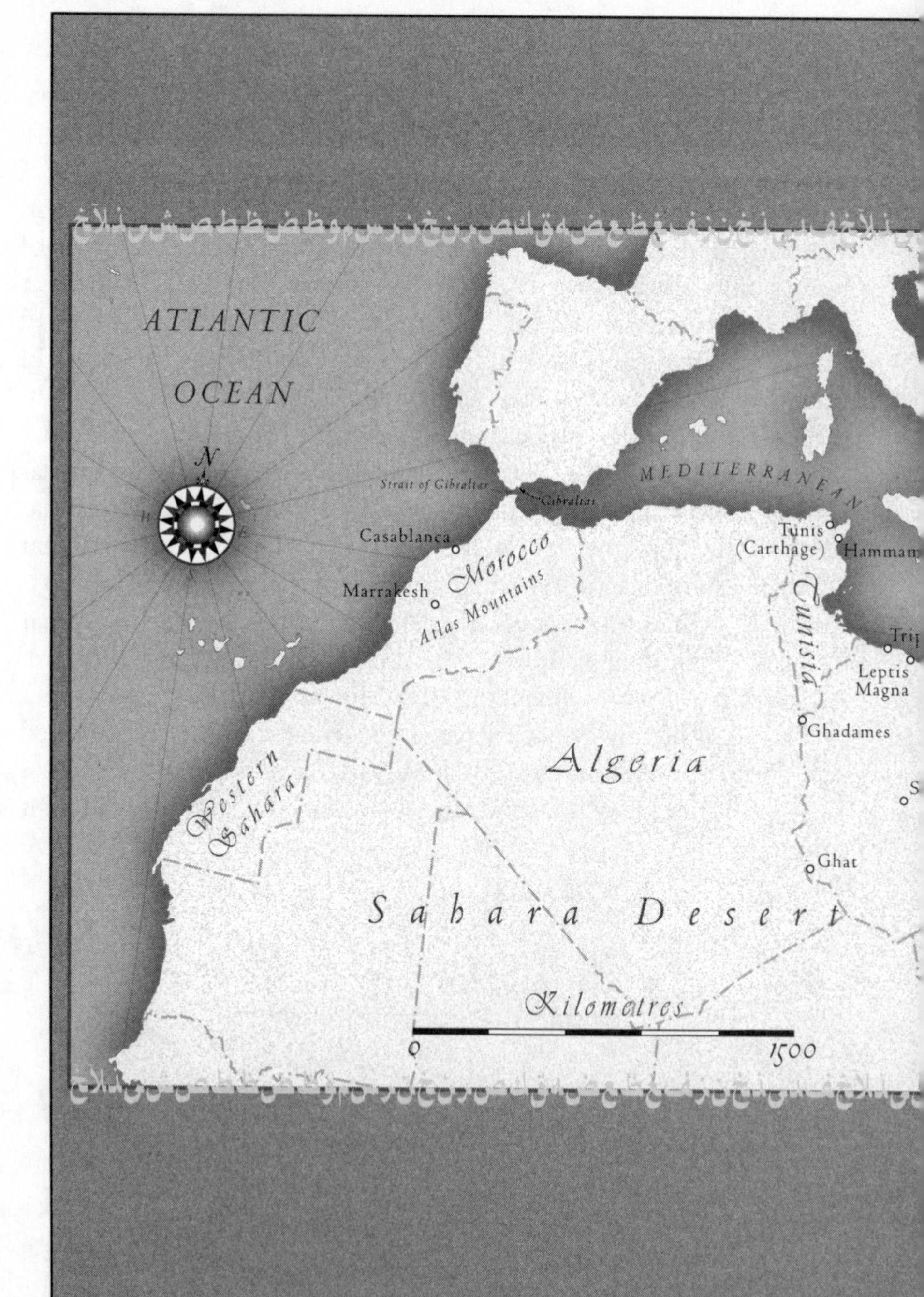

ATLANTIC
OCEAN
N
Strait of Gibraltar
Gibraltar
MEDITERRANEAN
Casablanca
Morocco
Marrakesh
Atlas Mountains
Tunis
(Carthage)
Hammam
Tunisia
Leptis
Magna
Ghadames
Algeria
Western
Sahara
Ghat
Sahara Desert
Kilometres
0
1500

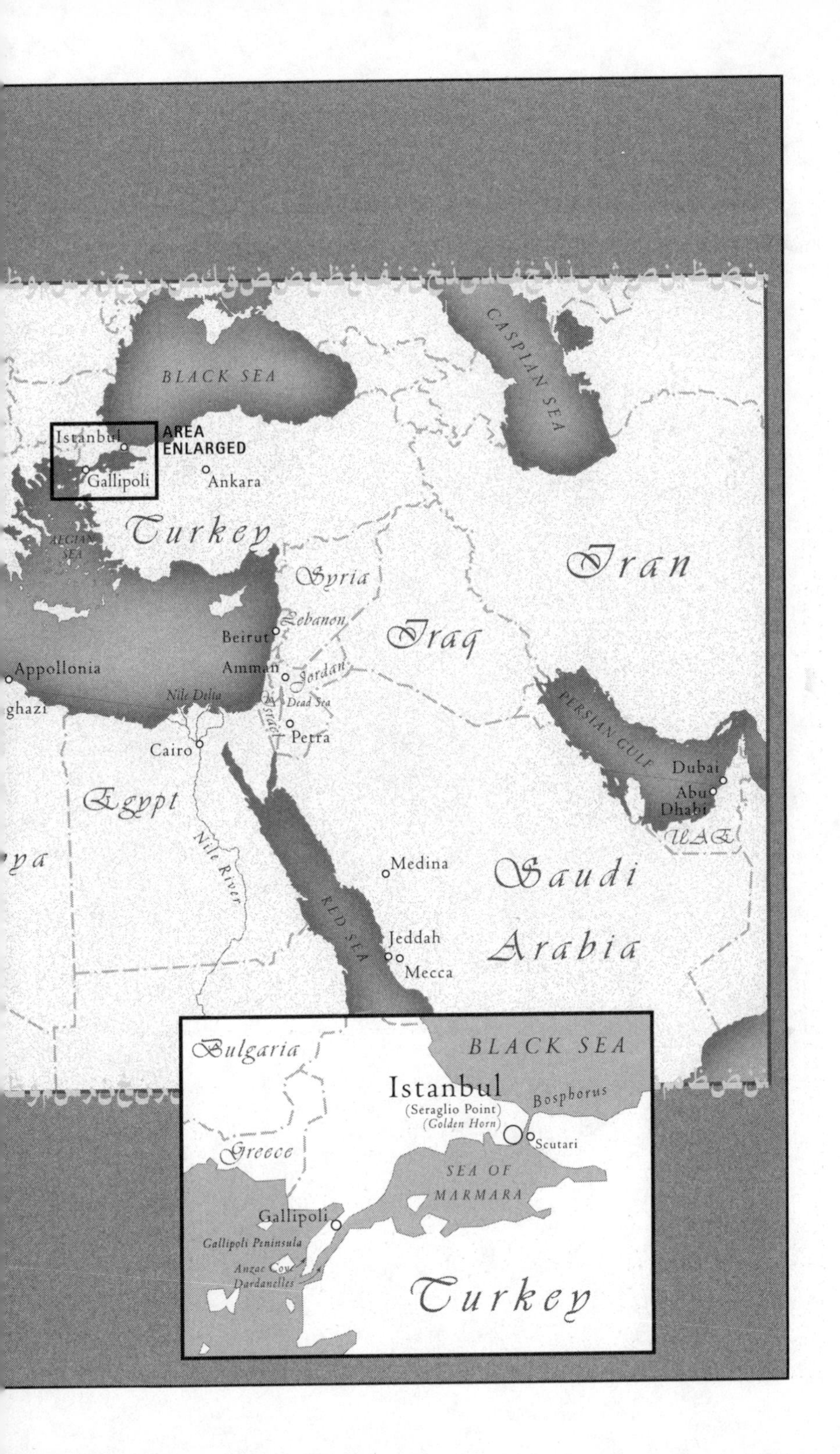
BLACK SEA
CASPIAN SEA
Istanbul
AREA ENLARGED
Gallipoli
Ankara
Turkey
AEGIAN SEA
Syria
Iran
Lebanon
Beirut
Iraq
Appollonia
Amman
Jordan
Nile Delta
Dead Sea
Israel
Petra
Cairo
PERSIAN GULF
Dubai
Abu Dhabi
UAE
Egypt
Nile River
Medina
Saudi Arabia
RED SEA
Jeddah
Mecca
Bulgaria
BLACK SEA
Istanbul
(Seraglio Point)
(Golden Horn)
Bosphorus
Scutari
Greece
SEA OF MARMARA
Gallipoli
Gallipoli Peninsula
Anzac Cove
Dardanelles
Turkey

Prologue

On ne voit bien qu'avec le coeur. L'essentiel
est invisible pour les yeux . . .
Antoine de Saint-Exupéry

AROUND 3 AM, A finger of night chill woke me. Instantly alert, I slipped out of my sleeping bag, swung my feet through the door of the two-man tent, stood up and looked about. The silence of the sleeping camp was riven only by the snores coming from under trucks that were silhouetted against the encircling walls of the protected basin in the desert. The moon was slung low in the sky, but its pale light was still bright enough to guide my way. Time to get going: I had an appointment I didn't want to miss.

The dunes of the Sahara, contoured and patterned by the wind, rose and fell around me. In the dark sands, occasional spots of phosphorescence gleamed, and a light breeze feathered across my face. The dunes by moonlight were creamy-mauve along their crests, deep purple in their shadowed dips. Amid their grand simplicity, it was easy to lose focus, to forget where I was – a real no-man's-land, and no woman's either, close to the border where Libya meets Algeria and Tunisia. I had to concentrate to pick out the stars and the line of the horizon which would guide my steps back.

The air was fresh, not cold, and I had become so used to these nightly solo excursions that I wore only a thin, Indian-cotton caftan and was barefoot. Given it was close to full moon, I didn't carry a torch, and I left my glasses behind in the tent. What I needed to see wouldn't require glasses.

By the time I had come to the end of my shadowed path some ten minutes later, I was well away from our little camp. I lay down on a flat stretch of sand and focused my attention on Heaven. This light show had become my nightly obsession since I had arrived in the Libyan Desert five days earlier. It was entrancing, especially for a woman who until this point had thought that roughing it meant a four-star hotel, and for whom camping out had been a distant memory from Girl Guide days.

But these nights were glorious, each one. Far from being frightened of the immense emptiness, I loved it. Alone here, I had a sense of peace and freedom I had never known before, and my forays had become addictive. I couldn't get enough of the silence, the space and the stillness of the Sahara. No wonder everyone from Moses to Jesus to the Libyan leader himself had made pilgrimages into deserts across these latitudes, nor that the Torah, the Bible and the Qur'an were all written by desert dwellers.

On the previous four nights, after a period of contemplation, I had stood up, realigned myself with my markers in the sky and landscape, and retraced my steps. But on this particular night, I hadn't paid attention to what I was doing, and hadn't faced the direction from which I'd come when I lay down. So when it was time to head back to camp, it quickly became clear as I was walking that I wasn't getting any closer to my tent; on the contrary, it felt as though I was going further away. The smell of benzine, which habitually announced the presence of our camp, was becoming fainter.

The markers I had chosen to guide me in the dark – a star cradled by a concave curve in the dunes – were suddenly less clear. I listened carefully. No snores, no night sounds, indicated the way back. In my ears instead was the rush of panicky blood. Fear clutched at my stomach and I could feel my bowels loosening. I didn't have a clue where I was or how to get back to camp.

Anger flooded through me as I realised that I had managed to get myself lost. I would have cried, but it occurred to me that I couldn't afford to waste the fluid.

It wouldn't be long until moonset and pitch blackness. How long till dawn? I started to think furiously . . . I might not have known where I was, but I did know that roaming about blindly would make things worse, not better. I sat down on the ridge of a dune, settled my ragged breathing. I started to shiver and wondered if I should dig myself into the sand to preserve body heat. Or was that with snow caves for mountaineers?

I tried to concentrate on where I was. Thousands of pinpoints of light pricked the dome of the sky; by squinting, I could sharpen dark dunes into focus as they rolled away to where Earth bled into Heaven. Sitting there in the chill, in the dead quiet, it never occurred to me to yell, to try to wake someone in the camp. That wasn't the way I was raised – in our family, everyone went out of their way not to make a fuss. You could be halfway to the undertaker or could have just won the lottery, but if somebody asked you how you were feeling, the proper response was always, 'Well, thank you.'

Lost in the desert, good manners and embarrassment in equal measure rendered me mute. They might also render me dead if I wasn't careful, I thought. I cast my eyes around the bowl of the night, and saw another bright star, another dip in the dunes. But they lay to the right, not the left like the ones I had been following. Was that the correct direction? How could I be sure? I decided this was the time to call for a little heavenly intervention.

'Bloody hell, Dad. Could you just give me a sign? Which way is it?'

And dear old Dad, dead for more than a decade, came good.

As I prayed, a shooting star appeared over the top of the bright star to the right. You wouldn't credit it, and neither did I. Since I couldn't believe my eyes or the timing, I called out again. 'Okay, thanks,' I said. 'That was good. No, it was great. But could we just confirm? If that was a sign, could I please have another one, Dad?'

You can see properly only with the heart. That which is essential is invisible to the eye . . .[1] The words of Antoine de Saint-Exupéry, a man who had once been well and truly lost in the Libyan Sahara himself, were oddly appropriate as I sat on that sand dune and pushed my luck with God and Dad. All I had to do to see fully was get my heart operating on the problem. It came down to a question of trust, so I stood up, dusted the sand off, and headed right towards that bright star.

Some time later, I staggered back into camp, slid sheepishly into my tent and then said nothing about how I had managed to lose myself. The question for me was not why I had got lost, but how it was that a middle-aged, middle-class woman from Sydney, like myself, with a natural proclivity for deep comfort and none at all for adventure travel, could find herself in the Libyan pre-dawn. It was hardly my natural habitat. Still, there I was, in the desert. Somehow I had turned into the owner of a sleeping bag, a stocked first-aid kit, hiking boots, a bush shower and a working knowledge of tent erection.

In September 2003, William Suganda, study tours program manager of the Centre for Continuing Education at Sydney University, called with an invitation: a tour of Libya was being planned for October 2004 – would I like to join a small group from the CCE on the preceding familiarisation trip, and then write a story about it to publicise the tour?

Until that moment, Libya was not a place I had ever considered visiting. What was there in that rogue state apart from Colonel Gaddafi, a haven for terrorists, great drifts of nothingness floating on the world's third largest oil fields, uncertainty and menace? Besides, the timing was bad: tension between the West and the Muslim world seemed explosive and could be seen nightly on the television news. It was just six months after the start of American occupation of Iraq, so a Muslim country was hardly the place I would be rushing to see.

And yet, I'd been dreaming of North Africa and the Middle East for years. A childhood spent watching *Ivanhoe* and *Robin Hood* on the television had led to a passion for King Richard the Lion Heart and Saladin, and driven me into the school library to pour over the stories of Scheherazade, *The Arabian Nights: Tales from a Thousand and One Nights* and the creation myths of pre-Islamic times.

There were even images to feed my obsession. Works by artists such as Jean-Auguste-Dominique Ingres (*Le Bain Turc*, 1862), Jean-Léon Gérôme (*Bain Turc ou Bain Maure: Deux Femmes*, 1870, and *Le Bain*, c. 1880–85) and Edouard Debat-Ponsan (*Massage in the Hammam*, 1883) depicted Turkish baths and harems as realms of luxury and sensuality – which was a long way from the straitlaced, Anglo-Celtic world I grew up in during the 1960s in Brisbane. To a sixteen-year-old in a Presbyterian and Methodist college for young ladies, they were the last word in exoticism.

I had been fascinated by the Orient and romanticised it long before I ever heard the word 'Orientalism' – or understood the negativity it often carries. Later, I devoured other real-life fantasies, stories about the Englishwomen who had adventured through the Middle East and North Africa in the late nineteenth century, women such as Isabel Burton, and her European counterparts Isabelle Eberhardt and Aimée Du Bucq de Rivéry. The adventures of TE Lawrence, Gertrude Bell and the writer Freya Stark came later.

But go to Libya? All that I had heard of the place – except for two things – made me inclined to say no immediately. But then William uttered the magic words: 'We will be camping with Touareg in the desert for five days.'

Touareg . . . The famed 'Blue Men of the Sahara' had peopled my imagination since I was a child. This matrilineal, hierarchical tribe, whose range stretches through the Sahara from Burkina Faso in the south and the Senegalese border with Mauritania in the west, and up into Algeria, Niger and Libya, has been the guardian of the Sahara for more than two thousand years. To spend time in the desert with these fabled people seemed an improbable fantasy.

William wasn't finished, though – 'We will be visiting Leptis Magna,' he added.

As for Leptis, the imperial city of the Roman emperor Septimius Severus, it was supposed to be the greatest Ancient Roman site in the world. 'Will we get out of Libya alive?' I asked him.

'Yes, why not?' wondered William, who would also be going on the trip.

Well, what about the suicide bombers, and kidnappers? It was a reasonable question: the itinerary William outlined took us deep into the desert, close to where, in February 2003, in the mountainous south-east of Algeria, fifteen Germans, ten Austrians, four Swiss, a Swede and a Dutch citizen travelling in a convoy of four-wheel drives and motorcycles were kidnapped by a group linked to al-Qa'ida.

'Libya is very safe, Christine,' said William.

The Blue Men and Leptis tipped the risk–reward ratio into the plus side of the ledger, so I said yes and got on with the travel arrangements, in secret. I couldn't tell my family where I was going – I wasn't sure they wouldn't try to have me committed if they knew the truth.

And so it was that four weeks later, I was in the Sahara. After a couple of days' travelling with our Touareg drivers and cook, I was able to work out who was who, and what the pecking order was. Béchir Trebelsi and his business partner, Ali Ali M Ettounish, had organised the trip and acted as our hosts here. Milad, the small, shy and softly spoken chief driver of the group, had travelled these dunes with his father since he was a boy. His face, weathered like the dry wadi beds that carved through the mountains of the Akakus, which edged the west of Libya, seemed ageless, but he was in his early fifties. Milad drove the lead car, with Salah Amura from Sand Ruins Tours in his front seat. Exquisitely mannered and with excellent English, Salah was a former pilot who had lived for many years in London and had recently come home to attend to family matters. He had a well-muscled body that other men in their early fifties would have paid a lot for at a gym, but he seemed almost free of vanity. I don't know how he did it, but last thing at night, first thing in the morning, Salah always looked as neat as a pin.

Masoud, the youngest of the drivers, was in charge of the truck in which William Suganda and I were travelling. Next to him, in the suicide seat (as the front passenger berth is often referred to), was Hakim, a 26-year-old specialist policeman who worked through each tourist season with groups of visitors. William and I soon discovered that Hakim and Masoud had a thing about personal freshness: every couple of hours or so, they would apply a blast of a local deodorant from a lurid spray pack. It kept them feeling nice and the Landcruiser perfumed.

Abu Bakr, the cook, was a passenger in Omar's hectic blue and dinted ute, the cook truck. He always seemed to have a headache, which required frequent trips to my first-aid kit and handfuls of Panamax to eradicate.

Finally, there was Omar himself. Each night, Omar would take to a mat next to the fire, where he made chai – hot, smoky, minty, sweet tea – with painstaking care. He poured and repoured the hot liquid, so that the chai developed a light, foamy head in each little glass. When he had finished, our gracious host would recline on one elbow, knees up, his ankles crossed like a Turkish pasha. Omar looked like a man who owned the world.

It occurred to me as I considered this party of men that I had taken something of a gamble coming on this trip. But Arab culture is renowned for its hospitality. I saw it in action whenever we encountered anyone walking in the desert. Our drivers would pass bottles of water out of their windows as they uttered their traditional greeting, '*Salaam alekum*' (Peace upon you). Muslim men have a reputation in the West for being chauvinists, but the six Libyans all treated me as though I were the queen of our little camp in the Sahara.

Even so, that trip to Libya raised several challenging questions, the most vivid of which was about perception and reality. My impression had been that this was a dangerous region, and that Westerners were targets for ransom and possibly murder, but I found a country where the fundamentals seemed the same as in my own: people worked hard, put their children through school, and worried about the future.

And what was the truth about women in Arab and Muslim societies? Whenever the Western media do stories about women in the region, they normally address one of the Big Four: the veil – always seen as a bad thing; polygamy – also a bad thing; female genital circumcision (or mutilation, depending on who is describing the surgery) – a perversion; and honour killings. But I wanted to know how prevalent these practices were through the Middle East and North Africa, and whether they were cultural rather than religious.

In Tripoli, on our return from the Sahara, I noticed women in the streets dressed in a variety of ways. There, the veil ranged from their being completely covered to completely bare-headed; yet, in the desert, I'd got used to the sight of women wearing traditional dress – sometimes a white burnous, anchored under the arms and between clenched teeth, occasionally a brightly patterned, coloured version shot through with metallic thread.

Men in the deep desert, poorer, more isolated and less educated than those on the coast in Tripoli, seemed to have a number of wives. As with the veil, the difference seemed regional rather than religious. In the urban areas, I never encountered polygamy. The Tripolitan men I asked about polygamous marriages looked as though they could barely handle one wife, let alone multiples.

Honour killing might occur in Libyan society, but no one I talked to had ever heard of it. And as for female genital mutilation, whenever I raised that with anyone, they looked sick and told me it was not Qur'anic, not Islamic, and that if girls were being circumcised in Libya, it was among the sub-Saharan Africans using their country as a conduit to jobs and money in Europe.

This went some way to addressing my questions on Muslim women but in the company of men, as I was on this trip, I was unable to ask the women we encountered about their lives and aspirations. I wanted to know more. So, after I came home and confessed to my family exactly where I had been – not an easy conversation – I started to read. I signed up for Arabic classes. And then Béchir Trebelsi invited me to go back, to join the Sydney University CCE tour of the Sahara, in October 2004. 'You are our family now,' he said.

It would have been impossible to say no, even if I'd wanted to. The Sahara had migrated into my very soul and I was longing to see it again.

Engulfed

Chapter 1

Bag Lady

One of the gladdest moments of human life,
methinks, is the departure upon a distant journey
into unknown lands. Shaking off with one mighty effort the
fetters of habit, the leaden weight of routine,
the cloak of many cares and the slavery of home, man
feels once more happy.
Sir Richard Burton

AFTER NEARLY A YEAR OF planning and strategising, revising and agonising, my return expedition to North Africa and the Middle East was arranged. I wanted to see the region for myself and get to know something of its culture, and so attempt to understand a part of the world that had always been so foreign, and yet so fascinating, to the West. My perceptions had already been challenged by my experiences in Libya in 2003; now, I approached the trip specifically as a subject for a book.

I was about to close the door on my safe, secure existence, move right out of my comfort zone and challenge myself physically and emotionally in a series of completely different cultures. But three hours from flight time, things were coming unstuck. Close the door behind me? I couldn't reach the door to open it, let alone close it.

There was a mound of luggage in the entrance hall, evidence, if any were ever needed, that here lived a woman with serious baggage. Packing had been complicated by the nature of the trip – research and work – its length and the different climates I would encounter. There'd be late summer in Dubai, where the temperature hovers at around 40-plus during the day and dips to a chilly 35 at night; early autumn in Turkey, Jordan, Lebanon, Morocco and Tunisia, where it turns out an Indian summer will linger through to the end of September; the heat of the day and the chill of the night in the deep Sahara; the humidity of Cairo and the dryness of the desert air.

Then there was the sheer variety of appointments and activities in the itinerary: planned interviews with a cabinet minister and businesswomen, and even a hope that I might score a session with Colonel Gaddafi. Appointments with the heads of national women's bodies in the Middle East and North Africa were also planned, as well as the couple of weeks in the desert with the University of Sydney group, where clambering over rocks and up dry wadi beds and hundreds of kilometres of walking were certainties. I had made bookings in some quite plush hotels along the way, and would possibly go to a formal drinks party or dinner or two. You try getting all that into luggage that weighs less than 40 kilos and not leave out the presents.

But my requirements were nothing compared with the baggage that women travellers and adventurers of earlier generations used to assemble to take on their trips. Indeed, there is an historical tendency to over-pack among women facing a journey to the Middle East. Lydie Paschkoff, for instance, went from Russia to Palmyra in 1872 with thirty-five camels, almost as many mules, and two-dozen donkeys and horses; while, nine years before this, Katharine Petherick travelled with her husband to the Sudan and wouldn't leave her custom-made piano (in two pieces for easier handling) behind.[1]

Emily Beaufort, who journeyed through Syria, Egypt, Lebanon, Turkey, the Adriatic, and Montenegro in the nineteenth century, listed some of the things she couldn't live without as an appendix to one of her books: aromatic vinegars for 'bad odours', smelling salts for fainting fits, high-laced boots to prevent attack by malarial mosquitoes, and a portable tin bath. A dragoman, who would function as her guide and translator, would provide Emily with an iron bedstead.[2]

Gertrude Bell, the archaeologist, explorer, ally of Lawrence of

Arabia and adviser to the British government on Middle Eastern affairs, was even more accustomed to her travelling luxuries. She turned up in Damascus en route from Syria to Mesopotamia with crates of crystal and china, silver, linen, a set of Shakespeare's works, Charles Doughty's seminal text *Arabia Deserta*, a collection of blank notebooks and a well-equipped first-aid kit.[3] In her wardrobe were fur coats, French dresses, hats, parasols, jackets and shawls, and a suitcase containing 'maps, cameras, film, binoculars, theodolite' . . . and a gun.[4] All of these last items would have been of interest to the Turkish authorities in the region, had they discovered the stash hidden among Gertrude's stays and other undergarments. Bell never seemed to pack enough, though, and once wrote home asking for a wardrobe top-up – which included crêpe de Chine shirts, chiffon evening gowns, and parasols.

I blamed my travelling companion on the first leg of my trip for some of my own excess. I met Cass Jennings through a mutual friend when I had first discussed my field-research trip for this book. Cass had lived in Dubai, in the United Arab Emirates, for some years and seemed an ideal contact for the start of my journey this time around. But she turned out to be far more than that. Since she was setting up her own tourist excursions in the Gulf region, Cass was able to give me a crash course in the Emirates and Emirati hospitality; and, even better, she decided to come along as well, to give me a personal, guided tour.

One of the lessons seemed to be that every person we were about to meet needed a present of some description. So into the grip went a dozen copies of my book and chocolates for everyone, from the hotel public relations directors to the locals we would encounter. This pressie bag weighed fourteen kilos on its own, and I wondered how on Earth I was going to get everything onto the plane without paying for the equivalent of a business-class seat at the check-in counter. The total weight? I didn't like to think.

But these were just peripheral concerns. In ten minutes time, I would be leaving home, and suddenly I was not excited anymore. Fear was pushing my stomach into my throat. The very thought of this trip now seemed ridiculous.

I had committed myself to a path from which there was no

turning back. I was about to take the night flight to Dubai and my anxiety level was so high I was finding it hard to breathe. Six months ago, this project had been as exciting as it was distant. Now immediate, it was suffocating.

I felt under-prepared for what I had committed myself to, similar to that feeling at university when a final exam is about an hour and a half away and the basic revision isn't finished. I was off to the Gulf, the Middle East and North Africa, travelling through different cultures and societies and trying to understand a world divided, at least in the media, symplistically along the lines of religion, into the Clash of Civilisations. Us versus them, Westerners against Muslims, the Third World competing with the First, the rich versus the poor, the liberal West pitted against the conservative East . . . Had I done enough study? I hadn't even finished the basic text, the Qur'an. Dread curled around my rising stomach and squeezed.

A dismal thought surfaced: a woman about to embark on this sort of adventure might have been better named something other than Christine. And it might be a drawback to be a citizen of a nation fighting alongside the Coalition of the Willing in Iraq. These worries were not without foundation. Gunmen in Iraq had just kidnapped two young Italian childcare workers and the gravest possible fears were held for their safety. I had tried not to watch the nightly news on television – the bombings, the beheadings, the blood running in rivers across the Middle East – but it was hard to block out such reports.

This last-minute nerve-storm was interrupted when Cass and her husband arrived. It was immediately obvious that she had gone large with the packing and had included a pallet-load of chocolate nuts. Those Emiratis were in serious danger of sugar shock. And I was about to have a quite different shock to the flesh.

Chapter 2

First Stop, Orientalism

A WALL OF WET warmth greeted us at the exit of Dubai airport. It was just after sunrise, and the weather was sticky, an indicator of what was to come. White heat bounced off the black macadam of the wide, straight roads into town, shimmered in Dubai Creek, reflected off the city's modern skyscrapers and wrapped around motionless palm trees, minarets and building sites alike.

Those sites were already at work: there was no time to lose. Dubai is in the middle of a boom, largely under construction and only half up, and the heat can get in the way of progress. When the temperatures are too high, the workers stand down until the heat subsides. Although it was a relatively mild September morning in the Emirates – it couldn't have been much more than 35 degrees or so at 8 am – the mercury was rising, followed by the humidity level, so the builders were working hard to get as much done as they could before the heat became unbearable.

A fretful haze enveloped the city. Tired and disoriented, Cass and I picked up our hire car, and drove the half an hour from the airport to Jumeirah Beach, Dubai's glamorous resort strip, which edges the clear azure waters of the Arabian Gulf (as the Persian Gulf is called in that part of the world). We checked into our hotel.

There's nothing like a suite – or two, in this case – with views of lush gardens and water to cheer up a tired traveller, and the junior suites at our hotel were very encouraging. Mine boasted a bathroom with a mosaic-covered shower recess, cable TV, internet access, excellent toiletries and a huge wardrobe. Behind a wall of glass, a large terrace led down to manicured gardens and on to the Gulf. There was just enough time to admire these features before we had to report to the hotel's particular jewel, the Oriental *hammam*.

I was determined that this second voyage into the Islamic world would begin with a very Islamic concept: the purification of a ritual bath. Cleanliness – moral and spiritual, as well as physical – is an important tenet of the religion, and the Prophet himself insisted on it, making it fundamental to the faith. (In contrast, consider Queen Elizabeth I in rainy old England. Hundreds of years after Mohammad, she was reported as saying she bathed once a month – whether she needed it or not.)

Through the Qur'an and the Sunna (examples from the life of the Prophet Mohammad), Islam requires believers to purify their entire way of life. For Muslims, cleanliness really is next to godliness. *Sura* 2:222 of the Qur'an, spells it out: 'God loves those that turn to Him in penitence and strive to keep themselves clean.'[1]

And so it was that at 11 am on our first morning in Arabia we reported to the front desk of the Turkish *hammam*, collected our keys and entered Paradise. This could have been the anteroom for a fashionable health club in the Western world, except Cass and I were equipped with small, white hip wraps to ensure our modesty. This was an Arabian dream of fantastic luxury, of blue tiles and misted heat, of day beds and cushions, of fountains and water spouts, rose petals and mint tea.

The Ottomans acquired the habit of bathing from the Byzantines, who had inherited it from the Ancient Romans and Greeks. But Islamic bathing rituals diversified. First of all, men and women do not bathe together, a custom that was observed only in part at our hotel's *hammam*: women were admitted in the morning; mixed couples in the afternoon; and men in the evening.

The emphasis of the Turkish steam bath became one of beautification and purification, and eliminated both the athletic and intellectual elements so obvious from the gymnasia and libraries attached to the Ancient Romans' baths. There is an element of sensuality and contemplation in Turkish baths. The *hammam* also served – and continues to serve – Islamic societies with an important social function.

Inside its rooms, news of who was in town, which girl was marriageable, which man was looking for a wife, was exchanged. Eagle-eyed mothers of sons could check out the form of potential daughters-in-law – no disguising child-bearing hips or lack of them when you're wrapped only in a small loin-cloth – and report back to their husbands so that they could start negotiations for a marriage.

There's no disguising anything much at all in a *hammam*, as Lady Mary Wortley Montagu discovered when her husband was posted to Constantinople (now called Istanbul) in the early 1800s. She was able to see herself as her Turkish sisters saw her when she appeared in the middle of the bath – and at the same time, she gained an insight into this world of women that had previously been hidden from the West.

In one of her famous letters home to England, Lady Mary wrote:

> The first sofas were covered with cushions and rich carpets, on which sat the ladies, and on the second their slaves behind them, but without any distinction of rank by their dress, all being in the state of nature, that is, in plain English, stark naked, without any beauty or defect concealed, yet there was not the least wanton smile or immodest gesture amongst them . . . There were many amongst them as exactly proportioned as ever any goddess was drawn by the pencil of Guido or Titian, and most of their skins shiningly white, only adorned by their beautiful hair divided into many tresses hanging on their shoulders, braided either with pearl or ribbon, perfectly representing the figures of the graces.
>
> So many fine women naked in different postures, some in conversation, some working, others drinking coffee or sherbet, and many negligently lying on their cushions while their slaves (generally pretty girls of seventeen or eighteen) were employed in braiding their hair in several pretty manners.
>
> In short, it is the women's coffee house, where all the news of the town is told, scandal invented, etc.[2]

In return, Lady Mary's bath-time companions were curious about her:

> The lady that seemed the most considerable amongst them entreated me to sit by her and would fain have undressed me for the bath. I excused myself with some difficulty, they being all so earnest in persuading me. I was at last forced to open my skirt and shew them my stays, which satisfied em very well, for I saw they believed I was so locked up in that machine that it was not in my own power to open it, which contrivance they attributed to my husband.[3]

This was a world of women forbidden to men, as Lady Mary noted: 'It is no less than death for a man to be found in one of these places.'[4]

Isabel Burton, wife of the diplomat and Orientalist Sir Richard Burton, was also entranced by her first visit to a *hammam*, in Damascus. She related the experience in *The Romance of Isabel, Lady Burton*, published in 1897:

> The Hammám, or Turkish Bath, is another feature of Damascus, and was one of my favourite haunts. First they lather you, then they wash you with a *lif* [loofah] and soap, then they douche [shower] you with tubs of hot water, then they shampoo you with fresh layers of soap, and then douche again.
>
> They give you iced sherbet, and tie towels dipped in cold water round your head, which prevent you fainting and make you perspire. They scrub your feet with pumice-stone, and move you back through all the rooms gradually, douche you with water, and shampoo you with towels. You now return to the large hall where you first undressed, wrap in woollen shawls, and recline on a divan.
>
> The place is all strewn with flowers, incense is burned around, and a cup of hot coffee is handed and a *narghíleh* [water pipe] placed in your mouth. A woman advances and kneads you as though you were bread, until you fall asleep under the process, as though mesmerized. When you wake up, you find music and dancing, the girls chasing one another, eating sweetmeats, and enjoying all sorts of fun . . .
>
> It is often said by the ignorant that people can get as good

> a *hammám* in London or Paris as in the East. I have tried all, and they bear about as much relation to one another as a puddle of dirty water does to a pellucid lake. And the pellucid lake is in the East.[5]

The pellucid lake at our hotel's spa was the Turkish bath experience. Although this *hammam* was modern in its plumbing (jacuzzis abounded), it followed the routines of the traditional *hammam*. After an introductory shower, Cass and I entered the antechamber. In the middle of the room was a pool, and around the edges were niches – a large one with day beds for relaxation, others with tables and chairs where the clients could take tea or water.

Here, my *hammam* destiny awaited, in the form of Rima, a solid Tunisian with a dazzling smile. Rima looked as though she could truly be counted on, which was a very good thing, since I was relying on her for the Truly *Hammam* Experience. I would be completely in her hands.

Rima ushered us into an internal chamber dominated by a domed ceiling over a large, raised marble slab. Cass and I were steamed in one of the saunas, and then taken to the slab for our first deep cleansing with black soap – an unpromising-looking sludge that works into a silky lather and exfoliates and moisturises while it cleans. We were washed down (at first, I kept trying to manage my bathers to cover my modesty, but in the end I just gave up), then scrubbed again with a loofah, steamed again, jacuzzied, and finally stretched, pulled and pummelled like raw dough until we were allowed out of Rima's palace of pleasure and pain, back into the antechamber. On the floor, at the steps leading down to the sunken pool, the *hammam*'s attendants had laid flowers.

All this pampering sapped Cass and me of any strength we had left, and although we'd been relative strangers only a matter of hours ago, we had now been united by an age-old tradition. Stripped of our clothes, our inhibitions had followed.

Eventually, the two of us – by now with the physical resistance of overdone pasta – left the *hammam* and headed towards the swimming pool in the garden. It was a stew outside, hotter even than in the sauna, so that sitting under an umbrella felt like being in a fan-forced oven. So we retired to our suites for a little lie down and to rest up before our next appointment.

By six o'clock, Cass and I had settled up on the rooftop next door to the hotel and were reclining on tented divans whose curtains were occasionally shaken by hot little gusts of wind blowing from the south. We ordered a couple of drinks: it was happy hour overlooking the Arabian Gulf. From our vantage point, we could just discern the outline of one of Dubai's most extraordinary man-made features – The Palm. Along with The World, and The World Two, this development is dredging up sand from the bottom of the Gulf (and quite possibly changing its currents forever) to build a new world shaped like a palm tree (the others are, unsurprisingly, shaped like a map of the world). Rod Stewart is rumoured to own 'England' in the first World development.

The modern Emirates is still freshly minted, just a little more than thirty-five years old. The first president, Sheikh Zayed bin Sultan Al-Nahayan, was born in a tent in the oasis of Al Ain, had no formal education and ended up at ease in international diplomacy and boardrooms representing one of the fastest modernising countries in the world.

The UAE is thoroughly grounded in an ancient culture. Its coasts and inland oases are known to have been settled since at least the third millennium BC. Then, a culture known today as Umm Al-Nar grew up near Abu Dhabi, and its influence spread into what is now the Sultanate of Oman. Persian traders came, then the Arabs, in 636. The Portuguese, never a group to miss a trading opportunity, arrived in 1498, but were gone by 1633.

By the mid eighteenth century, Britain was the world's supreme naval power and had come into conflict with the local tribal powers along the UAE coast, the Qawasim (whose descendants are now the emirs of Sharjah and Ras Al-Khaimah) and the Bani Yas. There was trouble between the European superpower and the nine local sheikhdoms until 1820, when the British installed a garrison and imposed a peace treaty on them. The area acquired a new, consolidated identity, and a collective name: the Trucial Coast. The British influence over the region remained until the Trucial Coast gained independence in 1971, and formed a federation under the presidency of the Emir of Abu Dhabi, the much admired, respected and loved Sheikh Zayed.

Sheikh Mohammed Al Maktoum, the ruler of Dubai, drives the city with seemingly endless energy. His contacts and relationships – one of his wives is Princess Haya of Jordan, daughter of the late King Hussein of Jordan and half-sister of the current king, Abdullah – put him in the heart of Middle Eastern politics. (It is one of the most potent paradoxes that the thoroughly modern Sheikh Mohammed is a traditionalist when it comes to polygamy. He has had a number of wives, but the privacy that surrounds the lives of women in the region makes it hard to work out how many there are now.)

Sheikh Mohammed's vision has created the powerhouse of growth, money and bling that Dubai has become. In the last three decades, it has developed from a small trading port at the mouth of Dubai Creek to the Hong Kong of the Gulf, and has become the face of modernising, Westernising, Arabia.

As in Saudi Arabia, oil has made all the difference to Dubai. Concessions were granted in 1939, but it wasn't until the 1950s that oil was found, and not until 1962 that Abu Dhabi began to export it. Almost overnight, the poorest emirate was on track to becoming the richest. Dubai continued to build its reputation for trade, but then in 1966, it struck oil as well.

Cass had arranged for us to meet Michelle Sabti, a former Sydneysider living and working in Dubai, and Michelle's then-colleague Mohammad Ghaffari, from Dubai's Department of Tourism and Commerce Marketing (DTCM). A live-wire with electric-blue eyes, Michelle arrived in a flurry, and the more low-key Mohammad followed. Michelle had been Cass's trainer in a course to become a fully fledged Dubai guide, and had organised much of the program we were going to follow over the next few days.

Michelle was a bluff, no-nonsense sort of woman in her late thirties, and had a young son. Mohammad had been studying engineering physics and astronomy at the University of Arizona when the Twin Towers came down and, immediately, along with every young Muslim man studying in the United States, he became a person of interest to the Federal Bureau of Investigation. When his apartment was raided by the FBI, he decided to get out of America – fast. When I met him, his parents still regarded it as too dangerous for him to return to finish his degrees, so he had enrolled in a master's in quality management at the Dubai campus of the University of Wollongong. When he finished that, in December 2005, he planned to start a doctorate in leadership development.

Mohammad didn't drink, and just as well, because he was about to drive – which is pretty much the most dangerous thing anyone can do in the UAE. Off we headed, Cass, Michelle, Mohammad and I, into the super-heated night, on marvellous roads. It was soon clear that these wide roads were populated exclusively by rally car drivers with no concept at all that anyone else existed. Bad manners on the road? More like no manners, particularly at the roulette wheels they called roundabouts, where cars were slung in like missiles and often exited from the inside lane.

Somehow we survived this nightmare of Dubai's traffic 'system' and arrived, grateful to be alive, at another Oriental dream, the Medinat Al-Jumeirah. This complex, styled to look like an ancient Arabian citadel, is in reality two boutique hotels, which owe their distinctive rooflines to the wind towers used to cool traditional Emirati houses. The hotels have thousands of rooms linked by meandering waterways to courtyard summer houses, a new souk, and the region's leading conference and banqueting centre.

The crowd at the Medinat Al-Jumeirah was a gender study in black and white: men in snowy white, women in funereal black. In their elongated overshirts, called *dishdashas*, the men looked graceful and cool. The traditional costume for Emirati men is typical of that favoured by Gulf Arabs: the shirt is worn over a sort of half-slip wrapped around the waist (men who don the more secure, elasticised versions of this were wimps, according to our new friend Mohammad), and with a *gutra*, or head dress, tied down with a two-stranded black cord called an *aqaal*. The look of these men, as they guided the women of their families through the winding alleys of the souk, was very Omar Sharif in *Lawrence of Arabia*.

The flights of black-clad women, who at first glance looked like nuns in their old habits, their wimples drawn close around their faces, their sleeves long over their wrists, gradually resolved into individuals. These women put a lot of thought into varying what appeared to be a uniform: a black coat, or *abaya*, to the floor, and a headscarf. Subtle beading picked out the cuffs of one coat; thread which reflected the light top-stitched the panels across the breasts of another, swelling and falling with the figure of the voluptuous woman enclosed within it. The fluttering hems of these graceful garments, trailing in the air behind the women who wore them, spoke more about sensuality than low-rider jeans ever could.

The women's headscarves were carefully arranged to show the designer labels over one ear. Sometimes they covered all the hair; others hid only some of it. The degree of coverage varied considerably. Some younger women – new brides, it was suggested – even appeared sporting a *yashmak*, or face veil, and clung close to their husbands.

Every woman at the Al-Medinat souk that night, having coffee, visiting the *oud* shop to buy some incense to perfume clothing over braziers at home, seemed to have a statement handbag. The marketing departments of luxury goods brands had done their work. Louis Vuitton, Prada, Hermès, Ferragamo and all the other up-market French and Italian luggage firms were represented.

When it was getting on for nine, the souk came alive. After the heat of the day, families were taking their evening constitutionals in the comfort of the centre's air-conditioning. Traditionally, souks are dark, mysterious, organic, crowded and labrynthine, and the well-lit Al-Medinat souk was different in every way except one: it was easy to get lost in. As a result, we arrived at the Moroccan restaurant we had been looking for somewhat late. No matter. When we went inside we found that nothing was happening in the kitchen. The generators of the centre had failed, and the stoves were out. The air-conditioning was gone too. The place was starting to cook.

Chapter 3

Dancing in the Desert

IF THE *HAMMAM* IS one Orientalist dream of the East, the belly dancer is another. She's been the focus of speculation and scandal for generations by Westerners who see her as a sex object, a woman who performs lewd dances – often bare-breasted, sometimes naked – in front of groups of men.

But the origins of the Oriental dance are rather more complicated. What is now a largely commercial entertainment in the Middle East or an innocent pastime among Western housewives trying to either spice up their sex lives or strengthen their pelvic-floor muscles was once a dance to celebrate fertility and a workout for young women to harness the muscles of the abdomen.

It's one of the West–East misconceptions that I became accustomed to in this part of the world. The belly dance was never intended to be what outsiders construe it to be – a dance of seduction. And neither does it use only the belly; it's far more extensive in its muscle-group workout. The Oriental dance (which translates from Arabic as 'the Dance of the Country') is one of the oldest forms of dance, its roots deep in pre-Judaic religious rites, worshipping the Mother Goddess and preparing young women for childbirth. It's not about sex itself, but about the consequences of sex – a very early form of instruction in the art of natural childbirth.

Bedouin and Berber women had to deal with childbirth almost every day in their communities. No doctors, no hospitals, no medicine . . . Just women, helping to deliver their sisters safely. Away from the gaze of men, they would encircle a woman in childbirth, and start their ritual. The aim was to hypnotise the labouring woman, to make her imitate the undulations of the dancers with her own body. By helping the mother to move in sympathy with them and her own body, the pains of the contractions were said to be minimised, and the birth easier.

Western male eyes saw the dance differently, however, and in response, the form became a vulgar sideshow. In *The Dancer of Shamahka*, Armen Ohanian recorded one exhibition:

> Thus in Cairo one evening I saw, with sick incredulous eyes, one of our most sacred dances degraded into a bestiality horrible and revolting. It is our poem of the mystery and pain of motherhood, which all true Asiatic men watch with reverence and humility, in the faraway corners of Asia, where the destructive breath of the Occident has not yet penetrated. In this olden Asia, which has kept the dance in its primitive purity, it represents maternity, the mysterious conception of life, the suffering and the joy with which a new soul is brought into the world.[1]

I'd seen a Libyan Dance of the Country the previous year during a music festival in Ghadames. The dancers had been veiled and covered, as they were when described by one nineteenth-century observer. He wrote about some Egyptian dancers, clothed in 'garments of black from head to foot, with silver stripes, while the braids on their head were very prettily made, terminating in many silver balls'.[2]

But as the custom was corrupted, the clothes came off. Some, for private performances, wore red nipple caps on their breasts; others stripped down to their undershirts and pantaloons. Others danced naked but, according to Wendy Buonaventura in *Serpent of the Nile*: 'they did not like to do so, and agreed to the request with considerable contempt. In such a case, the musicians were blindfolded and the Arab men were dismissed from the room.'[3]

Natasha, a belly dancer hired to entertain almost two hundred tourists as part of a 'Dinner in the Desert' experience that Cass and

I went to one evening, was more in the tradition of 1950s Hollywood than anything ancient. A fleshy forty-something with red curly hair tumbling past her shoulderblades, Natasha looked more Eastern European than Egyptian, but embodied what the image of belly dancers has become. She would have been familiar as a movie slave-girl type to any kid who grew up watching old Tony Curtis movies on the television on Sunday afternoons.

Natasha was a vision in silver-blue bra and matching hipster skirt of chiffon rattling with coins, and her routine was energetic and skilful – one leg extended and bent at the knee, she sketched circles in the air with her opposite hip. It was about as erotic as watching your grandfather jive, but she certainly got the men in the audience going. And then she had her revenge.

She made some of the noisiest of them get up and do their own version of a belly dance to amuse the rest of their dinner companions. The serpentine dance proved too much for these sweating, half-sozzled Westerners, and had the onlookers smothering shrieks. It was a different story when the women were made to do it, though. I was aware of a blow many of us had suffered, being separated from the power of our own bodies. Even Cass, who is lithe and had learned belly dancing before, looked a little awkward, but she was clearly having the time of her life up there on stage with Natasha – and at least she was having a go.

But I was saddened by an inchoate sense of longing. For what? For the way women could express themselves before custom and religion stripped them of their power? Yes, perhaps. To distract myself, I wandered away from the dining area to visit the camels and their Yemeni camel herders.

'You want a ride, lady?' asked one.

'I'd pay money *not* to ride one,' I said.

He looked interested. Money for nothing – that was something he apparently didn't often see.

When the Dinner in the Desert was over, Cass and I were herded into a car and set off back to the city. Our driver, Yamin ('Call me Yum-Yum'), was interesting. A Muslim who loved his religion, he said more than once during our long drive home from the desert that Islam was the religion of peace. And that it was forbidden by the Qur'an to kill, particularly innocents. I wondered if we could send Yamin to Indonesia, to help the Jamaa Islamiya members who had bombed the nightclubs in Bali in October 2002, killing over two hundred people, with their religious studies.

Yum-Yum talked about the Qur'an, Allah (who to him was 'the Generous One, the Bountiful, the Gracious, the One who is attributed with greatness of power and glory of status'), Esa (Jesus) and Maryam (Mary) all the way home. His parents had taught him to be a man of God, a good man, he said, a man of honour. And that meant he wouldn't go with women.

Did this 'go with' mean having sex with women? In Yum-Yum's culture, it might have meant simply to go out with them. Yum-Yum said that if he 'went' with women, Allah would send someone to 'go with' his sisters, and Yum-Yum wouldn't, *couldn't* allow that to happen. I couldn't bring myself to ask this ardent, observant man whether he was talking about sex or not. It might easily have offended him off the road, and he needed to concentrate on the task at hand.

Then he said something really unexpected: he reckoned that the Americans were right to remove Saddam Hussein. He was an awful man, a cruel man, with awful, cruel sons, according to this man of peace.

There was a lot to think about that night, but once back at the hotel I turned on the television to wind down and catch up with the world outside Dubai and the desert. The news was terrible. The Australian Embassy in Jakarta had been bombed. Nearly a dozen people, most of them Indonesians, most of them Muslims, among them women and children, had died in the blast. Jamaa Islamiya, the Indonesian group with links to al-Qa'ida, had sacrificed more innocents of their own faith in pursuit of terror. This wasn't the way of Islam, according to Yamin and his fellow Muslims dwelling in the House of Peace.

Chapter 4

Thank God, it's a Dry Day

AS THE GULF WOKE the next day, the War on Terror turned three years old. The satellite TV news was full of preparations in the United States to commemorate the al-Qa'ida attacks. Meanwhile, on the Arabian Gulf, life in the lap of luxury went on as normal. Peaceful, calm and well fed. Braving the thermal blast outside the sliding doors that lead onto the terrace (it was so hot outside and so chilled inside that the glass ran with condensation), I went for a swim in the clear waters off the Dubai coast and wondered which way Saudi Arabia was.

Afterwards, I met Cass downstairs for breakfast. Michelle Sabti joined us, and brought another colleague who worked with her at the DTCM, Sarah Shaw. Sarah sounded very, very English, but she was actually half British, half Emirati and totally Gulf. Her English name was her father's: her mother had married him before the laws forbidding Emirati women to marry outside the Emirates were promulgated.

Sarah was in her early twenties, a university graduate who had specialised in hospitality, and lived at home with her mother and stepfather, her sister and her two younger half-brothers. She had a foot in both her father's culture and her mother's, spending every summer holiday with her grandmother in Warwick, in England.

Sarah was wearing the veil, as she told us she always did when she was in public or company. 'My grandmother in England always wants to know why I won't take it off,' she said over breakfast. 'And I always tell her the same thing: my religion requires that I wear it.'

Like many of the Muslim women I spoke to, Sarah saw the hijab (the traditional Islamic dress for women) not as oppressive, but liberating – the exact opposite of the way women in the West might see it. Her covering demanded respect from other Muslims because she was making a declaration of faith linked with dignity and personal honour. At the same time, Sarah was released from the scrutiny of men who might be judging her on her physical attractiveness alone, thus making her a sex object. By veiling, she said, she declared that there was more to her than just her looks, and that the spirit and the mind of the real woman under the veil, inside the flesh, were what truly mattered.

Michelle was, like Sarah, wearing a headscarf, and an *abaya*, the long black coat worn traditionally by women in Dubai, which was also required national costume for women working in the DTCM office. Michelle loved wearing her *abaya*: 'It's great! Sometimes I go to work wearing my track pants, and no one knows. I still look professionally dressed.' She could even go to work in her pyjamas under her *abaya*, she added with a giggle. Instead of wearing a black headscarf, Michelle teamed her *abaya* with a colourful veil in the way of women in neighbouring Oman. It made an arresting contrast with her blue eyes and pale, freckled skin – which is not the intention of the hijab at all.

Very few things get as much attention in the outside world as those small pieces of cloth worn by some Muslim women. The word 'hijab' has the same stem as the Arabic word *hajaba*, which means 'to hide from view or to conceal', and can refer to either the headscarf itself or the whole costume which makes a woman properly veiled, according to Islam.

There are endless debates about modesty of dress and what is required of women who wish to be veiled correctly, but there are few references to the veil in the Qur'an. One of these refers not to any physical covering, but to a metaphysical one. In *Sura* 7:26, it says: 'O children of Adam, we have given you clothes to cover your shameful parts, and garments pleasing to the eye. But the finest of these is the robe of piety.' And that probably explains why high-profile Muslim women such as Queen Rania of Jordan, her step-mother-in-law, Queen Noor, and the Begum Aga Khan are often seen without a head covering – they remain modestly clothed in their womanly piety at all times.

Sura 24:31 continues the theme:

> Enjoin believing women to turn their eyes away from temptation and to preserve their chastity; not to display their adornments (except such as are normally revealed); to draw their veils over their bosoms and not to display their finery except to their husbands, their fathers, their husbands' fathers, their sons, their step-sons, their brothers, their brothers' sons, their sisters' sons, their women servants, and their slave girls; male attendants lacking in natural vigour, and children who have had no carnal knowledge of women.

The phrase 'except such [adornments] as are normally revealed' forms the basis for the differences within the Arab world regarding the headscarf. Practices are adjusted to local customs, it seems.

A third reference to the veil is found in *Sura* 33.59: 'O prophet, tell your wives, your daughters, and the wives of the believers that they shall lengthen their garments. Thus, they will be recognised and avoid being insulted. God is Forgiver, Most Merciful.' Another translation of the Qur'an has this a little differently: 'O prophet, tell your wives, your daughters, and the wives of the believers to *wrap their veils* around them' (my italics).[1]

To wear or not to wear the veil? To be properly dressed in an Islamic country seems to depend on which Islamic country one is in. For instance, after taking control of the Afghan city of Kabul in 1996, the Taliban – which literally means 'students' in Arabic – virtually locked away all the women of the country. They forbade women to work outside the home or go to school if they were older than eight. (Even for girls aged eight and below, the only text allowed in the schools was the Qur'an.)

According to the August 1998 report *The Taliban's War on Women: A Health and Human Rights Crisis in Afghanistan*, women in that country were not allowed to leave their homes 'unless accompanied by a husband, father, brother, or son' and 'In public, women must be covered from head to toe in a *burqa*, a body-length covering with only a mesh opening to see and breathe through.'[2] The report continued: 'Women are not permitted to wear white [it was the colour of the Taliban flag] socks or white shoes, or shoes that make noise while women are walking. Also, houses and buildings in public view must have their windows painted over if females are present in these places.'[3]

Failure to observe these rules of the Taliban earned summary justice: arbitrary beatings by the religious police, employees of the Department for the Propagation of Virtue and the Suppression of Vice.

In Iran, the women's coverings are black, and head to toe. A friend of mine who was visiting there a couple of years ago took her own glamorous version of the local dress code. But it was so light that it kept flying up and away in the breeze. She was taken immediately to the souk by her scandalised driver, who watched contentedly while she bought heavy, non-fly-away veils. 'They were polyester, and so hot!' she remembered of the weeks she stewed in the Iran hinterland. At least her driver was happy and she wasn't abused by outraged locals.

In the Gulf, women like Sarah choose to wear the veil, and she would have been offended if her stepfather or a man in her family tried to force her into it, just as she was a little offended when her grandmother tried to coax her out of it. But I saw some little girls of six or seven wearing the headscarf. They were hardly old enough to make such a decision or know what they were doing when they put it on. The hijab was something that belonged to puberty, a rite of passage for girls of twelve or thirteen. Why would a mere child be compelled to wear something that's connected to sexual maturity? In defence of the girl, apparently. 'It is easier to get them to wear it then, to get them accustomed to it,' said one man I spoke to. 'They like to imitate their mothers and their older sisters. By the time they are older, they are used to it and don't mind so much.'

The headscarf was a subject that I sought to discuss often, but first of all, Cass and I had to get through another hot day in the Gulf. It was hard enough without wearing the hijab; heaven only knows what it would have been like in one. We spent the day in a bath of sweat doing what Dubai has celebrated with a festival every January since 1996: shopping.

We went first to the fabric shops in Satwa, the Indian enclave of the city. We saw dreamy cotton voiles, broderies anglaises, Swiss cottons, heavy Japanese cottons, as well as silks, shot and slub, and sequinned fabrics. And we bought fabric lengths for prices close to theft.

Armed with our cottons, we then paid a visit to Cass's tailor, Mohammed Sadiq, who worked in a tiny shop down an alley that was far hotter than outside in the sun. The reason for this heat was the air-conditioning units that chilled the interiors of the shops, but pushed blasts of boiler-hot air into the narrow, grimy corridor between them.

Mohammed was a man with chocolate-coloured eyes and a bright, wide and Rinso-white smile. He was alone downstairs, but the whirring of sewing machines overhead indicated that there were machinists up there, hard at work in a shop that could not avoid the qualification 'sweat'.

We had a large number of clothes for him to make, but Cass first had to negotiate a ritual that she was well accustomed to. When would they be available?

'When are you leaving?' he countered. He wanted as long as possible; we wanted to make sure we were not dashing past his shop on the way to the airport.

Mohammed thought a particular shirt that I had requested – a knock-off of a linen Armani shirt I had – might take too much time because it was cut like a jacket, so I took it back. But when Cass and I were in our car, returning to the hotel, her mobile rang: he had changed his mind and could make it after all. The next day, the shirt and the fabric went back. Mohammed had either crammed more workers into his factory upstairs or was giving the existing staff inducements to work harder.

From the tiny tailor's shop, we moved on to Bur Dubai, and the fabulous silk shops where pure cashmere shawls, pashminas, are stacked by colour, fineness and price against the walls. If you asked, the assistants could doubtless find some shahtoosh, which are shawls made from the fine chin hair of an endangered Tibetan antelope known as the chiru.

After this, we trawled through the shopping malls – an architectural concept with which Dubai is enthralled. Already there are more than thirty malls (including the Ibn Battuta Mall, which commemorates the journeys of the fourteenth-century Moorish explorer through Andalusia, Tunisia, Egypt, Persia, India and China in the mall's six different architectural styles), but it's not enough, it seems. Dubai is now in the middle of building the biggest shopping centre in the world, the Mall of Arabia.

Cass took us to her favourite, Wafi Mall, part of Wafi City, in which there is a Raffles hotel, plush apartments and a convention centre. Wafi – the Arabic word means 'to satisfy everything you want' – is a cultural trip all of its own. The influence here is Ancient Egypt, and the theme is continued from the Sphinx restaurant (which one enters through its paws) to the twin, pyramid-shaped skylights over the escalators linking the mall to the car park, and the gilded papyrus, lotus-themed friezes around the walls.

Opened in 2001, Wafi Mall has more than two hundred shops, including sixty international luxury brands, a 3-D theatre, and a roller-blading rink – obviously to keep the kids happy while the mothers of Dubai take part in their own favourite indoor sport. I could have spent hours there, watching the local women shopping and interacting. (Seeing gloved, black-clad Muslim ladies in face veils chatting with black-clad, veiled Christian nuns was a particular thrill.) But we still had much to see. Our next destination was Bastakiya, an area in Bur Dubai that Persian merchants had built in the unusual vernacular architectural style of the old city: mud-walled houses with distinctive wind towers, the original air-conditioning of the Gulf. The towers, festooned with wet sheets hung on exterior poles, were built to catch the winds and push the cooled air down into the houses below. The settlers made the streets here long and narrow passageways, so they are always in shadow except when the sun is at its zenith.

This part of the city had recently been pulled down, but the old buildings were rebuilt to conserve the flavour and nature of the quarter. It's now best known for its men's meeting place, the *majlis*, a living treasure in the city of Dubai and our destination that evening.

When the old houses were demolished, and the new 'old' houses built to replace them, the residents were resettled throughout the city. But some of the men who had lived there since they were boys were unwilling to leave behind the friendships they'd had since childhood. Ten of these men, in conjunction with the local authorities, worked to maintain the *majlis* and continued to fund it.

Every night, the men of old Bastakiya meet in the simple structure. There is an open-air porch with sofas at one end and floor cushions at the other. Inside, where it's air-conditioned, there is a huge, flat-screen TV (probably tuned permanently to sports and news), cushions and bolsters around the walls, and low tables for playing dominoes and cards.

When we arrived, the veranda of the *majlis* was empty: all the men were in the mosque for the evening prayers, but they soon came back.

'Go in, go in,' said one of them, a tall man in a white turban.

'It's okay?' I asked Mohammad, who had joined us for the evening, along with Michelle.

'Sure. No problem. You'll see.'

We took our shoes off and left them at the front door of the *majlis*, among the leather sandals left by earlier arrivals. The four of us went into the men's room and then Cass, Michelle and I pulled up short on the other side of the door – we were the objects of interest for about twenty-five men scattered around the walls.

I hissed at Mohammad that we really shouldn't be there, and that clearly we were invading the privacy of these men.

'No, no,' he replied. 'You can talk to them. Ask them what you like.'

I started: 'Mohammad, could you please ask –'

'Why don't you come over here and sit with me? Then you can ask us yourself whatever you like,' said a handsome, grey-haired man with a clear face and a welcoming smile. It was the George Clooney of the Gulf and he was speaking perfect English. Like a cat looking for space out of the heat, I crept across the carpet, hoping to go unnoticed as I parked myself next to Mr Handsome.

Fat chance. But the awkwardness was only on my part; the men of the *majlis* could not have been more hospitable. My interview subject was Ahmed, an army major in his early forties who was moving into property. Ahmed said he had given 'twenty years for education, twenty for service to my country, and now the next twenty to take care of my family'. He was well educated, and spoke Arabic, English, Urdu and Farsi, the language of his Persian forbears.

Along with his friends in the *majlis*, he had once lived in Bastakiya, but now just visited two or three times a week. I wondered how his wife felt, with him off with his mates so often, but he pointed out that it was similar to the Western habit of going for a drink at a pub or a club after work. But he forgot one big difference: the husbands don't arrive home half molo from the *majlis*. They're obviously alcohol-free zones.

'You know, our wives are not locked up at home,' Ahmed told me. 'They go and visit their families, see their friends.'

Women's *majlis*? Children's *majlis*? That seemed fair. How did the men feel about visitors to their *majlis*?

'We welcome them. We want people to visit us, to speak to us.' Sometimes, when the tour buses of foreign visitors went past the *majlis*, he said, the men would beckon the tourists over and ask them to come in. They were rarely taken up on their offer. 'I don't know why,' he added. 'Perhaps they are frightened. Perhaps they are wary. But we want them to join us.'

The talk turned to politics, as it inevitably does in the Gulf, and I heard for the first time on my journey something of the dismay, frustration and anger of people in this part of the world about the way their countries are treated by Western governments. They might not have approved of Saddam Hussein, but at least he was a Muslim dictator, said Ahmed, not a 'Crusader' puppet, as so many rulers in the Middle East and the Gulf had been in the past one hundred and fifty years.

He was very careful to make the distinction between Western governments – whose actions he largely deplored – and Western citizens, however. He also voiced an opinion that I was to hear repeated many times over on my journey: 'You have a house . . . someone comes into your house as a guest. They overstay their welcome, and you ask them to leave. They will not. They force you out of your house. You can see them living in your house. And you decide to take back what is yours. Even if that means you have to fight.' This is an argument that Iraqis, looking forward to running their own country, could use; it is also one used by fundamentalist Islamists to justify terror attacks within Saudi Arabia.

Suddenly the mood was lightened by the rustle of tablecloths being unfurled. 'The dinner is coming,' said Ahmed. Because of approaching Ramadan, the Emirati president, Sheikh Zayed, had declared a 24-hour public holiday from six o'clock that evening, a Saturday. This meant that music was prohibited and that no alcohol would be served in the hotels, except to guests on room service. Since it was a special night, one of the *majlis* patrons had sponsored dinner for everyone. We started to gather our things, not wanting to intrude further.

'No, stay, stay. You must eat with us,' Ahmed insisted.

It was barbecued saltwater fish, served on a large bed of rice, and with a side order of salad. Ahmed picked out the sweetest parts of the fish and put them on my side of the platter. 'You must eat!'

We did as we were told. Back when I set off on this trip, I'd decided not to turn down any opportunity or adventure because of fear (not something I always managed to pull off, unfortunately). Besides, who was I to turn down an invitation to dinner from a military man who looked like a matinee idol?

Chapter 5

Sunday School

As one would imagine from their Arabic names, the Islamic world – *Al-Dar al-Islam*, or 'the House of Peace' – is different in many ways from the non-Islamic world – *Al-Dar al-Harb*, 'the House of War'. Just one of those ways can be seen in their places of worship. In Christendom, churches are generally open to all, provided you dress properly and go at the right times. In Islam, many mosques are forbidden to non-believers at any time and a strict dress code is enforced by those mosques that do allow non-Muslims to visit.

Almost all of Dubai's 560-plus mosques are closed to non-Muslims. But the pale and elegant Jumeirah Mosque not only welcomes visitors twice a week, on Thursday and Sunday mornings, but holds Islam classes to explain the basics. Over the past four days as we moved around Dubai, Cass and I had often seen the mosque and admired its illuminated minaret spearing the night sky. The mosque was always busy at prayer times, as the neighbouring streets clogged with the luxury saloons and SUVs of the faithful, who rushed to worship when the muezzin called.

On the Sunday following our evening at the *majlis*, in the quiet between dawn and midday prayers, when the usual attendees would not be disturbed by our presence, Cass and I found ourselves in the mosque for religious instruction with a difference. This open mosque and class is one of the initiatives of the Sheikh Mohammed Centre for Cultural Understanding, based in Bastakiya and opened in 1999. My journey into Islam, the religion, truly began when we were met at the door of the mosque by Michelle Sabti (who volunteers for the centre) and met a woman named Juwayryah Perez – known to all as JoJo – who would lead the class.

The mosque-visit program, according to its director, Abdallah bin Eisa Al Serkal, is a cornerstone of the cultural centre's program: 'A personal, first-hand experience allows more insight and understanding. It has always been the Centre's philosophy to create opportunities for cultural exchange through our activities.'[1] Under the patronage of Dubai's emir, Sheikh Mohammed bin Rashid Al Maktoum, the centre is aimed at familiarising expatriates with the local culture, and runs courses in Arabic language, lectures on Islam and guided tours to local homes.

This initiative is aimed at bringing people together instead of allowing differences to drive them into suspicious and belligerent camps. The world has been dividing itself along religious ground for thousands of years: pagans against Jews, Jews against Christians, polytheists against monotheists. Within religions, sectarianism is also a curse – and is often more about the advancement of temporal power of an elite than the spread of spiritual values.

Even though I had been in a couple Libyan mosques previously, I was still largely ignorant of Islam, just like the other visitors to the mosque that morning. JoJo and Michelle started slowly outside; with gentle words and manners, they clothed and veiled those in our thirty-strong group who had failed to observe the requirement for modest dress for the mosque visit.

JoJo explained the architecture of this particular mosque, which, like mosques all over the world, was based on a traditional design: an open space, generally roofed, with a *mihrab*, a semicircular niche from where the imam leads the prayers and orientates towards Mecca and the Kaaba (Islam's sacred stone), and a *minbar*, which is a seat at the top of steps that is used by the preacher as a pulpit.

The Jumeirah Mosque has a fine minaret, a feature of most mosques throughout the Islamic world. Minarets are seen by some Muslims as gates between Heaven and Hell, and they can be conical, cylindrical or polygonal. Stairs spiral up the inside of the shaft anticlockwise. There is a balcony on the upper section, from which the muezzin used to summon the faithful to prayer – but that is now done either from the body of the mosque or by prerecorded message. The minarets are covered by a roof-like canopy, and the level of decoration, or lack of it, means that each mosque can be easily identified in terms of place and era.

JoJo told us that the floors inside a mosque are covered by mats or carpets. It is here that ritual prayer is performed. Men line up in rows, elbow to elbow, shoulder to shoulder, and pray under the guidance of the imam. Beautiful as these structures can be, we learned, Muslims don't need formal spaces in which to worship. Mohammad himself declared that the Earth is a mosque. Women at home, busy with their families, put on their veils, lay out their prayer rugs and kneel towards Mecca to pray. Muslims away from a mosque pray wherever they are.

We left our shoes outside, and then JoJo explained the precise washing routine observed by Muslims before prayer. Inside the mosque, she opened with a basic discussion about the Mohammedian faith, before taking questions from the group about the religion, dress code, family life, and the role of women in Islamic society. Nothing was off-limits.

We formed a loose circle around her – some on the carpet, others on chairs – and prepared to learn. The first thing I realised was that JoJo looked better than any living human being has a right to when dressed in the hijab. Born in Switzerland of Spanish parents, she was rumoured to have converted to Islam when she married an imam. Her ability with languages and understanding others' concerns about her religion made her the perfect person to lead this discussion.

Muslims regard their religion as the final and perfect revelation of God's will. The Jews had the story first, the Christians second, and then Mohammad was chosen as God's ultimate prophet, and it was to him that the angel Gabriel revealed the Qur'an. Muslims consider Jews and Christians also to be people of the Book – all are children of Abraham. '"Look now toward heaven, and tell the stars, if thou be able to number them": and he said unto him, "So shall thy descendants be"' was the promise made to Abraham by God in Genesis 15:5, and so in Islam all the children of Abraham have a special position and deserve protection. (Just as the members of the three religions are all the progeny of Abraham, according to the Old

Testament we are also the sons and daughters of Cain. Many of us have been and are still involved in long-term efforts to reduce each other's numbers.)

Islam has three basic tenets. The first is that there is only one God, and he has many names, from Ar-Rahman, the source of all mercy, and Al-Haqq, the truth, to As-Sabour, the patient (*Sura* 20:8). According to one of the *hadith qudsi*, which are the sacred, direct revelations from Allah to the Prophet but expressed in Mohammad's own words: 'God has ninety-nine names, one hundred minus one. Whoever enumerates them enters Paradise.'

The second tenet is that Mohammad is the final messenger of God, the last of a long line that includes Abraham, Moses and Jesus (Esa).

And the third is belief in an after-life, following the resurrection of the dead and the final day of judgement.

Being a Muslim means practising the five pillars of the religion. These are as follows:

1. **The profession of faith.** The declaration is the acceptance of Allah as the one true God, and of Mohammad as his prophet.
2. **Prayer** (five times a day). Before dawn, the muezzin calls the faithful to prayer with the advice that it is better to pray than to sleep. There are also prayers just after noon, around mid-afternoon, just after dusk and finally after eight.
3. **The giving of alms.** In an enlightened instruction, Mohammad required his followers to give a portion of their earnings to others. The rate is around 2.5 per cent, but it can depend on circumstances.
4. **Fasting.** The faithful Muslim must observe the holy month of Ramadan, the ninth in the Islamic calendar, during which the Qur'an began to be revealed to Mohammad. During the Ramadan fast, the faithful abstain from sunrise to sunset. This means that if a person is capable of observing the fast, they should not drink or eat during the hours of daylight. Neither should they ingest any medicines or drugs. The chronically ill, children, the aged, and pregnant or menstruating women are exempt from the duty. However, menstruating women and

healthy men who somehow break the fast during Ramadan are expected to make up the lost days later in the year.

5. **Pilgrimage** (to the Kaaba in Mecca). Muslims consider this the site of the Garden of Eden. It is forbidden for non-Muslims to enter the city, and if a person 'reverts' to Islam (true believers think we are all Muslims, but some get off-track, so when they take up the religion, it is not a conversion but a reversion), they are required to show their certificate of reversion in order to get a visa to travel there.

   If a person is not well enough to go to Mecca, they can pay a pilgrim to go in their place. If someone is unable to complete the pilgrimage before their death, a member of their family can do it on their behalf. There are no limitations for this – great-grandchildren can undertake the pilgrimage on behalf of their ancestor, if they wish.

Misunderstanding is something that the Islam classes at the Jumeirah Mosque try to address, and it's something Muslims and visitors have been trying to overcome for centuries. In April 1717, Lady Mary Wortley Montagu was living in Constantinople when she wrote to the Abbot Conti, a cleric at Adrianople, regarding the things she had begun to understand about Islam:

> Mohametism is divided into as many sects as Christianity, and the first institution as much neglected and obscured by interpretations. I cannot here forbear reflecting on the natural inclination of mankind to make mysteries and novelties. The Zeidi, Kadari, Jabari, etc. put me in mind of the Catholic, Lutheran, Calvinist, etc., and are equally zealous against one another.
>
> But the most prevailing opinion, if you search into the secret of the effendis, is plain deism, but this is kept from the people, who are amused with a thousand different notions according to the different interests of their preachers . . .
>
> [I was assured] that if I understood Arabic I should be very well pleased with reading the [Qur'an], which is so far from the nonsense we charge it with, it is the purest morality delivered in the very best language. I have since heard impartial

> Christians speak of it in the same manner, and I don't doubt but all our translations are from copies got from the Greek priests, who would not fail to falsify it with the extremity of malice.[2]

Despite the many generations that have passed from Lady Mary's time to ours, many Westerners still have either an uninformed or an ill-informed idea of 'Mohametism', hearing only the calls to sharpen ploughshares into swords. But the Qur'an, which can give both the Torah and the Bible a run for their money in terms of bloodthirstiness, can also be lyrical. It begins in beauty with the first *sura*, 'al-Fatihah':

> In the Name of God, the Merciful, the Compassionate
> Praise be to God, Lord of the Universe,
> The Compassionate, the Merciful, Sovereign of the Day of Judgement!
> You alone we worship, and to You alone we turn for help.
> Guide us to the straight path,
> The path of those whom You have favoured,
> Not of those who have incurred Your wrath, nor of those who have gone astray.

And the Qur'an is full of surprises, like this recognition of equity: 'I will not suffer the work of any worker among you to be lost whether male or female, the one of you being from the other' (*Sura* 3:195).

The mosque visits provide an essential bridge between religions, cultures and individuals. In the West, Islam is seen as repressive to women – and that was certainly the tenor of some of the questions posed to JoJo that morning in the mosque. Is Islam a religion that liberates, or one that represses, women?

Chapter 6

Women of Islam

THE FIRST MUSLIM WAS a woman. But before we get to Khadija, we should start at the beginning of the story, with the Prophet. Mohammad was born around 570 into one of the poorer branches of the richest families in Mecca, the Quraishi. He was a post-mortem baby – his father, Abdullah, died before he was born, leaving his mother, Amina, in straitened circumstances. She died when Mohammad was just six years old, so his grandfather, Abd-al-Muttalib, of the Muttalib family, one of twelve clans making up the Quraish tribe, then took charge of the boy. But he died too, so when Mohammad was eight he was cared for by his uncle, Abu Talib. It was a pretty miserable start for a little boy.

Mohammad had to work to earn his living, and eventually joined a trading enterprise owned by a widow, Khadija. She was a socially and financially independent woman when she employed Mohammad, a man fifteen years her junior, to manage her business affairs and trading interests. Then, at the age of forty, she decided to ask Mohammad to marry her. Khadija sent a woman named Nefissa as her go-between. Nefissa's mission is described in *Al-Tabakat al-Kobra,* said to be the earliest comprehensive history of the Prophet, his companions and the nascent Arab nation: its author, Mohammad Ibn Saad, reported that Nefissa was sent secretly, instructed to propose that he marry Khadija.[1] Which is what he did.

The regard in which Mohammad held Khadija during her lifetime was obvious at the time of her death. He said of her that she had believed in him and embraced Islam when no one else had; and that she had supported him personally and financially when there was no one else willing to do so.[2] On top of that, Khadija was the mother of the Prophet's only surviving children, all daughters.

Mohammad had his first vision when he was around forty years of age, and was called to be a prophet and began to preach in public shortly afterwards, in around 613. Mohammad's earliest disciples, besides his wife and daughters, included his cousin, Ali, and his slave Zayed, whom he had adopted. Other converts followed, among them Abu Bakr, who would be the first caliph after Mohammad's death, and Uthman, who became the third caliph.

Within a few years, trouble mounted. The other residents of Mecca were not happy with Mohammad's message of the oneness of God, the resurrection, and the responsibility of the individual to God; they particularly disliked his disavowal of the trinity of goddesses whom they believed dwelled in the Kaaba. Opposition to the Prophet and his teachings went from disapproval to persecution, so, with his followers, Mohammad was forced out of the city to Medina, in 622. That exodus marks the year from which the Islamic calendar is dated.

Relations between Medina and Mecca grew increasingly strained and finally collapsed when the Meccans confiscated the property of those Muslims who had fled the city. In 624, Mohammad led a raid against a Meccan merchant caravan, and then the Meccans retaliated, sending an army column against Medina. At Badr, battle was joined. The Meccans were defeated, with forty-five men killed and at least seventy taken for ransom. The Medina contingent lost only fourteen men. In the light of his military successes, Mohammad became the virtual ruler of Medina.

He made a couple of forays to Mecca in an attempt to take the city, including one in 628, but finally, in 630, at the head of an army of nearly ten thousand men, he forced the Meccans to surrender and convert. Mohammad died in 632, leaving no named successor.

Women were fundamental in helping Mohammad to proselytise, and his attitude towards women was – in the context of the time – extremely advanced. Women were then in the front line of Islam, among the Companions of the Prophet (defined by scholars as members of the select group of early Muslims who saw and heard Mohammad at least once and died as believers), which was appropriate, since in God's word as revealed in the Qur'an, all human beings are equal. The first convert to Islam was Khadija; the first Islamic martyr was also a woman, Sumaiya, killed for embracing Islam and rejecting the polytheistic religion of her ancestors.

Islam gave new freedoms to women, who had previously been treated no better than cattle or slaves. One of Mohammad's earliest teachings was to forbid the killing of children, when it had long been the custom of his people to bury infant girls who were surplus to requirements.[3] The Qur'an declares that women can keep their own dowries, inherit property and support themselves if they need to. It also protects women against mistreatment, and limits the number of wives a man can have at any one time and sets out how they must treated. From the *sura* that deals specifically with the treatment of women (4:3) comes the following: 'And if you fear that you cannot treat orphan girls with fairness, then you may marry other women who seem good to you: two, three or four of them. But if you fear you cannot maintain equality among them, marry only one . . .'

While Khadija lived, Mohammad had no other wives, and their union – despite her age – produced two sons (neither of whom survived childhood) and four daughters, including Fatima. When Khadija died, the Prophet was still in his early fifties and he remarried, often for dynastic, political and social reasons, as well as reasons of the heart. While the Qur'an declares that men can have up to four wives, Mohammad was exempted from that particular limit.

The position of women in Islamic societies is often reviewed unfavourably in the Western media, and much is said about what the Qur'an requires, and what Mohammad himself said, regarding the role of women in Islam and the dominion of men over them. This is one of my favourite *hadith* from the Prophet, which speaks for itself: 'Among my followers the best of men are those who are best to their wives and the best of women are those who are best to their husbands. To each of such women is set down a reward equivalent to the reward of a thousand martyrs.' That is something that many wives of any religion or denomination would be grateful to hear!

It's worth noting that not long before the birth of Mohammad, in 584, Christians at the Council of Macon in France debated 'Are women human?' The ayes won, but only just: the final tally was thirty-two to thirty-one. At the time, many (presumably male) Christians considered women to be subhuman, with no souls, and less holy than men. Martin Luther, the German theologian, was apparently still under this impression in the sixteenth century. He is attributed with an astonishing statement about the role of women: they should stay home, sit still, occupy themselves with keeping house, and bearing and bring up children. 'Even though they grow weary and wear themselves out with child-bearing,' he is reported to have declared, 'it does not matter. Let them go on bearing children till they die.' That, after all, is what women were made for, he concludes.[4]

Aisha, the daughter of the first caliph, Abu Bakr, is believed to have been married to the Prophet when she was a child of eight or nine – a cause for great concern among critics of Islam. However, she was known for her strong will, logic and eloquence, and was one of the primary eyewitnesses to the life of Mohammad. She became a fierce warrior who fought in several wars and battles and was also, according to Islamic theologian Orwa Ebn El Zobeir, something of a polymath. He said: 'I have not seen anyone who is more knowledgeable in theology, in medicine and in poetry than Aisha.'[5]

Aisha was no 'yes' woman to the Prophet. She sometimes challenged him and was often reported to be unhappy when he married a new wife. On occasion, she rebelled, inciting her co-wives against Mohammad. She is reported to have challenged him in relation to one of the Qur'anic verses, in which Allah permitted Mohammad to marry as many women as he wished. ('Allah always responds immediately to your needs,' she is said to have commented.[6]) In the fifty years of her widowhood, Aisha became a teacher of Islam and transmitted more than two thousand *hadith*.

Aisha was not alone in fighting physically for the new religion. Nessiba bint Kaab is also said to have taken part in sword fighting next to Mohammad during the Battle of Ahad. She did not drop her weapon and abandon the fight until she had been wounded thirteen times. Mohammed was said to have held her in great respect, and that the position due to her was 'higher to that of men'.[7]

Some women also fought against Islam. Hind bint Rabia put on the mask and armour of a warrior at Ahad, and plunged her sword into Muslim after Muslim as she fought opposite Mohammad's ranks. During the battle, in which the Quraishi were victorious over the Muslims, she even offered an inducement for the life of Hamzah, the Prophet's uncle. As an Arab woman, Hind took a rather unusual course in life, insisting on personal freedom. She is reported to have told her father that she was a woman who held her life in her own hands and knew what she wanted.[8]

In the Battle of Badr, Hind lost three men of her family. After that, she swore to avenge them, taking an oath not to perfume herself or approach her husband until she was revenged. Hind eventually repented and converted to Islam.

Asma bint Abu Bakr was another daughter of the first caliph, and half-sister of Aisha, wife of the Prophet. One of the earliest people to accept Islam, she took part in the exodus from Mecca while heavily pregnant, and was later delivered of a son, Abdullah, the first child born to one of the faithful in their new home, Medina.

Rumaysa Bint Milhan, also known as Umm Sulaym, had been married before she converted to Islam, and her first husband was deeply unhappy about that development in her spiritual life. When he was killed, she accepted another husband – not on the basis of his gold and silver, but on the grounds of his conversion to Islam. His submission to God would be her dowry, she said. Umm Sulaym was renowned for her great courage and bravery. During the Battle of Ahad, she carried a dagger tucked into the waistband above her pregnant stomach while she brought water to the fighters and attended to their wounds. She was ready to defend Mohammad, too, when the battle turned against him. At one moment, Mohammad spied her with the dagger and asked about it. She is said to have replied: 'It is to fight those who desert.'[9]

Umm Sulaym was a constant comfort to Mohammad, who sometimes visited her and her husband, Abu Talhah, at home. On occasion, when the time for prayer came, Mohammad would pray on a mat provided by her; at other times, he would nap there. As Mohammad slept, she wiped the sweat from his brow. 'Umm Sulaym, what are you doing?' Mohammad once asked her when he woke in the middle of her ministrations. 'I am taking these [drops of perspiration] as a *barakah* [blessing],' she responded.[10]

Interestingly, one of the most influential women in Islam was not alive during the lifetime of Mohammad, and neither was she a Muslim. The most celebrated woman in the Qur'an is in fact Mary, the mother of Jesus Christ. She is mentioned more often in the Muslim holy book – where she has her own chapter, *Sura* 19, the Book of Maryam – than she is in the Bible. Muslim beliefs about Mary are close to those of Roman Catholics. According to Islam, Jesus and his mother were the only two people ever to live who were not 'touched by Satan' at birth – the Islamic expression for freedom from original sin.

In other ways, the Islamic Mary is close to the Mary of the Eastern Rites churches. According to both traditions, Mary was raised by her guardian, Zechariah, in the Temple, previously the domain of male priests. The Islamic Mary is said to have been brought food by Zechariah, who always found her already nourished, metaphysically (*Sura* 3:37). In a story recounted by the apostle James in his Infancy Gospel, the three-year-old child was taken to the Temple in Jerusalem, where she passed her childhood.[11]

In Islam, Mary is considered to be a woman who lived a holy life. This view is expressed in the Qur'an (at *Sura* 3:42–43): 'And the angels said: "O Mary, Allah has chosen you and purified you. He has chosen you above the women of all peoples. O Mary, be devoted to your Lord."'

Mary also appears in later Islamic theological works, described as having reached the pinnacle of 'servanthood', seen as the exemplar of how the individual can be transformed by selfless and pure love of God. For Mohammad, who is quoted in one of the *hadith* as saying 'Paradise lies at the feet of thy mother', Mary was the exemplar of what a woman, a mother, could be.[12]

As we walked out of the Jumeirah Mosque that Sunday morning, I was filled with hope that the gap between Islam and Christianity was not unbridgeable. I looked about me. The women were all dressed modestly in *abayas* and veils, looking like 21st century manifestations of the greatest Jewish mother, Mary, mother of Christ – Islam's Maryam. This was the same Blessed Virgin Mary whose kindly image I had loved during my childhood in the Church of the Little Flower, in Brisbane, helping to arrange the flowers around the feet of her statue. Mary, the highest expression of womanhood to Muslims? That was a turn up for the books.

Chapter 7

❀

Customs of the Country

AN ANXIOUS PAIR OF modern-day Blessed Virgin Marys perched over a counter of a busy shop in the gold souk in Deira, a suburb on the opposite side of Dubai creek from Jumeirah Beach. They had every right to be nervy: picking a suite of wedding jewellery, when there was so much on offer, with prices ranging from quite expensive to stratospheric, meant there was a lot riding on their decision. They straightened their hijabs, adjusted their jewellers' loops, and bowed their heads to inspect another avalanche of diamonds.

Cass and I had found the pair after a little adventure through the spice souk, tramping past the dhows that ply the Gulf from here to India and back again. Down on the quays outside the old spice market, away from the luxury hotel complexes and the skyscrapers of Sheikh Zayed Road, old Dubai is still visible on the edge of the creek, the saltwater inlet that curves into the city from the Gulf. Scruffy boats that travel between Dubai and Pakistan were sitting hard up against the wharves, their cargoes on the dockside. Lascars lazed on the top decks under bimini sails rigged over wheelhouses to provide protection from the blazing sun. It looked timeless until we peered a little, and spotted GPS navigation systems partly obscured by the dhows' sails.

Up and down the wharves the workers bustled, pushing their little trolleys in and out of the old spice market, as generations of them have over hundreds of years. Even the air in the narrow passageways of the market was redolent of the past: aromas of cashews, almonds, pistachios, frankincense, cloves, cardamom, cinnamon, incense, dried fruit and barbecued limes wafted out of open bags and mixed with the tang of saltwater from the creek.

It had been a relief to leave the solid heat of the spice market and wander into Dubai's fabled gold souk, which is covered from the sun, but there wasn't a breath of air there, either. It was being sucked up by the crush of locals and tourists out to make major purchases and heavy breathing at the very thought. There was certainly a mountain of goods suitable to satisfy any acquisitive shopper: earrings, rings, necklaces, bracelets, pendants; traditional, modern, bold, conservative, fine, chunky; pink, white or yellow gold.

It's said that there is nine billion dollars (US) worth of gold on sale in this market at any given time. And almost all of it seemed to have one-third off the normal price on the day we called in to see Cass's friend Arun, at his jewellery shop. There was frantic action at the counters downstairs, but the real drama in Arun's shop was up the narrow stairs, where our 'Marys' were making an initial inspection of the bridal jewellery – over-the-top sets of rings, earrings, bracelets and necklaces, which are part of the customary dowry in the Gulf.

'Madame would like to see some wedding jewellery,' Arun asked me with a twinkle almost as bright as those reflected by the shop's diamonds. He ushered us into his inner sanctum.

The concept of this jewellery is simple, even if the sets are not. At Emirati weddings, the brides' dowries are generally hung about their necks by the bridegroom and his family. Some of the brides have four or five sets for the different events that take place during the customary wedding festivities – which can really add up, given that the sets range in price from seventy thousand to more than a million dirhams. With an exchange rate of around 2.8 dirhams to every Australian dollar, that means more than twenty thousand dollars for a basic suite.

The UAE government gives every national couple a starter set, costing seventy thousand dirhams, for their first wedding. And if the bride is older than thirty and has been married before, she gets a premium: a bridal suite worth one hundred thousand dirhams. (A premium for age and experience? Brilliant!) For those readers tutting and thinking, *How silly! Wouldn't a house be better?*, stand by for the news . . . The happy couple also gets half a million dirham from the government to buy a house.

These bridal sets never become community property; the bride's dowry is considered hers and remains that way during the life of the marriage. She might be inclined to bankroll her husband into a venture using the bridal suites as surety, but he always has to ask nicely.

Arun started us off with the seventy thousand dirham sets, which looked quite nice until he upped the ante with even more refined (and expensive) sets. His assistant started to raise a sweat, pulling one kid-lined leather box after another out of the strong room, where the really top-of-the-line sets were kept. All these top-quality sets are made in Italy, to Arun's designs, and freely adapted from designs by Chopard, Chanel, Graff and Bulgari, among others.

Yellow diamonds with white diamonds, white diamonds with yellow sapphires, emeralds, rubies and blue sapphires all winked out of their luxurious homes. Apparently there's no concept of 'too much' when it comes to Emirati bridal jewellery – the brides see over-the-top and aim higher. Cass was in heaven, happily hanging hundreds of carats around her neck.

Arun was discreet, and wouldn't discuss the palaces he often called on with his suites. Apparently the sheikhas (daughters of sheikhs) in Dubai don't like to go out, not even into the gold souk. Visiting them instead was always worth Arun's while, however, since a sale was guaranteed. The sheikhas could never *not* buy a set: it was a matter of saving face.

We got out eventually, but only because we were on the hunt for something else, namely the history of Dubai. On the surface, this emirate – with its obsession with biggest, tallest, most expensive, most astonishing and newest, manifested in places as various as its huge malls and its IT and communications centre called Knowledge Village – might seem like a place with more future than past. But Dubai is a blend of old and new: camel races, an ancient local passion, are still popular, but the boy jockeys are being replaced by robots. Other ancient Arab passions, such as horses and horse races, are particular favourites of Dubai's emir, Sheikh Mohammed Al

Maktoum, whose renowned Godolphin stables winners are celebrated in a museum at the Nad Al Sheba course. The track has a full racing calendar, and the renowned Dubai Cup, with its purse of four million US dollars, attracts runners and observers from all over the world.

I was beginning to fall in love with one particular custom of Dubai: the Ladies Line. This is a custom found through the Middle East and North Africa, from shops to airline queues, but one I had encountered for the first time when I was in Ghadames for the annual music festival the year before. There, it was writ large, because the ladies-only line was a ladies-only stand at the football stadium. 'The ladies, they do not like to be jostled,' my friend Salah had said when I remarked on the tranquil oasis the local women and their children had created.

A year later I learned that non-jostling of ladies had been formalised in Dubai. Those Ladies Lines were all over Dubai, according to Sharon Garrett, a Brisbane-raised public relations director who had opened several of the city's best hotels. 'You can find them in supermarkets, at petrol stations,' she explained over drinks that night. 'I love them. And when I can't find one, I really miss them.'

Sharon was also full of stories about the young blades of Dubai in their sports cars – 'They'll throw their cards and their phone numbers into the cars of women they like the look of!' – and how to pick a good man here. 'Check out the sandals,' she said. 'Just as you can always tell a lot about a man in the West by his shoes, here, it's all in the sandals.'

A little later, Sharon took me to meet Emira, the half-Iraqi wife of a local sheikh, and her English mother, Annabel. Emira, a tiny, charming, pretty woman in her early forties, had a master's degree in modern literature and had been deciding whether to go to New York to become a banker when she was introduced to the man who would become her husband. He was so smitten that every weekend he flew over from the Gulf to London, where she was living, to take her and her friends out.

'I didn't know he was travelling so far until he said he couldn't afford to keep doing it and that we really should get married,' she said with a smile.

And that's what they did, when Emira was twenty-six. Their eldest child, Farah, was fourteen when we met, and they had three other children, including Ataa, who was six.

'The youngest children sleep with me . . . Don't ask me where my husband sleeps!' she said with a laugh.

The sheikh was a financier, I learned. Emira had her own business, which dealt only with women, so she could work in the office. Her life was fairly circumscribed, so how could she be out in a hotel that night, wearing Western clothes, and without her hijab? I asked.

'Nobody recognises me here,' she replied. 'If I were recognised, I couldn't come.'

But she was out with her mother and three women friends – surely there couldn't be a problem with that?

'It doesn't matter. My husband is always alert to problems that might damage his reputation through perceptions of me.'

Annabel, her mother, was a vital, red-haired English woman who had married Emira's father when she was nineteen and then moved to Baghdad. Sometimes, she remembered, the whole family drove from London to Iraq, through Belgrade, Sofia, Istanbul and Ankara. As she spoke, nostalgia swept over all of us for the romance of a simpler time now long gone.

Despite the restrictions that controlled aspects of her life, Emira was happy with her lot. 'Women rule the world,' she said. 'The men think they rule everything, everywhere, and they actually decide nothing, anywhere. Women arrange things.'

Ottomania

Chapter 8

Kidnapped

I am going away . . . to an unknown country
where I shall have no past and no name,
and where I shall be born again
with a new face and an untried heart.
Colette

WE ARRIVED AT ISTANBUL'S Atatürk International Airport at night, en masse. Indians, Africans, Emiratis, Arabs, a bloc of New Russians . . . The Cold War might have ended, but the elbowing between former Communists, unreconstructed capitalists, modern entrepreneurs and traditional carpetbaggers continued. A clot of impatience formed at the immigration gates. A maul of Russians turned on one of their own, telling a supercharged Slav trying to push in to push off. 'It's worse than India here,' said one woman, who had clearly had enough of the heat and the press of flesh at passport control. As for me, having farewelled Cass earlier that day, I was already starting to miss the refined life of ease the two of us had been enjoying in Dubai for the past week.

Soon enough though, I handed over twenty US dollars for my visa, squeezed through, and there I was. Outside passport control stood a man with my name on a sign. The driver had been organised by a friend of a friend, and I was relieved that the man had waited for the delayed passengers to arrive and not just given up and left without me.

'Welcome to Turkey,' he said as he took my hand luggage, helped me collect my bags (only slightly diminished by my time in the Gulf) and shepherded me towards the exit. As we walked away, I heard something above the general hubbub of the airport.

'Is someone paging me?' I asked.

'Yes?'

'Listen . . .'

'Yes?'

I heard it again. 'Paging Madame Christian Hooligan,' the tannoy repeated softly.

'That's me. Christine Hogan.'

'Yes?' My escort kept moving. Nothing was going to stop the man with my luggage, so I followed. He deposited me with two more strangers and disappeared.

'Someone is paging me,' I said to the older of the two men who now had hold of my luggage and so custody of my person.

'Welcome to Turkey. I am Nebi Yaşa Tan. I will be your guide.'

'Please. Can I answer the page?'

'I hear nothing,' said my new companion in lightly accented English. The good news was that, like generations of Western visitors to Byzantium (later named the Ottoman Empire and now Turkey), I had my own dragoman; the bad news was that he, like the first line of my reception committee, seemed to be deaf.

I was bustled out of the terminal and deposited in the back seat of a small Ford. It became clear that I wasn't being kidnapped but was a victim of over-planning: there were two reception committees to meet me off the plane. The one I hadn't been expecting, from the Turkish Department of Tourism, got there first. The unanswered page was Mustafa's.

On the drive into Istanbul, I wondered how Cass was doing. I had left her at noon in Dubai, full of excitement because she was going to stay with a friend, the wife of another local sheikh – a man so rich and eccentric that his extensive gardens provided cheetah with luxury digs. I considered my new companions. Ayhan Demir, the driver, spoke no English, while my guide, who I would later learn to address formally as Nebi Bey, spoke excellent English but preferred French, the language of diplomacy – and love. Since he had been posted around the world with Turkish Tourism, to

Barcelona, Paris, Moscow and Anatolia, he had a number of languages, but none of them pleased him quite as much as French when it came to communicating with non-Turkish speakers who were also francophone.

Struggling to make myself understood after some time away from French conversation class, I was silenced when a vision appeared on my right. In the inky blackness, dozens of lights rode low in the water.

'The Sea of Marmara,' said Nebi. 'And those are the maritime walls of the city to the left.' The lights belonged to freighters and tankers waiting to go up through the Bosphorus, a stretch of water linking the trade routes of the Mediterranean and the ports of the Black Sea that have been so sought after across the millennia.

The air was fresh, the breeze off the water clean and alive, as Nebi Bey and Ayhan deposited me at my new hotel, and promised to come back first thing in the morning to start my Turkish adventure. I was getting used to this luxury travel lark: a vizier, if not a sultan, would have been pleased with my room, where trays of baklava, Turkish delight and sliced fruit were waiting next to ewers of fresh fruit juices. The snowy-white linen on the bed was scattered with rose petals. The curtains were open, giving a glittering view of a football stadium, the Bosphorus and, beyond, the other half of the city – the Asian side. Welcome to Turkey, indeed.

Nebi was on the job early the next morning, taking me straight to the number one site for tourists and Orientalists alike: the Topkapi *sarayi*, a palace of dreams, and, for some, nightmares.

First stop on our visit was scheduled to be the famous harem, but since it was a little early, the women's quarters were not yet open to the public. Nebi Bey and I settled on a low stone bench outside the Imperial Council Chamber – the Ottoman Divan. Here, for hundreds of years, generations of ambassadors and supplicants to the sultans had sat, waiting to be received. The Topkapi is a series of buildings, rather than a monolithic palace, and the buildings edge a series of courts. The first court, the most remote from the sultan's private realm, was empty on the morning of our visit. The second, which was where we were sitting, had been built by Süleyman the Magnificent in 1524.

We were directly outside the third court, the inner administrative sanctum of the palace, with its exquisite library and treasury. The fourth court lay beyond that again, and there, we would discover, the mood changed to one of pleasure. There were kiosks, tulip gardens and a marble terrace and pool, which looked out from Seraglio Point over the Golden Horn on one side, and the Bosphorus on the other.

It was crisp and quiet inside the palace walls. The tourist buses were already pulling up outside, but Nebi and I were alone as pale sunlight bathed the palace forecourt with a ghostly glamour.

I took a closer look at my host as he gave me a background briefing and oriented me in the courtyard. Gravely spoken and perfectly mannered, he was a different man from last evening, when the long wait for the plane had shredded his nerves a little. He was dressed beautifully; his tie silk, his grey hair neatly standing to attention, his shirt crisp, as befitting a former head of the Department of Tourism. He had a gallant, courtly air, and as he spoke it became clear this was going to be a very interesting day.

The bench we were occupying was just outside the happily named Gate of Felicity, also known as the Gate of the White Eunuchs, which leads from the second court of the Topkapi Palace into the third. The gate forms the portal where the sultans habitually met their foreign visitors – a guest list that included the willing, the less willing and the completely reluctant. Marie Martha Aimée Du Bucq de Rivéry would definitely have been in the final category.

Between the gate and the divan, the rooms and terraces where the viziers traditionally received their guests, is the place where the Ottoman ruler – the Caliph of the Faithful, the Padishah of the Barbary States, Shadow of the Prophet on Earth – would sit on state occasions on his splendid throne. It was also here that obeisance was made and tribute to him laid.

Among the tributes deposited to Sultan Abdül Hamit I on one particular day in 1784 was Marie Martha Aimée Du Bucq de Rivéry, a young woman whose story was to become the stuff of legend, perhaps even myth. Little more than a convent schoolgirl when she saw the Gate of Felicity for the first time, she could never have expected to find happiness behind it – let alone a long and extraordinary life that saw her become the most powerful woman in the Ottoman Empire. Degradation, rape and murder were probably what she was looking forward to.

Born into a planter family in Martinique, Aimée, as she was known, was beautiful and well connected: her cousin was Joséphine Beauharnais, the future wife of Napoleon. Aimée had been taught by the nuns of the Order of Les Dames de la Visitation at Nantes, in France. By the time she was twenty-one, thanks to the war between England and France over the American colonies, she'd been stuck in the convent for more than eight years. It was decided she'd had enough of the regimen of light schoolwork and needlepoint, and was suitably accomplished. It was time for her to go home, find a husband, put theory into practice and start filling the nursery of a plantation house.

With her on the ship home to the West Indies was her governess. In front of them lay two months of tedium interrupted only by some books and conversation. A couple of days out of port, the ship ran into a heavy storm. Not being particularly seaworthy, the vessel started to come apart at the seams. It shipped water, began to list, and finally started to sink. As the passengers and crew were busy abandoning ship, the sails of a Spanish merchantman appeared on the horizon. This trader was heading to Majorca, in the Balearics in the Mediterranean, somewhat off-course for Martinique. Still, it was better than going straight to the bottom of the sea, and the rescued passengers were delighted to be sailing to safety.

However, it soon became evident that they were being hunted by Algerian corsairs, the feared denizens of the Barbary Coast of Africa. These pirates, who had safe and secret harbours among the inlets and islands of the coast, from Tangiers in modern Morocco to close to Tocra in today's Libya, operated under the tacit approval of the Turkish sultans.

Piracy was a well-established tradition – and so was slavery. Sub-Saharan Africans, with their exotic ebony flesh, were particular favourites in Constantinople, the Ottoman capital (now Istanbul). There was also trade in young boys, to fill the ranks of the black eunuchs of the seraglio, and in fair-skinned Circassians and appealing Greek, Georgian, Romanian and Syrian women.

Once the pirates had taken their ship, slavery was exactly the fate that awaited beautiful, blonde Aimée. The pirate captain spotted her and, to preserve her from the attentions of his crew and keep her safe for his overlord, the Bey of Algiers, he locked her in his cabin. On reaching land, Aimée was taken first to Algiers, and into its kasbah. The ruler was delighted with his new captive and recognised her as a rare pearl, one who would do him much credit were he to give her to his sultan.

A new ship suitable for a sultan's favourite was luxuriously fitted out in Algiers, and Aimée embarked in fine style on her final Mediterranean cruise, this time towards Constantinople. In the city where Asia meets Europe, the two parts of her life – the European and the Oriental – would collide, and she would meet her unexpected fate.

That destiny couldn't have seemed too promising on Aimée's first morning ashore when, dressed in the Ottoman style and heavily veiled, she was bustled off the ship and across the quay. From the harbour, she would have seen the dominating bulk of the palace on Seraglio Point.

The agglomeration of buildings that formed the Topkapi Palace was, according to estimates based on the provisioning records of the kitchens, home to around twenty thousand people. There were palaces and libraries, kiosks and pleasure gardens, pools and fountains, barracks, prisons, torture chambers, school rooms, even a dedicated hall in which the sons of the sultans were circumcised. This immense complex must have seemed more dreadful with every step Aimée took towards it through the busy streets of the city.

When she finally entered the second court, an enormous black man bore down on her to inspect this gift to his master, Abdül Hamit I. The man's headgear (a turban topped with flamingo plumes) indicated his station as Chief Black Eunuch. This was the Kizlar Aga, known as 'His Black Highness'. In his feathers and a flowing cloak lined with ermine, he must have seemed terrifying to the young woman. The scene could not have been enhanced for her by a further tribute, in the background: a pile of severed heads, some still bleeding. At the Gate of Felicity, Aimée was not happy at all; indeed, she promptly swooned.

In her unconscious state, Aimée would hardly have been aware of another portal, one that would assume far greater importance for her – that of the harem. These were the luxurious quarters of the sultan's women, presided over by his mother, the Valide Sultan, and populated by his wives, his concubines and their guardians, the eunuchs.

The Valide Sultan exercised considerable power, presiding over her son's harem and managing the family business. She organised marriages for the princesses and other females of the harem, and groomed concubines for her son. She also worked outside the harem, supporting certain factions by marrying her daughters to men of high office in the government, such as the viziers, or the military or religious establishment. These sultan mothers held an elevated position, summed up by a popular Turkish proverb: 'A man might have many wives but has only one mother.'

At any one time, up to one thousand concubines inhabited the sultan's harem. There was a strict hierarchy: at the top was the sultan's mother. Then came the *kadines*, women who had also given birth to royal children. The *kadines* with sons outranked those with daughters and could hope to become Valide Sultan themselves.

After the *kadines* were the women who had attracted the attention of the sultan and had slept with him, but had not yet become pregnant or safely delivered a royal child. Then there were the women who had attracted the attention of the sultan but who were yet to be led down the Golden Way – the alley that runs from the harem to the sultan's apartments – and deflowered. The alleyway is said to owe its name to a custom whereby each newly installed sultan would throw gold to the staff as he entered the harem for the first time, as an adult man.

Aimée was admitted to the school for royal favourites, which taught the newest recruits to the harem how to dress, how to behave and, above all, how to please a man. Or rather, one man. With her long blonde hair, fair skin and pale eyes, it wasn't long before Abdül Hamit selected her for his couch.

But when the time came for the Kizlar Aga to take Aimée down the path to meet her lord in private, she created an unprecedented fuss. The Kizla Aga was aghast at the violence of her outburst. This was the sultan's realm, a place in which he was never rebuffed and never had any competition. But if Aimée continued in this way and was dragged to the sultan, she might be dangerous and attempt to harm him. Then the Kizlar Aga's life would be on the line, and he could look forward to strangulation with a piece of bowstring. If he didn't deliver the girl, though, he would also be in trouble. Faced with this dilemma, the senior eunuch took himself off to consult one of the *kadines*.

She understood the problem immediately and counselled Aimée to face up to her fate. There was no escape, she pointed out. Very few women left the seraglio who were not dead or about to be so (many who fell from favour or who were discovered to be unfaithful were sewn into weighted sacks and thrown off Seraglio Point into the Bosphorus below). And besides, if she didn't comply, the power of the unpopular chief *kadine*, Ayşe Seniyeperver, could not be curtailed – because, with Sultan Abdül Hamit's own mother long dead, the mother of his eldest son effectively filled the role of Valide Sultan.

Aimée paid attention: she laid back, thought of Martinique, and became the royal favourite. Renamed 'Nakşidil' (the Beautiful One), she fulfilled her duty and became the mother of Mahmut II within a year. That was 1785, and Abdül Hamit I's reign had less than four years to run.

The pleasures of the flesh proved Abdül Hamit's undoing. After Aimée, he became deeply enamoured of a new favourite, Ruşah. 'My mistress, I am your bound slave,' he wrote to her in a letter that is preserved in the Topkapi Museum. 'Beat me or kill me if you wish.' As it happened, she loved him to death. He had a stroke and died at the age of sixty-four in 1879, and was succeeded by his nephew, Selim III. As custom dictated, the new sultan immediately locked up Abdül Hamit's sons, Mustafa, aged ten, and Mahmut, who was nearly four. The two boys were incarcerated in the Cage, the infamous rooms of the palace where the brothers, nephews and male cousins of the sultan were kept until they succeeded, died or (most likely) were murdered.

Selim ruled until 1807, when he abdicated in favour of his feeble-minded cousin, Mustafa IV, who by that time had spent eighteen years inside the Cage. But the Cage seemed to have a revolving door at times. In 1808, Mustafa was deposed and returned to it – and the 23-year-old Mahmut was installed in his place. His mother, Nakşidil, the former convent schoolgirl, unexpectedly became Valide Sultan. Her triumph was complete, and a lifetime away from the day she entered the Gate of Felicity.

As we walked through the rooms of the palace, the private quarters of the women, the school rooms of the sons of the sultan, and the *hammam* of the Valide Sultan, Nebi Bey proved to be a fund of information and a charming, urbane host. With him, the past came vividly to life. He showed me the library, the kitchens, the circumcision room (a whole room for such a small piece of flesh), the kiosk, the view of the Golden Horn from the top of Seraglio Point, the relics of the Prophet, the portraits of the sultans, their war museums, and their magnificent treasures. The more he showed me, the more I understood how overwhelming it must have been for a woman like Aimée to be suddenly thrust into this, one of the most opulent and sensuous courts in history.

As Nebi talked to me in his measured French, I was half-seduced by the sensuality and the secrecy of the place. And that's to say nothing of the wonder of the tiles and the taps in the windows of the sultans' private refuge, a world that existed largely without men.

In *Inside the Seraglio*, American writer John Freely declares that this romantic story of a French girl who became the mother of a sultan is apocryphal. Whether or not the story of Aimée Du Bucq de Rivéry is true, it deserves retelling.

There were many women like Nakşidil, stolen from their homes and families, sold in the principal slave markets of the Ottoman Empire – Constantinople and Cairo – and destined for the Golden Way of the sultan. A few of them, through their sexual power over the ruler, or through their sons on the throne, became some of the most powerful women in the world.

Chapter 9

Ladies of Letters

ONE MORNING, KNOWING MY curiosity about harems, Nebi Bey took me to visit Dr Nevzat Kaya, director of the Süleymaniye Library and an expert on the Ottoman sultans. I asked him about the most powerful women in the empire and how they became so.

According to Dr Kaya, the Valide Sultans made their position by a combination of good works and politics. Good works? Wasn't that contrary to the Western belief that the harem was a den of iniquity, a dangerous and secretive place?

'There are no records of what went on there, and what information we do have is gleaned by the purchasing orders of the kitchens,' Dr Kaya explained. 'Up to 1839, the Topkapi and the other palaces were modest, well-run places. But after 1839, overspending ruined the system.'

The word 'harem' translates as 'closed' or 'refuge', a world forbidden to men. Paradoxically, much of what the modern world knows of the Ottoman harem of the early eighteenth century comes from a European woman. Those letters by Lady Mary Wortley Montagu, whose adventurous life stretched from 1689 to 1761, provide a vivid and entertaining look inside the sanctuary of the sultans – and the realm of women stolen or bought, enslaved and then made the wives or mistresses of members of the Ottoman court.

As the wife of Edward Wortley Montagu, the British ambassador-designate to Turkey, Lady Mary arrived in 'the city of the world's desire', Constantinople, in 1716, and was determined from the start to write a true account of the Ottoman Empire. With unprecedented access for a foreign woman – and, more importantly, egress

– she recorded her adventures with a sharp eye for detail.

For this vantage point, she was indebted to her birth as well as her marriage. Born in 1689, Mary was the eldest daughter of Lady Mary Fielding and a wealthy Whig peer, Evelyn Pierrepont (later the Marquess of Dorchester and Duke of Kingston). Like other women of her class at that time, Mary was educated at home. Unusually, she was an ardent student, and would spend up to fourteen hours a day in her father's library, reading and secretly teaching herself Latin. By the time she was fourteen she was familiar with French and English authors such as Dryden, Molière, Aphra Behn and Congreve. (Later in life, Mary continued her contacts with the literati, becoming close to her cousin Henry Fielding and corresponding with Rousseau, Voltaire and Montesquieu.)

By the age of twenty-one, she had translated Epictetus's *Enchiridion* and was so confident of her work on the Stoic philosopher's handbook for living that she sent a copy to a bishop, taking care to include a letter advocating a woman's right to formal education. At this time she also embarked on a correspondence with Edward Wortley Montagu, a Whig member of parliament like her father. She fictionalised their relationship, claiming it was as much her wit and independent thinking as her physical beauty that had won Edward's attentions.

Her father and fiancé negotiated the terms of the marriage settlement on economic grounds – an arrangement that included no input from Lady Mary herself. She later complained that marriagable women of her rank were simply commodities, and that she had no idea what price had been set by her father.[1] When Wortley Montagu would not agree to the terms and conditions, however, the marquess forbade the match.

That interdict ensured that Mary and Edward could do nothing else but marry. They eloped in 1712, and their son was born the following year. By 1714, Wortley Montagu was junior commissioner of the Treasury and the three were living in London, where Lady Mary worked with the poets Alexander Pope and John Gay.

During the following year, she suffered from smallpox, a disease that left her permanently scarred, without eyelashes. Her beauty was ruined. She took the loss of her looks philosophically, writing in an essay, 'The Nonsense of Common Sense' (published in 1738), that prettiness was the consolation prize women received for being locked out of the decision-making processes of life.

Lady Mary's illness seems to have had two effects: she came to appreciate the anonymity of the veil, and she became an advocate for smallpox inoculation. When her daughter was born in 1718, she had both her and her son inoculated and, on her return to England, published her brief 'Plain Account of the Inoculating of the Small Pox' in the *Flying-Post* in 1722.

Mary's marriage was not a great success. But when Wortley Montagu was dispatched to Turkey, Mary's twin careers as foreign correspondent and anthropologist were born. Her letters from the British Embassy in Turkey reflect the life of the Ottoman court through the prism of her keen mind and demonstrate the truth in her claim that she didn't think like most girls of her age. Indeed, she was witty, fresh and frank, as the following extract shows.

> I am well acquainted with a Christian woman of quality, who made it her choice to live with a Turkish husband, and is a very agreeable sensible Lady . . . She is a Spaniard, and was at Naples with her family when that Kingdom was part of the Spanish dominion. Coming from thence in a felucca, accompanied by her brother, they were attacked by the Turkish admiral, boarded and taken; and now, how shall I modestly tell you the rest of her adventure?[2]

Mary then related the story of the woman, whose brother and his entourage rushed to Spain to collect the ransom, and sent it to her Turkish captor:

> The Turk took the money, which he presented to her, and told her she was at Liberty. But the lady very discreetly weighed the different treatment she was likely to find in her native country. Her Catholic relations, as the kindest thing they could do for her in her present circumstances, would certainly confine her to a nunnery for the rest of her days. Her

> infidel lover was very handsome, very tender, fond of her, and lavished at her feet all the Turkish magnificence.[3]

The Spanish woman told her kidnapper that the only way he could restore her honour was to marry her, and asked that he accept the ransom as her dowry. She would have 'the satisfaction of knowing no man could boast of her favours without being her husband'.[4] The admiral returned the ransom to the lady's family, 'saying he was too happy in her possession'; the two were subsequently married, and 'as she says herself . . . she never had any reason to repent the choice she made'.[5] When the admiral died, she became one of the richest widows in Constantinople, but could not 'remain honourably a single woman' and so decided to marry the new *Capitan pasha*, her late husband's successor.[6]

Mary believed that her friend had not fallen in love with her ravisher, but 'acted wholly on principles of honour', although the author did concede that perhaps the Spanish lady had been 'reasonably touched at his generosity, which is very often found amongst the Turks of rank'.[7]

In her dress and behaviour, Lady Mary herself was something of a scandal, taking snuff and dressing like a man – a *Muslim* man. She was also impressed by the beauty of the women of the Turkish sultan's harem. 'They have naturally the most beautiful complexions in the world and generally large black Eyes,' she wrote to her sister. 'I can assure you with great truth that the court of England (though I believe it the fairest in Christendom) cannot shew so many beauties as are under our protection here.'[8]

An avid student of her new world, Mary learned Arabic, read Arabic poetry and discussed Islamic practices with key Turkish personalities of the time. Impressed with her new surroundings, she thought the women of the seraglio in a better position than women of her own country; they were 'perhaps freer than any ladies in the universe'.[9]

It is hardly a surprise that when the time came for the Wortley Montagus to leave Constantinople, Mary deeply regretted having to go. Used to the air and familiar with the language, she noted, 'I am easy here.'[10] To 'the admirable Mr Hill', a contemporary writer who had claimed that Turkish women were confined, she wrote:

> It is also very pleasant to observe how tenderly he and all his brethren voyage-writers lament the miserable confinement of the Turkish ladies, who are (perhaps) freer than any Ladies in the universe, and are the only women in the world that lead a life of uninterrupted pleasure, exempt from cares, their whole time being spent in visiting, bathing, or the agreeable amusement of spending money and inventing new fashions. A husband would be thought mad that exacted any degree of economy from his wife, whose expenses are no way limited but by her own fancy. It is his business to get money and hers to spend it, and this noble prerogative extends itself to the very meanest of the sex.[11]

Mary's life after Constantinople was no less full of movement and drama. She ended her days in London, after travelling widely in Europe. She died of cancer there in 1761, not long after her estranged husband. Her family, notably her daughter, Lady Bute, tried to prevent the publication of her letters, but they were printed in 1763 and were widely read and appreciated. They give a unique view of life for women inside the harem, one quite at odds with the Orientalist view that came to prevail, that these harems were dens of endless iniquity for debauched Turks and Arabs.

Isabel Burton, the wife of Sir Richard, the diplomat, also travelled extensively in the region, though more than fifty years after Lady Mary. She was another who recorded her impressions of the harems she saw:

> I found them very pleasant; only at first the women used to ask me such a lot of inconvenient questions that I became quite confused. They were always puzzled because I had no children.
>
> One cannot generalize on the subject of harems; they differ in degree just as much as families in London. A first-class harem at Constantinople is one thing, at Damascus one of the same rank is another, while those of the middle and lower classes are different still.
>
> One of the first harems I visited in Damascus was that of

> the famous Abd el Kadir . . . He had five wives: one of them was very pretty. I asked them how they could bear to live together and pet each other's children. I told them that in England, if a woman thought her husband had another wife or mistress, she would be ready to kill her and strangle the children if they were not her own. They all laughed heartily at me, and seemed to think it a great joke. I am afraid that Abd el Kadir was a bit of a Tartar in his harem, for they were very prim and pious.[12]

While European painters depicted lives of ease in harems, the reality was rather more bracing. In the early 1600s, newly admitted women to the harem led lives characterised by a strict monasticism. There was no luxury for them: they endured harsh and coarse woollen bedding, and the lamps were left burning all night so that the older women guarding them could see what they got up to.

Still, traditionally, women in this part of the world were highly valued. According to Ibn Battuta, a wandering Moor who visited the region in 1336, just as the Ottomans were consolidating their power, the wives of the Tatars and the Turks were accorded high social rank and even held a more 'dignified' position than men.[13]

And there was a time during the Ottoman Empire when women actually ruled, albeit through their sons. For around one hundred and thirty years during the sixteenth and seventeenth centuries, the women of the sultan's harem wielded unprecedented political influence and, in some cases, real power. Now called the Sultanate of Women, it's an era that some (generally male) historians say was the beginning of the end for the Ottoman Empire.

The power of these women originated in the harem, but spread throughout the empire. Their enemies constantly warned succeeding sultans about the perilous practice of listening to women too much and taking their advice. Around the same time, on the edge of another continent, the Scottish firebrand John Knox was beating the same drum. Alienated by the usurpation of power by Mary Queen of Scots, he fired off a treatise that declared: 'To promote a woman to bear rule, superiority, dominion, or empire above any realm, nation, or city, is repugnant to nature; contumely to God, a thing most contrary to his revealed will and approved ordinance; and finally, it is the subversion of good order, of all equity and justice.'[14]

But some extraordinary women carved roles for themselves out of the hidden world of the harem, as we have seen in the story of Aimée de Rivéry. The picture emerging from the archives is not of a collection of rapacious concubines, self-seeking and self-serving wives and mothers managing useless regent sons. In fact, the women had roles to play in the court, to further the interests of the Royal House of Osman, and were often in contact with European courts. Nurbanu, the mother of Murat III, dealt with Catherine de Medici when the Italian-born queen of France requested a giraffe, other exotic animals and twelve Abyssinian slaves. Safiye Sultan, the mother of Sultan Mehmet III, was in correspondence with Elizabeth I, who sent presents, including a coach and an organ, the last of which arrived with its maker and was installed in the porticoed garden of the Topkapi's privy chamber.

The Valide Sultans also filled military coffers from their own purses when the Treasury came up short. In addition, many women of the harem were the patrons of architects, and thus changed the built environment of the capital and provincial centres with their endowments. Turkish historian Professor Lucienne Thys-Şenocak lists some of their beneficence as 'Mosques, baths, soup kitchens, markets, palaces, and fountains'.[15] From the bustling spice bazaar of Eminönü to the striking double bath on the grounds of the ancient Hippodrome, through their many buildings, the sultans' women continue to have a highly visible presence in Istanbul's landscape.

They also donated further afield: the Valide Sultan Hürrem endowed a soup kitchen in Jerusalem, locating it on the site of a pilgrim's hospice said to have been built by Helena, the Christian mother of the Roman emperor Constantine. Hürrem, who was originally known as Roxelana, was the best known of the sultans' consorts. Süleyman the Magnificent already had a chief wife – Gulbahar, 'the Rose of Spring' – and a son, Mustafa, when he first encountered Hürrem. But he became increasingly enthralled with her. At the same time, he was interested in the talents of Ibrahim, another of his slaves. Ibrahim quickly advanced to grand vizier, and Hürrem ('Laughing One'), the captive Slav Roxelana, became Süleyman's wife.

To consolidate her power, Roxelana moved first against the vizier, Ibrahim, who had been raised to the rank of commander-in-chief and was campaigning in Persia. When he returned, Ibrahim was strangled. Roxelana then worked to rid herself of Mustafa, Süleyman's firstborn son. It was a matter of protecting her blood: if he succeeded to the throne, Mustafa would commit fratricide and murder Roxelana's own sons.

She got Mustafa's mother, Gulbahar, away from court and arranged to have her own son-in-law, Rustem Paşa, appointed as grand vizier. Rustem reported that Mustafa was so popular that his troops wanted him to overthrow Süleyman and lead the empire. Mustafa was summoned to Süleyman to explain, and in his father's tent found death in the customary manner: strangulation by bowstring. Left standing at the end of the civil wars that followed was the most useless of Roxelana's sons, Selim the Sot, whose reign marked the beginning of the Sultanate of Women.

Roxelana was widely admired for her generosity and beneficence, and is now best remembered for the buildings she commissioned. Sinan, considered the finest Ottoman architect of all, created a complex for her around the Süleymaniye Mosque in Constantinople, a collection that includes a madrasah, a public kitchen and bath, and a hospital which functions to this day. Roxelana is still there, entombed near her husband in a garden of roses behind his mosque.

Her reputation grew over the centuries outside the empire as well. The sixteenth-century Valide Sultan would be celebrated over the coming years in Europe in plays such as *Roxelana* and *Sultane*, as well as in François Couperin's sonata *La Sultane* (1726) and Rossini's opera of 1813, *Italian Girl in Algiers*. In addition, her face inspired painters such as Titian, who imagined her in a double portrait with her husband.

Historians generally mark the beginning of the Sultanate of Women with Roxelana's time as favourite, in 1557, and its end with the death of Hadice Turhan, Mehmet IV's mother, in the late seventeenth century. The story of Hadice Turhan and her mother-in-law, Kösem, is perhaps the most alarming of all the tales that have emerged from the shadows of the Topkapi harem.

Kösem was born on the Greek island of Tinos, where she was Anastasia, the daughter of a Greek Orthodox priest. Captured by slavers, she was taken to Constantinople, where she soon became the favourite of Ahmet I, and the mother of his sons, the future sultans Murat and Ibrahim. When Murat ascended the Ottoman throne, Kösem became Valide Sultan. But Murat's reign was troubled from the start. The standing infantry, the Janissaries, revolted in 1631, entering the Topkapi Palace and murdering the grand vizier as well as the sultan's favourite page, the Grand Mufti, and a number of other high officials.

Initially, Murat followed the orders of his troops, but within six months he retook the government, executed the vizier he had been forced to accept, and had more that five hundred Janissaries strangled and their bodies thrown into the Bosphorus. Cruel and strong-willed, Murat had his brother Beyezid murdered for unseating him in a joust, then had two other siblings killed. He would have murdered his brother Ibrahim had their mother not convinced him that Ibrahim was mad and no threat.

Although an able administrator, Murat was a maniac who managed to execute an estimated twenty-five thousand of his subjects during his reign. To reduce the opportunity for sedition, he closed coffee houses and taverns, and banned alcohol and coffee, threatening execution to those found drinking them, even though Murat himself continued to indulge in both.

The Valide Sultan Kösem tried to make sure her son was not waylaid by women or procreating; instead, she flung boys in his way, so he ended up a total misogynist. Once, when a boat full of women sailed too close to the harem walls, his gunners were told to open fire. The boat sank, and the women drowned.

Despite Murat's many sins, Kösem still worried about him. She wrote a complaint universally familiar to all mothers, about how her son kept such long hours and was risking his health.

During his final years, she had even more to worry about. Murat was not only a murderer but also an alcoholic, and he eventually died of cirrhosis of the liver. That happy release for the Ottoman Empire brought his sole surviving brother, Ibrahim, to the throne.

Kösem had to coax him out of the Cage to take up his reign but, once he was on the throne, the demented Ibrahim started to make up for the time he had lost. His mother acted as regent, which freed up Ibrahim for more priapic pursuits. Kösem kept him busy by supplying virgins and increasingly fat women to sate his appetites.

In 1641, Hadice Turhan, one of Ibrahim's concubines, gave birth to his first son, Prince Mehmet. Meanwhile, his madness raged on. When he was told that his one of his concubines had been with another man, he had some two hundred and eighty of them sewn into sacks and thrown off Seraglio Point. He spared only two, Sechir Para and Hadice Turhan. It was a brief reprieve for Sechir though: Kösem, jealous of the younger woman's influence, invited her for dinner and had her killed.

When Ibrahim had fathered six sons, he had served his dynastic purpose. He was deposed by another revolt of the Janissaries and then murdered. The end of his reign, in 1648, should have marked the end of Kösem's period as Valide Sultan. But she wanted to hang on to power, so when Ibrahim's seven-year-old son, Mehmet IV, became the new sultan, she simply refused to move to the old dower palace to make way for the boy's mother, Hadice Turhan. Then, after much plotting and taking of sides within the royal household, Kösem was eventually murdered by her enemies.

Hadice Turhan was triumphant. Since her son Mehmet was still a child, she took control of his sultanate. It couldn't have been easy at first, since she was not a sophisticated woman and was unversed in affairs of state. But a decade in the harem, close to the administration of the empire, had given her an education in how the system worked. She was a quick study, as one of her viziers discovered when she sent an envoy to check on the state of the navy. In a subsequent letter to the vizier, Hadice Turhan included a chilly reproof: the vizier was not to think she could be fooled, nor that she didn't know what was going on.

Like Roxelana, Hadice Turhan was a builder. Among her works are a number of fortresses at the Aegean entrance to the Dardanelles, and the Yeni Valide Sultan Mosque and its adjoining Egyptian Bazaar in the heart of the Ottoman capital.[16] With her death in 1687, the Sultanate of Women came to an end, leaving present-day historians to try to assess its impact on the Ottoman Empire.

Chapter 10

The Longest Day

THE PALE SUNLIGHT OF early autumn filtered through the leaves of a large tree, dappling the lane below. Casually looking up towards its source, Ayhan was galvanised. '*Incir!*' the driver muttered and leapt into action.

'Figs,' translated Nebi Bey, as he helped harvest the fruit overhanging the car. Our little party – Ayhan, Nebi, Mustapha, our local Gallipoli guide, and myself – were starving, so this feast was manna from Heaven. We settled down to an impromptu late lunch of unexpected luxury after a hard morning in the battlefields.

This skinny back street of Bigali, a hamlet close to the town of Eceabat on the Gallipoli Peninsula, remained free of gunfire as we chewed our way through the juicy fruit that Ayhan continued to pull enthusiastically off the boughs.

Nebi Bey gravely handed me another fig. I split the outer, pale green, velvety skin. The flesh inside caught the sun and glowed like fire.

What a difference ninety years makes. In World War I, Bigali was the local headquarters of Mustafa Kemal – later known as Atatürk, the founder of the modern Turkish nation – during the long and bloody Gallipoli campaign. The place would have been heaving then with the comings and goings of soldiers and officers, and it was easy to imagine the driver of Atatürk's staff car idly picking figs while waiting to take the commander to the ridge at Chunuk Bair for a dress-circle seat overlooking warships at sea and the fighting on the beaches and in the trenches.

Our historical view of Gallipoli is far removed from the living

Hell of battle: to us, it's theory. It's hard to reconcile this place now – beautiful, quiet and sunny near the bright-blue Aegean – with the smoke, fire and daily obscenity of violent death back in 1915. The thump of distant explosions from the beachheads echoing up and down these lanes would have provided the soundtrack to Atatürk's days. We, however, heard birdsong as we sat outside the house the Turkish commander used as his peninsular headquarters.

Atatürk arrived in Bigali in late winter, 25 February 1915, to head the 19th Divisional Command and stayed for ten-and-a-half months. Upstairs in his study, he would have pored over reports and maps from the front. His desk is still there, and I found it difficult to imagine so great an enterprise being directed from something as insubstantial as this spindle-shanked, spavined table, but this was a field base, not some well-equipped operations room in the Turkish War Office.

Adjacent to the study is Atatürk's monastic bed chamber; directly downstairs is a kitchen, and besides that, a dining room. The carpets and cushions looked as though the commander and his lieutenants had just got up from them and gone out into the courtyard for a breath of air.

My day had started in the pre-dawn gloom, when Nebi and Ayhan collected me from the hotel. After an hour's driving, heading west on the E80, we escaped the suburban sprawl of Istanbul and its thirteen million denizens and stopped for breakfast at a *borek* restaurant in Tekirdağ, a good-sized town on the edge of the Sea of Marmara.

Dawn broke over the boardwalk funfair as we tucked in to our meal. For whippet-thin Ayhan, breakfast was *puf borek*, deep-fried pastries stuffed with cheese and chunky marmalade, a cigarette, and a cup of Turkish coffee. I had apple tea as Nebi pressed little sweetmeats on me. They were *helva*, a confection made from semolina, and the oldest pudding in Turkish cuisine.

'You remember what the Ottomans always said?' asked Nebi, former diplomat and consummate flirt. 'Eat sweet and talk sweet!'

A few hours later, we arrived at Eceabat, on the eastern side of the peninsula. Nebi Bey informed me that in Turkey, Gallipoli is called Gelibolu, while the site of the World War I campaign is known as

Çanakkale. We were to collect Mustapha, our battlefields guide, just before lunch, but since he seemed to be missing in action I wandered down to the wharf from where the vehicle ferry crosses to Çanakkale, fifteen hundred metres away in Asia. These were the Narrows of the Straits of the Dardanelles, a name drummed into the skulls of Australian school children for generations. I don't know what I expected . . . something bigger, perhaps, and terrifying, to match the resonance of the name in my mind. But this dark, choppy passage glittering in the noon sunlight, with its flotilla of container ships and tankers, was neither big nor terrifying.

The Dardanelles, 61 kilometres long and from 1.2 to 6.4 kilometres wide, divides European Turkey from Asiatic Turkey – or, in earlier times, Thrace and Anatolia. Linking the Aegean to the Sea of Marmara, this is the shipping lane that the world's merchants must pass through to get to the Bosphorus and on to the grain- and oil-rich Black Sea ports of the Ukraine, Romania and the Caucasus.

The Ancients called the strait the Hellespont, Helle's Sea, to commemorate Helle, a mythical Boetian princess who drowned in it after she fell off the back of the ram with the golden fleece. It was a fatal shore, too, for Leander, according to mythology. The handsome young man fell in love with Hero, a beautiful priestess of Aphrodite who lived in a tower overlooking the Hellespont. Every night, Hero was said to have put a light in a window of the tower, inviting Leander, who lived on the other bank, to come over.

Things went swimmingly that summer, when the strait was calm. But one night as the winter closed in, Hero felt the need for a little body heat. Despite the dicey weather, she put the lamp in the window to summon Leander. He saw the light and made an attempt to reach her. The following morning, the unsatisfied Hero looked out of her high window and saw Leander broken on the rocks below. Horrified, she jumped to join him in death.

The weather was obviously better in 480 BC, when the Persian king Xerxes I had a pontoon bridge thrown across the strait on his way to invade Greece. Showing he had learned something from history, Alexander the Great did the same in 334 BC when he was marching to invade Persia.

Some sixteen hundred years later, the Ottomans began to acquire territory in the region. The first of the great land-grabs happened on the European side in 1354, under Sultan Orhan. The acquisitions spread across to Çanakkale, on the other side of the Dardanelles, during the time of Murat I, in 1362. The Ottomans garrisoned and fortified the region: Kilitbahir ('Lock of the Sea') Castle was built in 1452 by Murat's relative, Mehmet II, and by 1463, a castle directly opposite it at Çanakkale was up. There were thirty cannons in each castle, which could hurl cannonballs straight across the Dardanelles, making it unpassable.

By the time Atatürk took up residence in Bigali, the fortifications of the strait were fragile, suffering from age and stress. The first line of defence were four forts at the entrance to the strait; seventeen kilometres further up were other forts and a line of mines strung from shore to shore; and the huge stone fortress from the fifteenth century were the third line of defence. It looked good on paper, but the materiel was old-fashioned and ineffective.

The Turks had previously been allied with the British to hold the Dardanelles and deprive Russia of her Mediterranean access, but a couple of disastrous diplomatic decisions, combined with the assiduous courting of the Turks by the Germans, meant that Enver Paşa, the war minister and Ottoman commander-in-chief, was in the camp of the Central Powers (Germany, Austro-Hungary and Bulgaria). He signed a secret alliance with them on 2 August 1914, the day after they declared war on Russia. By 4 August, the Central Powers were at war with the member nations of the Entente Cordiale (Britain, France and Russia). The British, who wanted to get aid through to Russia's Black Sea ports, launched a massive attack on the Gallipoli Peninsula. The Turks were determined to hold the line, and their land, at any cost. And so the disaster of Gallipoli was set in motion.

The tone of our big day out, which had begun as a light-hearted road trip, grew sombre after Mustapha joined us: it became a pilgrimage to some of the powerful sacred sites that tie the people of the Turkish Republic to those of Australia and New Zealand. For Nebi, it was a personal pilgrimage as well. His grandfather died on this narrow, hilly peninsula, which stretches some eighty kilometres from the European mainland to its tip at Cape Hellas.

There are some thirty-odd Allied cemeteries dotted along its length, more than twenty of them close to Anzac Cove, which sits on the narrow waist across the middle of the peninsula. (The two main Anzac war memorials are at Lone Pine, slightly to the south of Anzac Cove, for the Australians, and Chunuk Bair, inland and to the north-west of the cove, for the Kiwis.) The Turkish war graves are less formally presented, but generally indicated by groves of cypress trees. Most of those who died here, though, whatever their nationality, are not buried in marked graves.

We began at Cape Helles, where the monolithic Martyrs' Memorial (some 41 metres high) dominates the land- and seascape for kilometres. There's a garden cemetery, full of Mehmets – Mehmet from Benghazi, Mehmet from Edirne, Mehmet from Bursa – just some of the estimated quarter of a million Turkish servicemen who died defending their motherland.

Thinking about that generation of destroyed promise, among them Nebi Bey's grandfather, was overwhelming. The Gallipoli Memorial was inscribed in 1934 with Atatürk's message for those who died here and those who loved them: 'Those heroes who shed their blood and lost their lives, you are now lying in the soil of a friendly country . . . After having lost their lives on this land they become our sons as well.'

We continued on through the British and Canadian cemeteries, and then we got to the place called Hell Spit, the southern end of Anzac Cove. The Anzacs had been aiming for Gabatepe, a wide beach and a soft landing, but missed. Instead, on 25 April 1915, they arrived 1.5 kilometres further north, at Ari Burnu, the spot now known as Anzac Cove. Twenty thousand Anzacs landed on this beach in the two days following the first assault, and they faced Atatürk's well-armed and well-entrenched forces. Thousands died, and many of them were buried in Hell Spit.

From April to December, the Aegean ran red. Among the Anzacs, more that fifteen thousand men were recorded killed in action, some ten thousand went missing in action, and a further twenty-one thousand died of disease. Typhus, lice, gangrene, lack of fresh water, and poor food and sanitary conditions took their toll.

The annual Anzac Day ceremony at Anzac Cove now attracts

attendances of up to twenty thousand, so large a crowd that a new site has been developed to accommodate them and minimise damage to the cemeteries and their surroundings. These people attend despite the difficulty of access to the Gallipoli Peninsula: the only way for most visitors to get there is a four- to five-hour drive from Istanbul. It's worth the effort, though.

By the time our little group made it to the Australian Memorial at Lone Pine, the sadness of the place and the knowledge of the pathetic futility of the war was overwhelming. As I sat on a stone wall near the famous, eponymous tree, I watched a young Turk, a boy of perhaps seventeen or eighteen, dancing across the top of the stone at the memorial where the soldiers' collective epitaph is recorded: *Their names liveth for evermore.* I felt unsettled, offended by the teenager at first, but was almost immediately grateful that he was alive and able to dance when so many like him – some as young as sixteen, and buried in the ground here – had never had that chance, and when generations of their children remained unborn.

The memorial was silent, and it was impossible to avoid reading the names of the men interred there and wonder about them. Sergeant Shepherd, who died on 29 November, not long before the withdrawal, was just eighteen. Private Maas, who died on the same day, lies next to him for eternity. He is under a headstone that reads: *God is Love.*

Having grown up with Anzac Day ceremonies over the years, I'd thought I knew about Gallipoli – all those grainy black-and-white images of the battleground, of Simpson and his donkey, of Turkish soldiers in their distinctive headgear, of pine-covered trenches. I'd read the Australian official war historian, Charles Bean, and had imagined Anzac Cove the way he saw it: a convoy of dead soldiers washing in and out on the beach break, as the living struggled to survive long enough to get across the sand and under cover; when they got there, they discovered that to survive the landing and then die by inches was no bargain. As it turned out, though, I hadn't even known the true name of the place. And nothing could have prepared me for the immensity of the experience, of the connectedness with humanity that swept over me for men dead ninety years.

The sadness of Gelibolu clung to the day as we drove the two hundred or so kilometres back to Istanbul. Back in my hotel room, I took off my dusty clothes, slid into a hot bath and let tears of sadness and exhaustion fall into the rose-oil-scented water. Cleansed, I wrapped myself in the thick towelling robe, pulled up an armchair and from my window watched the ships that had come through the Dardanelles that afternoon heading up towards the Black Sea. The lights of Asia twinkled through the darkness as I picked idly at some of the *helva* that Nebi had pressed on me as he said goodnight. Then I climbed into the crisp, white cloud of my bed, pulled the covers over my head and fell asleep wondering about the vicissitudes of life. Today, I had a brief visit to Hell; tomorrow I was to get a glimpse of Heaven.

Chapter 11

Sufis Unto the Day

ONE AFTERNOON, NEBI BEY and I were seated in Galata Mevlevi Lodge, an eighteenth-century building in Istanbul's Tünel district. It was once the monastery of the main sect of the Sufi mystics, the Mevlevi, and a centre of music and literature, until the beginning of the twentieth century. Calligraphers, composers and scholars, among them the poet and scholar Galip Dede, studied in the building, which is now preserved as a museum of classical Ottoman poetry. Traces of mosque design can still be seen in the *mihrab* in the back wall orientating towards Mecca, and an adjacent *minbar*.

There was something in the air that afternoon when Nebi and I arrived and joined the seventy or so other visitors. It was the quiet expectancy of a place of worship just before a ceremony begins.

On the last Sunday of every month, that stillness is ruffled when the Whirling Dervishes – as these Sufis are commonly known – perform for the tourists, and give a brief insight into their practices. In the lower gallery, Nebi and I were bathed in the last of the afternoon light. Sunbeams slanted through the high windows behind the upper minstrels' gallery, lit up motes of dust dancing in the air, and pooled on the octagonal wooden dance floor.

Suddenly, it started. An orchestra of women, their eyes modestly cast down, filed quietly into the space in the centre of the floor and began to play classical music from the Ottoman period. Then the dervishes themselves appeared – twelve men, dressed for the afterlife of the ego, their brown woollen cloaks representing graves; their white shirts, skirts and trousers their shrouds; and their conical hats of camel-hair felt shaped like tombstones.

With their arms crossed, their bodies representing the number one and the unity of God, eleven of the men started to walk slowly around the room, stopping in the rotations to salute the chief dervish, who was sitting on a sheepskin rug opposite the front door of the building. As they began to whirl anticlockwise, the dervishes' arms opened, their right hands pointing skyward to receive God's kindness and their left hands turned downwards, towards the earth. In this attitude, the Sufis believe they can convey God's spiritual gifts on his people. Whirling, revolving around the heart from right to left, they embrace all humankind, all of God's creation, with love.

Sufism, the mystic path of Islam, has been dividing adherents of the religion since it began to spread across Asia, through Asia Minor and the Middle East, and into North Africa. One of the earliest Sufi sects dates from Yemen in 657, when the archangel Gabriel is said to have instructed Üveys El-Karani to abandon material existence and choose the spiritual life. Simply put – and there seems to be nothing really simple about the tradition – Sufism's goal is to reach God in this world, as well as the next, via the Spiritual Path, or way towards God, by means of love and devotion.

What the West mainly sees of Sufism are these Whirling Dervishes, who seem to have twirled themselves into an ecstatic trance for the benefit of tourists for hundreds of years. But in reality, the performances for tourists are just for show – the real trances are achieved when the Sufis whirl to worship in the privacy of their own orders.

The performance Nebi Bey and I saw was long, repetitive and followed a definite pattern. First came the eulogy to the Prophet, then a drum sound, signifying the divine order of the creator. Then there was music, symbolising the first breath, which gives life to everything. After that, the dervishes greeted each other in a circular walk, repeated three times around the hall, which symbolises the salute of soul to soul concealed by the shapes and bodies.

One of the Sufis explained to Nebi and me afterwards that the ceremony in fact contains seven parts of the mystic cycle to perfection. It begins with a salute to mankind's birth to truth by feeling and mind, and continues to the annihilation of the self in the higher being. The purpose of the dance that follows the walking, he told us, is not to achieve ecstasy, but for the dancers themselves to realise, and then submit to, God.

According to the late Dr Celaleddin B Çelebi, a twenty-first generation descendant of the founder of the Mevlevi Sufis, the ceremony follows a strict order. After the first three parts – the eulogy to Mohammad and the drumbeat; the music; and the dervishes' repeated circular walk – the dance begins. It breaks into four movements of different rhythms (mankind's birth, recognition of God, submission to the will of God, and finally unity with God), so making the seven parts that the Sufi had suggested.

At the end of the ceremony, the Qur'an is recited, particularly *Sura* 2:115: 'To God belong the East and the West, and wherever you turn is the face of God. He is the All-Embracing, the All-Knowing.' A prayer for the souls of all believers and prophets follows, after which the dervishes retire to their rooms for a period of contemplation.

To quote Dr Çelebi:

> The whirling causes the mind to participate in the shared revolution of all things. It's a mystical journey of man's spiritual ascent through love to the perfect, kemal. Turning towards the truth, he grows through love, deserts ego, finds the truth, and then arrives at the perfect. Then he returns from his journey as a man who reached maturity and a greater perfection and can love and be of service to the whole of creation without discrimination.[1]

Were women allowed to be Sufis? I asked our Sufi friend.

'Yes, of course,' came the reply. 'But they do not take part in pubic performances.'

There have been famous Sufi women in history, like Rabi'a of Basra, one of the earliest and greatest mystic ascetics of Islam. Born into poverty in around 720, she is believed to have been orphaned, captured and sold into slavery. As a slave, she was taught the flute and became an accomplished musician. Always devout, she worked through the days and was often praying when dawn came.

One warm night, her master couldn't sleep, and looked out into his courtyard. There, under a lamp, was Rabi'a, again at her prayers. He could just make out that she was apologising to God: she had been so caught up in her domestic duties, he heard the slave say, that she was late in her duty to Him.

Then, as her master realised that the lamp was hanging without a chain, a radiance filled the house. Recognising this as a sign, he became certain that such a person should not be a slave and set her free. Rabi'a is then said to have retreated to the desert to live a life dedicated to God and prayer. Rejecting many offers of marriage, Rabi'a became a noted teacher. Her scholarship and piety wiped out any sense of her gender from the mind of her pupils, at the same time prompting enormous respect for her sincerity.

Rabi'a is best remembered for the emphasis she placed on the selfless love of God – rather than love of God and accompanying good works in the hope of eventual reward in Paradise. She is credited with having written this prayer: 'O Allah! If I worship You for fear of Hell, burn me in Hell, and if I worship You in hope of Paradise, exclude me from Paradise. But if I worship You for Your Own sake, grudge me not Your everlasting Beauty.' That's a view which might be anathema to those doing good works to build credit points for the hereafter, or suicide bombers planning on meeting their seventy-two dark-eyed virgins in Paradise.

Nebi and I were standing in the garden after the performance with the head of the museum when I looked down to find cats surging around the two men's feet. In fact, there were cats everywhere! They lounged around the flagged path, wrapped around the legs of the visitors, and when they were bored with that, the cats did a little whirling themselves around the headstones of the graves of past Sufi masters. The cats have a respected position here, as the head of the museum discovered when he took up his posting. He had tried to reduce their number by not putting food out when the horde descended for its previously informal daily feed. 'They make a terrible mess,' he told us.

But his was a lone voice in the wild cat kingdom of his garden. The locals first complained about him, and then menaced him in public when they discovered he did not have the same passion for the cats that they did. As a result, the feeding program was resumed.

'We are cleaning up the garden now, and we have discovered old entrance stones, in the shape of hats, at the entrance,' he said happily, his mind off the furry fiends for a minute.

Nebi Dey and I left the lodge and walked down what used to be the Grand Rue of Pera, the neighbourhood where foreigners in Constantinople congregated, removed from the functionaries of the Ottoman court and ordinary citizens. Lord Charlemont, the eighteenth-century Irish archaeologist and traveller, noted that Pera was: 'a large city entirely peopled by Franks and Greeks who live together in the most sociable manner and, with the public Ministers [ambassadors] for a society as pleasing as possible . . . scarce an evening passes without balls, concerts, or assemblies at all which the intercourse between the sexes is as easy as can be wished.'[2]

Nebi again played tour guide. He took me to see the famous Hotel Pera Palas, built to receive travellers on the Orient Express, and where Atatürk frequently stayed. Room 101, Atatürk's favourite, is now a museum to him. The hotel was also the meeting place and melting pot of the rich and famous. Among the guests since its opening in 1892 have been King Zog of Albania, Shah Reza Pahlavi of Iran, Edward VIII of Great Britain, King Ferdinand of Bulgaria, King Carol of Romania, President Tito of Yugoslavia, Jacqueline Kennedy, Agatha Christie and Yehudi Menuhin.

Nebi pointed out the location in Pera that were the scenes of the most violent terrorist attacks in Turkey's recent history. In mid November 2003, a car bomb and a truck bomb went off at the Beth Israel and Neve Shalom synagogues, killing an estimated twenty-seven people and wounding three hundred others. Five days later, two more blasts – one at the British Consulate, the other at the Turkish headquarters of the HSBC bank – killed thirty people, including the British consul-general, and wounded close to four hundred others.

We walked on through the balmy, romantic evening, through cooking smells outside the old flower market, and on towards Taksim Square, Ayhan and the car. The street was full of tourists as well as locals.

Nebi tucked my hand into the crook of his arm as he took me through a gate, across a courtyard and towards the church of

St Anthony of Padua, the largest Catholic church in Istanbul. Saint Anthony, the patron saint of Assisi, is the one I still pray to when I lose something. He never fails, so I was pleased to see churchgoers hurrying towards him for Mass.

Nebi asked me what I wanted to do the next morning.

'Man proposes, God disposes, my dear Nebi,' I said.

'Man proposes, *woman* disposes, *ma chère* Christine,' he replied.

It was all the same, we agreed. A higher being was involved, both times.

At midnight, after a session in my hotel's *hammam*, I was back on my balcony, a little unsettled by the day, despite the masseuse's ministrations. Nebi Bey was filling my days with unending stimulation and he was starting to take hold of my nights as well. I was becoming far too accustomed to him.

A sliver of the new moon hung in the sky over the Bosphorus and the Çirağan Palace. It was another moment to commit carefully to memory.

Chapter 12

At Home with the Amazons

LIKE WASHINGTON DC, ANKARA is a company town. Since the modern Turkish state was founded, in 1923, the business of this city in the heart of the Anatolian plateau has been government. I had arranged to go to the capital to interview the Turkish Minister of State for Women's Affairs, Mrs Guldal Aksıt. I dressed with particular care for that meeting in Ankara, which my personal weather forecaster had warned would be cooler than Istanbul. I put on a cream trouser suit under a long, black Italian fine-knit cardigan, along with some serious pearl earrings to give me a bit of corporate clout.

At 7.20 am, Nebi Bey and Ayhan were waiting.

'Ah, Nebi,' I said greeting my guide. 'There you are . . . the last person I see at night and the first person I see in the morning.'

'Ah, Christine,' he echoed. 'You are always so fresh and so beautiful.'

It was gratifying that he noticed and I set off to Ankara with quite a spring in my step.

However, when Egemen Moral, from the Ministry of Press and Information, met me at Ankara airport, he had bad news: the arrangements for the day had changed. Members of the Turkish government had more pressing matters to attend to that day than to talk to an Australian writer. Overnight, a Turkish hostage had been murdered in Iraq. Mrs Aksıt was in ministerial crisis talks.

Egemen, a gentle and reserved 25-year-old and recent university graduate, was my new dragoman, and he was a man with a plan. We would start at the Museum of Anatolian Civilisations, Ankara's renowned archaeology museum and winner of the European Museum of the Year Award in 1997. It was an unexpected treasure house, and encompassed the history of Anatolia from Stone Age to current times, the breadth of its collection attesting to the fact that the Anatolian plateau was one of the earliest crucibles of human civilisation.

People built their houses, farmed their fields (though it must have been hard going as Ankara sits in what looked from the air like a treeless dust bowl) and worshipped their gods here as long ago at 7250 BC. At the archaeological dig at Cayonu, close to modern Diyarbakir, which is the main city in south-eastern Turkey, relics of the first farmers of Anatolia have been found.

The most striking element about this museum was the number of female figurines that have been found here on Turkey's central plateau. Hundreds of them have been unearthed: fertility symbols, almost always naked, sometimes reclining, sometimes sitting, generally in the process of giving birth. These are among the earliest traces of the Mother Goddess cult, from which archaeologists have deduced the existence of a matriarchal society.

From around 7000 BC, the influence of this Earth Mother spread. She was eventually named Cybele by the Ancient Greeks, becoming identified with their Rhea, the mother of the gods, and Demeter, the goddess of fertility. In Ancient Rome, she was associated with Demeter's equivalent, Ceres.

By the Bronze Age, Anatolia's 'Kybele' was the goddess of caverns, the primitive Earth, and nature and fertility, presiding over mountains and fortresses. Her crown was in the form of a city wall.

The Hittites, an Iron Age culture, called her Kubaba. They arrived in Cappadocia, a region of Anatolia, in around 1800 BC, and set up their capital at Hattusas, north of modern-day Ankara. Theirs was a busy, productive kingdom, which gave particular freedoms and rights to its women. Queens such as Puduhepa, the wife of Hattusilis III, and the last queen of Suppiluliumas I, ruled alongside their husbands.

Some historians believe that a matrilineal system once prevailed in Anatolia, and that this formed the basis for the legend of the

Amazons, a nation of female warriors said to have originated in the Caucasus and to have founded a town (modern Terme) on the Black Sea coast of Turkey. They would replenish their numbers with the assistance of a neighbouring town, from whence they borrowed men for a mating period. Boys born from these unions were either murdered or sent back to the village of their fathers; girls were trained to become Amazons. Another Amazon legend relates that the women kept men in their community, but relegated them to the dual role of begetter of children and domestic drudge.

Like the consuls of the Roman Republic, two Amazons shared the rule of the nation: one took care of defence, and the other, internal affairs. The Amazons bore arms to defend their home ground, but also made forays into neighbouring countries. Devoted to Artemis, the goddess of the hunt, and skilled in the martial arts, they fought on foot as well as horseback (they were said to be the first humans to ride horses) and carried crescent shields, spears, bows and battle-axes. The Amazons were said to remove the right breasts of girls in order to improve the draw back on the bow and the flight of the javelin. One popular legend had them founding Ephesus – Efes in modern Turkey – and naming it after their queen, Ephesia.

Among the famous Amazons are Antiope, the queen kidnapped by Hercules, brought to Athens and given as a bride to Theseus, the mythical king of Athens. Hippolyta, the sister of Antiope, was considered the greatest Amazon queen, the paragon of women of her time. The daughter of Ares, the god of war, she wore the golden girdle which signified her station and became the object of the ninth labour of Hercules.

Omphale was the Amazon queen said to have ruled southern Libya. According to the legend, she bought Hercules in a slave market and put him to work weaving, spinning and carding wool. Every time he made an error, she smacked him with her sandal. After tiring of that game, she sent him packing to Greece.

These women warriors went everywhere. Penthesilea fought for Troy and went one-on-one with Achilles in single combat, but was finally overcome. Thalestris took a group of three hundred Amazons to visit Alexander the Great while he was on campaign in Asia, in the hope that they would all breed children as brave and as intelligent as the Greek general. The regiment stayed with him for thirteen days, but there is no record of how Penthesilea's breeding program worked out.

Anatolian women might have been revered as powerful Earth Mother goddesses and Amazon queens in the past, but it's a different story in today's rural communities. It's there – not in Istanbul – that the fault line of fundamentalism lies.

Eastwards from Ankara, life is different for the women of Turkey, and the signifier is the headscarf. One sound bite from a news report I'd been watching a couple of days earlier summed up women who did not wear the headscarf: 'They're all bitches and prostitutes,' a shepherd was quoted as saying, and it was interesting to note that he lived and worked close to cosmopolitan Istanbul, not regional Ankara. Chris Morris, the BBC World News correspondent who presented the piece, went on to quote the same shepherd again in a book he wrote about modern Turkey: '"Just a little bit like this," said Hasan, tugging at his forelock, "if just a little bit can be seen, it's like committing adultery."'[1]

While I was travelling in the region, the headscarf was one of the issues getting Westerners in a twitch as Turkey waited to hear if it could begin the process of joining the European Union. My guide Nebi Bey was very glum about the prospect: he was sure the vote would be 'no'. It seemed impossible to believe that Europe would vote to keep out the seventy million Muslims on their doorstep, when the West needed to show the world what a moderate Islamic democracy could be.

But the Turkish prime minister, Recep Tayyip Erdogan, had put the cat among the EU pigeons by supporting plans to criminalise adultery. In the process of reforming Turkey's criminal code – including increased penalties for violence against women and for torture – he inserted the proposal, which pleased Islamic conservatives. But as the hue and cry mounted among Europeans and Turkish secularists, the pragmatic politician withdrew the plan.

The question of the headscarf was also providing a lightning rod in Turkish politics. The veil has been on the outer in Turkey for decades: it fell victim to Atatürk's program of Westernisation and secularisation in the 1920s, and then in 1999 it was banned from universities, schools and public offices (including parliament) as a form of politicised religion. The ban has led to some strange habits. Observant Islamic female students attending Turkish universities find themselves putting on a skull cap, then a synthetic wig over the top, to satisfy both their personal belief system and the government edict. This stratagem must be hideously hot.

The question of the veil was put to the test in April 1999 when 31-year-old Merve Kavakci, the divorced wife of a Jordanian Islamic activist, was elected to the Turkish parliament. Mrs Kavakci was expelled from her swearing-in ceremony at the Turkish Grand National Assembly, however, held the following month. The reason? She was wearing a headscarf. A US-educated computer engineer, Mrs Kavakci refuted accusations from the speaker of the Turkish parliament that she'd used her headscarf as a political symbol.

She was accused of being an agent provocateur, and an investigation was launched to see if she had incited religious hatred – something that could have resulted in a long prison sentence. Unfortunately for Kavakci, the press delved into her background and discovered that she had become a US citizen six weeks before she was elected to parliament, and had failed to notify the relevant authorities. Her Turkish citizenship was revoked, and she now lectures in culture and international affairs at the George Washington University's Elliott School of International Affairs, in Washington DC. According to the school's website, 'her main expertise is in the area of democratization of Muslim society and the role of religion in secular Muslim states.'[2] Her right to wear the headscarf in a US university was unimpeded.

Turkey's ban on the veil results in some odd situations. Emine Erdogan, the wife of the prime minister, is banned from many functions that her husband hosts or is invited to, because she wears the veil. The secular president of Turkey, Ahmet Necdet Sezer, banned himself from the wedding of the Erdogans' daughter, Esra, in the summer of 2004; King Abdullah II of Jordan, Pakistani president Pervez Musharraf and the Greek prime minister Costas Karamanlis were among the honoured guests, but Sezer sent his apologies. Too many headscarves, apparently.

According to *The Economist* magazine, Prime Minister Erdogan was taking a less Islamic line on the headscarf. He had promised the secular generals who controlled the Turkish military that he was 'in no hurry to assert the right of women to wear headscarves in public places', and had decided that in municipal elections in March 2004, no 'ladies in scarves' would represent his ruling party in safe seats.[3]

At the same time, however, Erdogan had been making moves that would have pleased the great reformer of Turkish history, Mustafa Kemal Atatürk. In February 2004, parliament approved a draft law that outlawed discrimination against homosexuals, and another one whereby crimes committed in the name of family honour would be treated as severely as any other, similar crimes.

Around the same time, there was a further change of heart, when a message was delivered from the pulpits of Turkey's mosques during Friday prayers. Honour killings – the murder of women by male members of their families who consider they have dishonoured the family reputation, sometimes by nothing more than going to the movies with a man who is not a member of the family – were described as not just a breach of civil law, but also of Mohammad's teachings on clemency. Almost fifteen million Turkish men were told that honour killings were a sin and that women had the right to life.

Mustafa Kemal Atatürk is the colossus who bestrides modern Turkish history, and he was next on Egemen Moral's schedule for me. The Anitkabir is the mausoleum and museum dedicated to Turkey's founding father – his name means 'Father of the Turks' – and the secular state he created from the rubble left after the Central Powers lost World War I.

Given that Atatürk was a soldier before he was a nation builder, it was appropriate that Egemen and I arrived at the Anitkabir in time for the changing of the guard. With military precision under a bone-bleaching Anatolian sun, the guardians of the secular traditions of the Turkish Republic observed their traditional rite. It was an impressive sight.

Atatürk was also a champion for women's rights. 'There is a straighter and more secure path for us to follow [than the one we have been],' he once said. 'This is to have Turkish women as partners in everything, to share our lives with them, and to value them as friends, helpers, and colleagues in our scientific, spiritual, social, and economic life.'[4] For that alone, he deserved all this respect, I thought, as Egemen and I stood in the enormous hall of remembrance on Monument Hill that houses his mortal remains.

Atatürk's attitude to women was reflected in women's suffrage. In 1930, for instance, just two years after the women of Great Britain and Ireland were fully enfranchised, Turkish women gained the right to stand in municipal elections and the right to vote; and by 1935, eighteen women had been elected into parliament. He also supported the education of women, and declared, back in 1925: 'We shall emphasize putting our women's secondary and higher education on an equal footing with men.'[5]

As a result of Atatürk's vision for equality in Turkey, women now hold 30 per cent of all professional positions, comparable to many Western countries. Some 14 per cent of women have graduated from university, and the participation rate of tertiary-educated women in the urban labour force is 78 per cent. An estimated 42 per cent of all students at Turkish universities are now women.[6] The picture from the rural areas is different, however, where schooling for girls often comes second to their work on family farms.

Turkey had a female prime minister in the early 1990s (something some Western democracies are yet to have – Australia among them), in the person of Tansu Çiller. She was a controversial figure in Turkish politics before she became premier, and was initially greeted by feminists as a role model, then attacked when it became clear that women's issues were not on her agenda. Attractive and US-educated, Çiller appealed to the West using Margaret Thatcher's combination of personal power, sex appeal and intellect. She was elected to the Turkish parliament in 1991, and in 1992 she was voted Woman of the Year in Turkey. Other women imitated her style: they affected the flowing neck scarves she favoured, and wore her fragrance – Estée Lauder's Beautiful. Libya's Colonel Gaddafi described her as 'a model for all Islamic women'.[7]

In 1993 Tansu Çiller became prime minister at the head of the True Path Party, a position she held until 1995. She then formed a coalition with the Welfare Party, and stayed in office for another two years, as both deputy prime minister and foreign minister. Çiller proved herself more than equal to any man when it came to political opportunism, according to her critics.

There were one hundred and one questions I wanted to ask about women in Turkish politics and society, but Minister Guldal Aksıt, whom I had been due to meet, was still not out of her meetings. What would the minister would have made of a story in the *Turkish Daily News*, for instance, about a woman in Iran who was beaten every day by her husband? According to another daily newspaper, Teheran's *Aftab-e Yazd*, Maryam had petitioned a court to tell him to beat her only once a week. 'Beating is part of his nature and he cannot stop it,' she was reported as saying.

And would Aksıt have any comment on a claim made in the same day's *Cumhuriyet*, that the prime minister's insistence on outlawing adultery had tarnished Turkey's reputation in the EU?

Since there was no possibility of talking about women's affairs, I talked about men's affairs with Egemen over lunch. He was on the age-old quest for love, using a high-tech weapon: the internet. A habitué of chat rooms, he had spoken to more than two hundred young women and had met a few of them.

'Some of them thought that I was ugly, and I thought some of them were ugly,' he said ruefully. And some of them wore a headscarf, which was something not revealed over the net. That was a problem. His was a family of secular intellectuals who had inherited Atatürk's vision of the separation of mosque and state. 'My family would not agree with my being with a girl like this,' he said, happy to admit that he had a new, scarf-less, prospect on the boil.

Egemen and I had eaten our way through an enormous amount of food as we waited on the minister, but it became increasingly clear that the meeting wasn't simply postponed, but cancelled.

Back in Istanbul, Nebi Bey was waiting for me at the airport. I asked him what he'd been doing all day while I was hanging out with the Amazons and the fertility goddesses of Anatolia.

'Fixing your problems, *ma chère* Christine,' he replied.

Now that was a perfect day, I told him, as Ayhan dropped me back at my hotel.

Chapter 13

❀

Nebi Storms the Barracks

THE NAME 'SCUTARI' HAS been engraved in my brain since primary school, when we learned about the heroic exploits of Florence Nightingale. The famous nurse saved thousands of soldiers in the Crimean War in her hospital at Scutari, a suburb in the Asian port of Constantinople. I was extremely keen to visit the sacred Nightingale site.

'Üsküdar,' Nebi Bey corrected me when I requested the trip.

'Not Scutari?'

'Üsküdar,' he repeated. 'It's the Turkish name for Scutari.'

It turned out that I had been looking at Üsküdar every night from my hotel. On top of a small hill sat the Selimiye Barracks, built by Mahmut II in 1828, and where Florence Nightingale nursed, and developed many of her theories that formed the basis of modern nursing.

But when we arrived at the barracks, there was a problem. As the barracks are still in use, and are a military installation home to the Turkish First Army Group, personal details of visitors need to be sent forty-eight hours ahead, for approval. No visitors without permission, Nebi reported. I could hear him explaining the situation to the extremely pleasant soldiers manning the entrance. I was becoming used to the Turkish for 'journalist, from Australia', but Nebi was talking sixteen to the dozen, taking on the Turkish army for me.

'Passport,' he shot at me. 'Could you please give me your passport?'

'I can't.' I felt as though I had let him down. 'It's in the hotel safe.'

'But it is no use to you there,' he said, looking a bit cross – which was unusual since I was used to only approval from him – and continued his conversation with an increasing number of soldiers.

Eventually, we had permission. Our bags were secured in lockers, and we were given the keys and handed over to one of the most handsome young Turks I'd ever seen. Our military escort accompanied us up the hill, through ordered gardens and into the barracks themselves. Wide, cool verandas with marble floors looked out across the parkland to the Bosphorus and Europe. He walked us past wall fountains to the tiny little Florence Nightingale museum, tucked into a corner of the enormous building.

On the ground floor of the museum, behind locked doors, were dioramas depicting modern Turkey as forged from the events of the past, and erupting from the ruins of the old Ottoman Empire and World War I. 'Of course, we won that war,' the young soldier said. 'But our allies did not, and so we lost as well.'

But before the Great War, Turkey had been an ally of Britain and France as they fought the Russians at the Crimea from the end of 1854 to early in 1856. Russia had demanded to be recognised by Istanbul as the protector of the orthodox Christian communities in the Ottoman Empire. Istanbul refused, so Russia occupied the central European territories of Wallachia and Moldavia. Britain backed the Ottomans when they declared war on Russia, and the British and French fleets sailed into the Black Sea and besieged the strategic Crimean port of Sebastopol.

The Black Sea turned carmine; the air reeked of saltpetre. The fighting was cruel and the casualties enormous on both sides. In this Hell on Earth appeared one of the most respected women of the nineteenth century: the eminent Victorian, Florence Nightingale, 'the Lady of the Lamp'. 'In the middle of the muddle and the filth, the agony and the defeats, she brought about revolution,' wrote her biographer, Cecil Woodham-Smith.[1]

She was born in 1820, in Florence, the city of the Medici, from which she was given her name by her parents, William and Frances Nightingale. They were a wealthy pair, and had embarked on the Grand Tour following their wedding. Away for two years, the

Nightingales had their first child, Parthenope, in Naples (whose Ancient Greek name was Parthenope), followed by Florence a year later.

The family returned to England doubled in size, and took up residence in Derbyshire during the summer, and in Hampshire during the winter months. The sisters were taught at home; Italian, Latin, Greek, history and mathematics were on the curriculum. Florence was the academic, while Parthenope excelled at the skills required for a gently brought-up young woman of the time: embroidery, needlework and painting. In 1837, when she was seventeen, Florence received what she later described as her 'calling'. She knew that God had spoken to her and had asked her to do his work, but she had no idea what that meant.

She developed a keen interest in matters of social justice and, as did many wealthy young woman of the time, she made the rounds of the sick in her local villages. She also began to look at hospitals and the possibility of becoming a nurse. Her parents were against the idea: it was not work for an educated gentlewoman. Nurses were even suspected by some of being loose women, and little more than whores with bandages.

Florence's mother had still more reason to be unhappy with her life choices: in 1851, Florence is said to have received and rejected a proposal of marriage from Richard Monckton Milnes. A poet, and the first Baron Houghton, he was eligible, but Florence was convinced that marriage would interfere with her plans for nursing. The brilliant society life that Mrs Nightingale saw for her daughter was fading fast.

With the issue of her future unresolved, Florence joined two married friends on a tour of Europe. Together they visited Italy, Egypt, Greece and Germany. During the trip, Florence visited Pastor Theodor Fliedner's hospital and school for deaconesses at Kaiserswerth, near Düsseldorf. She returned the following year to undertake her initial three-month training as a nurse. When she went to London in 1853, she started work at the Establishment for Gentlewomen During Illness, in Harley Street. Graduates with similar training to Florence's started to replace older, less educated nurses.

When the Crimean War broke out in March 1854, newspaper

reports soon criticised medical facilities for the wounded. The Minister for War, Sidney Herbert, a friend of Florence who knew of her work in Harley Street, appointed her to oversee the introduction of female nurses into the military hospital at Scutari.

There was, inevitably, resistance from doctors, who did not appreciate the presence of the nurses and refused to ask for their help, but by November 1854, Florence was walking these very marble verandas at the Selimiye Barracks at Scutari in the company of thirty-eight nurses, including her aunt, Mai Smith.

Florence and her nurses found the hospital in a shocking condition: overworked staff cared badly for the sick and wounded soldiers who had managed to survive the trip from the battlefields in overcrowded and unsanitary troop transport ships; there was poor hygiene, mass infections and no equipment to process food for the patients. The nurses set to work, first cleaning the hospital and the equipment, and then reorganising patient care.

Florence was a stickler for compliance with the rules of sanitation. She believed that infection spontaneously developed in dirty and poorly ventilated places, an erroneous belief that did, however, result in improvements in hygiene, which in turn created healthier living and working environments.

The army doctors of the time did not necessarily agree with her. And she had problems not only with them, but also with senior army officers, men who could not conceive of a woman (and a nurse at that) telling them about taking care of the injured. The reputations of the nurses were blackened – Florence was only there to be closer to her lover, the gossips whispered.

But within two weeks of her arrival, Florence's enemies were forced to rethink their position. The Battle of Inkerman had started on 5 November, and the fighting was ferocious. By 8 November, the first losses were being tallied in a battle that would stretch into March of the following year. A *London Morning Herald* correspondent reported on the casualties from the Crimea during those few days:

> Our total loss is 38 officers killed, 95 wounded, and 2400 rank and file killed and wounded – in all, upwards of 2500 men, which just now we can ill afford.

> The French lost 12 officers killed, 35 wounded, and 1500 rank and file killed and wounded. The Russian loss is far beyond what was first estimated. At the lowest computation it seems rather over than under the enormous amount of 20,000 men. Up to this evening, 5000 corpses have been interred, and there still remains as many more upon the field.[2]

With the Inkerman casualties about to arrive at Scutari, it was a case of all hands on deck – no matter that some of them belonged to women. Florence soon became known as 'the Lady-in-Chief', and was seen as a ministering angel by the men in her care. She acted as their nurse, their banker, even their scribe, often writing home on their behalf and sending their wages to their loved ones. She set up laundries and reading rooms in her hospitals, and organised classes, wholesome food and recreation for the soldiers. Florence's introduction of nurses to military hospitals was such a success that a public subscription was organised in 1855 so she could undertake the reorganisation of civilian hospitals in Great Britain.

The most dramatic two years of her life, as the Lady of the Lamp, are celebrated in the Selimiye Barracks, where she worked and lived. Upstairs in the museum, in a tower room on the northernmost corner, some of her furniture has been kept, and her rooms re-created. We saw her bag, bottles of tinctures, books she wrote and her modest desk. Around the walls were framed copies of some of her letters – Florence was a constant correspondent, and covered page after page with her flowing handwriting. In one of these letters, she'd written:

> What does 'being a woman' mean, when it is said in contempt? Does it not mean what is petty, little selfishnesses, envy, small meannesses, foolish talking, gossip, love of praise?
>
> Now while we try to be women in the noble sense of the word, each of us fights bravely against womanly weakness.
>
> Let us be anxious to do well, not for selfish praise, but for honour and advancing the cause, the work that we have taken up . . . Not to be clever . . . but let it be our ambition to be good women.

When Austria joined the Crimean War on the side of England and France, the end was assured. Unfortunately it came too late for the quarter of a million men who had died on both sides.

But the Crimean War left a number of legacies. During her time at the Selimiye Barracks, Florence the mathematician applied systems to record-keeping. She then used the data she collected to back her favourite theme: that the mortality rate (which ran at around forty-seven per cent of all patients in the military hospitals taking the wounded from the Crimea) decreased as sanitary methods improved. Her measurements resulted in another Nightingale invention – polar-area charts, or pie charts, which are used to this day. For her work in the field of objectively measuring social phenomena and submitting the data to analysis, Florence Nightingale would become the first female Fellow of the Statistical Society, in 1860.

By the time the war finished, Florence had improved not only the efficiency of nursing, reducing sepsis and cross-infection, but also its professional image and the lot of the ordinary soldier. Before her involvement, the foot soldiers were seen as simple cannon fodder; by the time the Lady-in-Chief was finished, they were seen as subjects of Her Majesty Queen Victoria and entitled to care and respect.

Florence returned to London from the Crimean War late in the summer of 1856, some four months after the peace was agreed, but she secluded herself. Her heart was still with the men she had left behind at the hospital, some five thousand of them buried in the barracks' British cemetery, and she thought of them often.

In a private note at the end of that year, she wrote:

> Oh my poor men who endured so patiently. I feel I have been such a bad mother to you to come home and leave you lying in your Crimean grave. Seventy-three per cent in eight regiments during six months from disease alone – who thinks of that now? But if I could carry any one point which would prevent any part of the recurrence of this our colossal calamity then I should have been true to the cause of those brave dead.[3]

In the last period of her life, Florence Nightingale devoted herself to the other work she is famous for – educating nurses. 'No man, not even a doctor, ever gives any other definition of what a nurse should be than this – "devoted and obedient",' she wrote in 1859. 'This definition would do just as well for a porter. It might even do for a horse. It would not do for a policeman.'[4]

Greatly influenced by her experiences in Turkey, she set about defining what a nurse should be. With money from the Nightingale Fund, she set up the Nightingale Training School for Nurses at St Thomas's Hospital in London. It's astonishing that a woman, banned by her gender from university education, was able to affect the world so fundamentally, both in science and social science. And, as we have seen, in Turkey, where her greatest opposition came not from Turkish, but British, men, she laid the foundation for the work that saved lives and has since changed the lives of millions of people.

From the gatehouse of the Selimiye Barracks, as Nebi, Ayhan and I waited to retrieve our stuff from the lockers, I could see the landing stage at the foot of the hill where the injured were disembarked and then carried up to the Lady-in-Chief and her nurses. Across the water loomed Seraglio Point, while Florence worked here among the bloody wounded and the dying, life went on as it always had in the harem of the Topkapi Palace. What would those pampered and immured women have made of their sisters in the barracks?

It was almost more than my mind could take in for one day, but it wasn't even lunchtime. Nebi had further plans: he was taking me to Kiz Kulesi, the Maiden's Tower, right in the Bosphorus itself. The present tower dates from the eighteenth century and occupies an islet sitting just up from the landing stage for the hospital of the Selimiye Barracks, so Nebi, Ayhan and I travelled there by ferry. The restaurant in the base of the tower was empty, and the staff were preparing for dinner, so visitors were amusing themselves by climbing the tower or sunning themselves like lizards beside it. Nebi and I did the latter; Ayhan, as usual, moved downwind and lit up.

There has been a tower on this tiny island since the fifth century BC. The original was constructed for the Athenian statesman and general Alcibiades, as he secured the grain trade out of the Black Sea. Later, it was converted by a Macedonian admiral into a mausoleum for his wife, and it entered mythology as the Tower of Leander when the legend of Hero and Leander was relocated from the Dardanelles to the Bosphorus. Another legend gave it the name 'Maiden's Tower', after a king of Scutari was said to have locked his beautiful daughter up in the tower to preserve her virtue.

By the fifteenth century, the Byzantine emperors were counting on a tower built on the site and another nearby at the southern end of the Golden Horn to help repel invaders. Chains were stretched between the two towers to stop ships from trying to enter the Bosphorus without permission. The strategy didn't work, and the empire fell when the Turks conquered Constantinople. The new landlords used the wooden tower to imprison the opposition before they were sent into exile.

In 1726, that tower burned down, and was replaced with a stone structure, which was improved and extended into its current baroque form in 1830. In its long history, it has been a fort, a tomb, a lighthouse, a prison, a quarantine station and – most unusually – a movie set, when the tower was cast as the lair of Elektra in the James Bond film *The World is Not Enough*.

Nebi and I sat in the sun and talked and, if Nebi's internal body clock hadn't declared it time to eat and eat sweet, we might well have been sitting and talking until sunset. So Ayhan took us away from the gleaming waters of the Bosphorus to a narrow street in Sultanahmet, around the corner from Nebi's kiosk. While the feral cats of the city scratched, hissed and brawled under the tables of the Akdeniz Restaurant, Nebi Bey taught me a little Turkish.

'*Akdeniz*. It means "the white sea". It's what you call the Mediterranean.'

He looked happy, as, having disposed of the meat course, he could get on with the serious part of lunch. He spooned in another mouthful of crème caramel.

'What do you think *Karadeniz* means?' he asked, pointing at the name of the kebab restaurant next door.

'Something sea?' I suggested.

'Yes!' It was getting quite *My Fair Lady* as I played Eliza to his Henry Higgins. '*Akdeniz* is "the white sea" . . . *Ak Sarayi* is "the white palace". *Kara*? *Karadeniz* is . . .?'

'*Karadeniz* means "Black Sea"?' I guessed.

It was the 'By George, I think she's got it!' moment of our day. Nebi gave me a spoonful of his crème caramel to celebrate and then walked me down to the Basilica Cistern.

There are thought to have been underground cisterns here in Constantinople during the reign of the Roman emperor Constantine (306–37), but this immense vault (only two-thirds of which is on show – in the nineteenth century, part of the cistern was walled up) was laid out in 532, during the time of Justinian, to supply the needs of his nearby palace. When the Turks invaded, it was some time before they twigged what was under their feet near the great Byzantine church of Hagia Sophia, and they only worked it out when they discovered locals lowering buckets through holes in the ground and coming up with water and, occasionally, fish.

'I can remember when I was a boy, you could hardly see anything of the cistern,' said Nebi, as we descended the steps. 'It was almost filled with rubbish. But there has been some serious work done here in the last twenty years.'

The shimmering glory of the Basilica Cistern came into focus. Into the half-gloom stretched an unexpectedly romantic sight. Three hundred and thirty-six columns, all more than eight metres high, buttressed the vaulted ceiling of the cistern. Light played across the water, colouring it from diamond-clear to transparent amber, melting away into the dark. Visitors had used the pools as wishing wells, hurling silver coins to glint in its shallows; shoals of fat fish lazily finned around the supports of the wooden walkways that wound through the columns. Inevitably, perhaps, Baroque music was playing. Water dripped.

Nebi took me up to the far end, to show me a particular column of note, with its capital, a head of Medusa, upside down in the drink. She was one of two, and she was head over heels. I had joined her: I was gone a million on Istanbul.

The East is Pink

Chapter 14

❀

The Road to Petra

To awaken quite alone in a strange town is one of the pleasantest sensations in the world.
Freya Stark

IF YOU SAT NEXT TO a terrorist on a plane, could you tell? Or would you be inclined to assume that everyone is suspicious and be very, very careful? Me, I'll talk to anyone, particularly if I'm feeling a bit low. Blame Nebi Bey. In the car on the way to Atatürk International Airport that final night, things had become a bit tricky when he declared it was time for a dangerous confession.

'Perhaps not, Nebi.'

'Ahh . . . Perhaps not then, Christine.'

He helped me get all my bags on to the flight and sat with me until it was time to go.

Then I kissed him and walked towards the gate. It wasn't until he'd disappeared from view that I stopped smiling. As I waited to board the plane, I tried to read Nebi's parting gift to me – a copy of *The New Life*, by Turkey's most celebrated contemporary writer, Orhan Pamuk. I blinked to get the words to focus and wondered what Nebi's confession might have been.

So when the man sitting next to me on the flight started to chat, I thought, Why not? In the way of strangers, we began with the basics. He asked about me, and that was all pretty conventional. But then it was his turn.

'Where are you from, Allen?'

'Los Angeles,' he replied.

I had another peek at him. He looked as though he belonged in a landscape of bare, rugged mountains and endless, flat deserts, not California's beach and celebrity culture. I tried it another way. 'What are your origins?'

'I am an American.' Then he took pity on me. It turned out that Allen had been born in Teheran, studied engineering in Germany and France, worked for the United Nations in Kuwait, and at the time of our flight was working for the US Department of Defense, overseeing large civil engineering projects in Baghdad.

He had just been on a break to see his wife, who had been spending some time in Teheran with her family. They'd met in Antalya, one of Turkey's sapphire-blue Mediterranean port cities, and now he was going back to life in the Green Zone. Since this was the first time I'd had access to a first-hand account of what living in Baghdad was like, I shut up and listened.

With the other US contractors, Allen was billeted inside the Green Zone, the fortified area of the city where the embassies and foreign personnel worked. He shared a dormitory with a dozen men, and they worked and lived in the compound, constantly under guard. 'It's not so bad,' he added. 'But the snoring is terrible.'

Every so often they encountered some of the children of the city and, like American personnel in every war, uniformed or not, handed out lollies to them. But even that was getting dangerous: suicide bombers, recognising a new opportunity to kill the occupying troops, had started to drive their cars near to groups of Americans and Iraqi children.

Allen was going back through Amman, into Jordan, into Baghdad, as it was the only way by air. The overland route was not a possibility for him. Too dangerous. And even then, to get from the airport in Baghdad to the Green Zone, he would have to travel along Route Irish, a four-lane stretch of road said to be the most dangerous commute in the world. Almost ten kilometres of critical supply line into Iraq, it was traversed every day by US military convoys, Iraqi and foreign businessmen, journalists, aid workers – and engineers like Allen. Despite banks of US military checkpoints, Iraqi insurgents found ways to stake out this stretch of 'target-rich' road. Ambushes and murders demonstrated every day the bloody holes in the existing security measures. Hundreds of people had died on the horror stretch of Route Irish in the past couple of years.

'I was thinking of going to the Dead Sea tomorrow,' Allen said.

'I was thinking of going to Petra.'

'Perhaps we could do both.'

We could, and we would. After sharing a taxi from the Queen Alia International Airport into Amman itself, thirty-two kilometres to the north, we confirmed our date for later that morning and parted company.

Allen came to collect me within hours, and we set off through the stony streets of Amman for Petra, an archaeological site about three hundred kilometres south-west of the capital. The site's 700-plus monuments add up to Jordan's most popular tourist attraction; it is a city built by the ancient Nabataeans which was lost, then found. This place, carved into the rock of the Jordanian desert, had been in my imagination since I was a schoolgirl, when I heard part of the 1845 poem 'Petra' by English Oxford undergraduate poet, and later divine, Dean John William Burgon:

It seems no work of Man's creative hand,
By labor wrought as wavering fancy planned;
But from the rock as by magic grown,
Eternal, silent, beautiful, alone!
Not virgin-white like that old Doric shrine,
Where erst Athena held her rites divine;
Not saintly-grey, like many a minister fane,
That crowns the hill and consecrates the plain;
But rosy-red as if the blush of dawn,
That first beheld them were not yet withdrawn;
The hues of youth upon a brow of woe,
Which Man deemed old two thousand years ago.
Match me such marvel save in Eastern clime,
A rose-red city half as old as time.[1]

Petra sits in the Wadi Musa, the Valley of Moses, named to commemorate the time when the prophet Moses tapped the stony ground there with his staff and caused water to flow. I had never thought for one moment I would be in Petra, and as we walked down the narrow gorge from the entrance, it became more and more possible that I might not actually make it. The city lies at the end of the fissure in the rock, which sometimes closes to just five metres wide; in places, walls two hundred metres high overhang the route. It wasn't good for my claustrophobia, this journey into the ancient caravan city.

As Allen, our guide and I avoided the carriages and the horses and the kids and the donkeys and the other tourists, I decided it wasn't for the faint of heart, this kilometre-plus walk. It was warm, around 28 degrees, which was fairly mild for this region at the end of September. It wasn't so bad, but with every step down, there would be a corresponding step back up. I mopped my forehead and pressed on, wishing I could have hitched a ride on one of the moth-eaten horses. As they did every day, they mizzled up and down the gorge, occasionally stepping up from a walk to a canter, their hooves hammering out a hollow, echoed beat.

At the end of the gorge is the fortress city, carved into the red sandstone itself – hence the name Petra, for 'rock'. Suddenly, the passage turned slightly to the right, and there was the Treasury. It's amazing the way things look like their photographs, and Petra looks exactly as it should. What the photographs never show, though, is the shimmering, rosy glow in the air as the gorge opens to the light.

Petra is a marvel, sometimes called the Eighth Wonder of the Ancient World. Created in the third century BC, it commanded the caravan trade routes from Arabia to Damascus. Then, Petra was a prosperous caravanserai surrounded by cliffs and nestled in an easily defended basin that measures about sixteen hundred metres long and some nine hundred metres wide.

The Romans moved in and took over towards the end of the first century AD, and administered the city through the second. But Petra was displaced as a trading axis when sea routes superseded the land route from Arabia, and it was then lost to the world until 1812, when the Swiss explorer Johann Ludwig Burckhardt rediscovered it. Allen and I followed in his footsteps, past the Treasury and the Street of Facades, to the weathered theatre and the royal tombs. We missed the High Place of Sacrifice (forty-five minutes up stone steps were easy to refuse) and were soon back in front of the Treasury among the gangs of urchins who busied themselves with the tourists. These children, all Bedouin, were super-traders. One sold me a piece of jewellery for ten Jordanian dinar which I later discovered in a shop for four of the same.

A Bedouin boy was ready with more beads.

'*La, shukran.*' No, thank you, I replied. '*Shu ismak?*' What is your name?

Sleman was not interested in helping me practise my Arabic, but he did want to polish his English. Sitting on the steps of the Treasury, he was happy to talk about his life. He was fifteen years old, one of twenty-two children.

'My father is married twice,' he said in good, unaccented English. 'He has two families.'

Would Sleman marry twice?

'No. One wife is enough.'

Would he have many children?

'Never!'

Sleman went to school in the mornings and worked selling trinkets to tourists in the afternoons, but he was a young man with ambition. 'I want to be a tour guide when I leave school,' he told me.

Our tour guide looked startled at this: he was doing his doctoral thesis on the coins of the Nabataean civilisation, and he obviously thought Sleman had an impossible road ahead.

We left the boy dreaming of a better future in the pink of Petra to face the walk back up to the car. I was determined to do it, if only to spite the horse touts.

'Tell your husband you want a carriage,' shouted one.

'My husband's wife is in Teheran,' I told them. They let out catcalls of appreciation to Allen for his sheer manliness.

The sun was high in the sky, getting higher and hotter. Dust swirled lazily around the exhausted horses, their cracked bridles caked with sweat, grime and boredom.

Back in the car, we visited some of the places that mark the high points of the Bible: the River Jordan, where John the Baptist baptised Christ; and past the peak that is said to be Mount Nebo, the summit of the Moabite Range, where Moses was buried. It was from here that Moses looked across the Jordan Valley to the Dead Sea and saw the Promised Land for the first time. This was also where Jeremiah was supposed to have put the Ark of the Covenant in a huge cave, and Egeria, a Spanish pilgrim nun of the fourth century, had walked;[2] and perhaps too where Saladin had followed in Christ's footsteps.

Along the way, we bought figs and grapes from boys on the sides of the road. Very organic, this produce, I thought, as I turned misshapen forms in my hands.

We reached the Dead Sea at sunset and could see the lights of the West Bank settlements coming on with the darkness. There were security checkpoints everywhere and, according to our driver, even the Dead Sea had been secured. 'The Israelis have set electrical cables in the water to keep themselves safe,' he said.

We got out of the car for photographs and to watch the sun set behind the West Bank. In the late afternoon, the view was idyllic – right up until it was blocked with swarms of sticky desert flies. We retreated to the car, but they came too. Then Allen and the driver spent half an hour trying to blow them out the back of the Merc, which kept us amused until we arrived at the public beach.

The water was crammed with bodies, and it was like swimming between the flags in January at Surfers Paradise, except there was an entrance fee. At the bottom of the steps was the Dead Sea, the lowest point on the face of the Earth, and so saline that it burns the eyes and requires a shower afterwards to wash it off.

Almost all the women we saw were veiled. Imagine going to the beach fully dressed and wearing a *yashmak* while your husband and children can feel the evening breeze on their faces.

Pleased with our day, we made plans to go to the souk the following morning. Allen was distracted, though. He had been unable to contact his office in Baghdad. 'I must tell them I am coming,' he said. 'They have to send the cars.'

Cars?

'There are several armoured vehicles in every convoy.'

That night, back in my hotel, I saw on the news just what he was heading into. Four US troops had been killed in Iraq; US war planes targeted Falluja, where a hospital spokesman said women and children were among the injured and the seven Iraqis killed. The Iraqi government decided to press on with elections in the coming January. A delegation of British Muslims was headed for Baghdad to try to secure the release of Ken Bigley, the 62-year-old Englishman kidnapped and threatened with decapitation by a group led by the Jordanian Abu Musab al-Zarqawi.

Early the next morning, my new travelling companion called: his plane was leaving at around midday, so he couldn't make our date for the souk. 'I am very sorry,' he said. 'But I am very happy to have spent my time in Jordan with you.'

Me too. 'I want to hear from you, Allen, not about you!'

He laughed. 'I have spoken to the people in Baghdad,' he continued. 'They will send five armoured vehicles for me.' This fact, I felt, was cause for concern, not reassurance. 'You must be careful,' he added.

Wondering if that meant I shouldn't hare off on trips into the desert with men I had just met, I carefully set off to the souk. Out alone for the first time in a couple of weeks, I felt exposed, odd, and frightened. Who would carry my bags now?

The taxi dropped me on the edge of Downtown, the old Islamic quarter, and as the day and the shops opened up, I was surprised to discover I was enjoying being alone. It would be hard not enjoy Amman, though. It is one of the oldest cities of antiquity, with archaeological finds dating back to 3500 BC. But it also has a bloody history. King David, feeling insulted by the Ammonite king, sent an army against the city in around 900 BC; the victorious Israelites then threw many of the city's inhabitants into a kiln and burned them alive.[3] In 30 BC, King Herod took the city, which, despite its brutal past, had been renamed Philadelphia ('the City of Brotherly Love') some two hundred years before by its Ptolemaic ruler, and thus brought it under Rome's control.

Modern Amman is almost a completely new construction. The Roman city had declined so much that, by 1878, it was just a small village. Then, a town was established on the site. By the beginning of the twentieth century, Amman was home to some two thousand souls. But when the emir, Abdullah I, made it his headquarters in 1921, it became the centre of the region then called Transjordan. Originally built on seven hills, like Rome, Amman now loiters untidily across nineteen, so it is a city not designed for walking around in. If you don't die of a heart attack climbing those hills, you'll get sunburn and heatstroke before you find any shade.

Downtown, with a large Palestinian refugee camp on its fringe, was chaotic, frenetic and friendly. Live animals and birds sat in cages along the kerbs, juice sellers pushed sugar canes into grinders, and baklava and sweets shone from cake-shop windows. The smells of spices and nuts rose on currents of warm air. In the markets, the sellers hustled the buyers, shouting and teasing money out of their wallets. The carriers were eager for attention: 'Take my photo, Miss!' 'No, Miss, take mine!'

I spotted a scarf shop and, deciding it was time to take the veil, plunged across the street, jaywalking through the unpredictable traffic under the nose of a policeman. If I was skittled, at least there would be one official witness.

The *shela* shop was tiny. Above the counter, there were endless additions to a woman's outfit to ensure her modesty – and maintain a high body temperature. There were plain headscarves, patterned headscarves, headscarves with matching *yashmaks*. I bought three sets in neutrals: black, white and cream. Also available were knitted-cotton skull caps of the type JoJo had worn under scarf in Dubai, as well as tennis-visor-shaped things, which, worn under the veil, ensure height from the forehead. As well, there were fake sleeves, like gloves for the forearms.

Below the counter was another story, one aimed at raising the temperature not of the wearer, but of the observer. The shopkeeper, a man, was selling some of the most outrageous underwear found outside of the sex shops in Las Vegas. The packaging showed photographs of women modelling these skimpy bits of nylon and lycra, provocatively pouting for the camera.

There seemed to be an inherent paradox here: the modest veils above the counter, the raunchy underwear below. And all sold by a man. It was certainly counter-intuitive to my upbringing. In my childhood, just being in a shop with a man selling skimpy smalls would have been unseemly. Back then, the only people who staffed the counters in David Jones's underwear department were middle-aged matrons. But here, of course, women, middle-aged or otherwise, simply don't work in shops. I had no idea how these concepts worked together.

The shopkeeper gave me a discount for bulk scarf buying, and with the purchases in my bag, I wandered back into the narrow alleys of Downtown and through the garment district. Row after row of sewing machines lined the sides of the narrow lanes where workers sewed and chatted. It was morning tea time, and some had broken for chai and pide bread.

'*Sabah Al-Kher*,' I said. Good morning.

'*Sabah Al-Noor*,' they replied. Day of light. '*Kief halik?*' How are you? one of them asked me.

'*Kwayyis, ilHamdu Lillah.*' Good, thanks to God.

'*Tifadfali*,' they chorused. Please join us. '*Tifadfali!*'

Not wanting to spoil their fun and having mined all my available Arabic pleasantries, I declined with thanks, bought some grapes and took a taxi back to my hotel. I had to do some preparation before I met two of Jordan's most interesting women, and to make some phone calls. I called Nebi Bey. He was out.

Chapter 15

A Question of Honour

IT WAS JULY IN Jeddah – hot. A hard sun hung in a pitiless sky. In a public car park, a young woman bowed her head in submission. Behind her stood a man, a pistol in his hand. Quickly, he raised the gun and pumped a volley of six shots into her brain. The first bullet knocked her forwards. She was dead, if God was merciful, before she struck the ground.

This was murder, but here in Saudi Arabia, it has another name: honour killing. A family's honour was being restored but the debt hadn't been paid completely. Another executioner took five blows to slice the head off the man who died with the woman that day.

These were no ordinary citizens. She was a princess, the great-granddaughter of a king, the great-niece of another, and the daughter of a man who would be king. The 1977 murders of Princess Mishaal bint Fahd bin Mohammed and her lover, Khalid Muhallal, brought the custom of honour killing dramatically into the open.

The incident was made into a docudrama entitled *Death of a Princess*, and it revealed exactly how the House of Saud – the rulers of Saudi Arabia and allies of Western governments – dispensed rough justice within their own family and country.

The truth of the story is slightly blurry, as are the secret photographs that recorded the murders, but it seems to be this . . . Princess Mishaal, a great-niece of King Khalid, and Muhallal, the nephew of General Ali Shaer, Saudi ambassador to Lebanon, fell in love. Mishaal and Muhallal, who was a student at the university in

Riyadh, fled to Jeddah, where they spent several days in a hotel together. Then Mishaal faked her own death by drowning. She cut off her hair and, disguised as a man, attempted to flee Saudi Arabia with Mulhallal.

They were caught at the airport, and Mishaal, one of an estimated two thousand princesses in the Saudi royal family at that time, was returned to her own clan. Her grandfather, Prince Mohammed, the older brother of King Khalid, was an arch-conservative and traditionalist who exercised political power within the royal family. Mohammed – who because of his bad temper and alleged drinking problem was known as 'Mohammed of the Two Evils' – insisted on his right as the head of the family to correct the injury done to his family honour by Mishaal. It was also, doubtless, an act devised to keep the other women of the family in line. He was clearly a believer in the 'kill one, educate a thousand' theory of punishment.

Mohammed initially demanded a public execution, which King Khalid refused. Khalid would have preferred the executions to be carried out behind palace walls if they had to happen at all, and well away from any witnesses who might attest to the fact that the House of Saud was not quite as modern as his friends in the White House and Whitehall had been hoping. To make the king's position worse, Saudi Arabia's supreme religious court would not hear the case, thus confirming to many Saudis the belief that the runaways had married and so Muslim law had not been broken by the elopement.

Mohammed and King Khalid reached a terrible compromise: the princess and her husband would not be killed in the main square, the customary location for judicial executions in Saudi Arabia. They would be bundled instead into a car park and hastily despatched. No public announcements followed, another break with tradition, and the dead were not officially identified.

Unfortunately for the king, a British expatriate was also at the car park that day, and took photographs with a hidden camera. Eventually, British journalist Anthony Thomas became interested in the story, and began to research the film that became the 1980 TV docudrama *Death of a Princess*. Twenty-five years later, Thomas talked about why his interest in the story grew. He had intended to do the film as a drama, he told a television interviewer, but discovered on his travels through the Arab world that everyone he spoke to held strong opinions about the event; from conservative Saudis to radical Palestinians, people in the region identified with the murdered princess. 'She'd become a myth,' he said.[1] And so he decided to make 'faction' – a documentary crossed with drama.

The Saudis objected to the film and the Islamic press interpreted it as an attack on Islam itself. The Saudi government asked the British ambassador to leave the country. They also went to great trouble to try to persuade the US government to suppress the film, but were unsuccessful.

The dispute within the Saudi royal family seems to have revolved around the question of primacy between two particular forms of law: one tribal, which Prince Mohammed invoked to restore his own honour, and the other sharia, or Islamic. Tribal law won.

Princess Mishaal might have become a myth, but women are still the victims of honour killings in the Middle East, and it remains one of the region's greatest shames. According to the United Nations Population Fund, some five thousand women around the world every year are murdered in the name of honour.[2]

Jordan is one of the countries most often linked with the crime. In 2003, the Committee to Defend Women's Rights in the Middle East reported on two particular Jordanian cases.[3] In one, the victim, nineteen-year-old Asma, was stabbed more than forty times by her eighteen-year-old brother. He murdered his sister and then turned himself in to the police, telling them he had killed to cleanse his family's honour. In the other incident, a man confessed to killing his 23-year-old married sister. Her family had first reported that she'd been accidentally killed when she was run over by a water tanker, but the mother of the victim knew her sons had been plotting to murder the woman, and told the police. The brother then confessed that he had deliberately killed his sister. The dead woman, who had been twice divorced and was the mother of a four-year-old child, had been returned to the family home that same morning by her husband because of 'immoral behaviours'.[4]

Honour killings shame the countries in which they occur, but they are a boon to publishers. In 2003, a Palestinian woman known only as Saoud, published her story, *Burned Alive*. At age seventeen, she fell pregnant to the man who had promised to marry her. When he then abandonded her, Saoud's brother-in-law doused her with petrol and set her alight.

Another account of an honour killing in Jordan galvanised the world's interest when it was published, also in 2003. Norma Khouri, a writer living in Australia, recounted the story of the life of her childhood friend Dalia in *Forbidden Love*. When they were in their twenties, Dalia and Norma had dreamed of setting up a hairdressing salon in Amman. But Dalia, a Muslim, fell in love with an army officer, a Christian called Michael. The young pair began to conduct an innocent, if clandestine, relationship. When their liaison was discovered, Dalia was killed by her father – he stabbed her a dozen times.

Fearing for her own life, Norma fled Amman for Athens, where she started to write her book in the city's internet cafés. When it was finished, she offered the story to an agent in New York. The agent sold the story to Simon & Schuster in the United States, and to Random House in the UK; the latter then sold on the rights to its subsidiary in Australia. The book sold more than two hundred thousand copies here and was published in more than fifteen countries.

The dark-eyed, dark-haired Norma, mother of two, became a literary sensation with her memoir, and a fixture at book festivals. She also became a pin-up among women's groups fighting against honour killings.

But there was a problem with *Forbidden Love*: it was a lie. There was no Dalia, no Michael, no dream of a hairdressing salon, and no author who had grown up in Jordan. Norma's literary hoax was revealed in the *Sydney Morning Herald* in July 2004.[5] The exposé's writer, Malcolm Knox, had been on Norma's trail for nearly eighteen months. He had been alerted to problems in the text by the secretary-general of the Jordanian National Commission for Women, Dr Amal Al-Sabbagh, in February 2003, and had had numerous telephone calls and email contacts with her during the subsequent ten months. And it was this same Dr Amal Al-Sabbagh that I was due to meet on my second morning in Amman.

On the stone terrace in front of the 75-year-old house where she had grown up, Amal talked to me about how she had tracked down the truth about Dalia and Norma. When she first read *Forbidden Love*, she told me, alarm bells started to sound.

'We began to check, trying to find this murder, which was said to have happened in 1996. We couldn't find it,' she said. 'Then we went looking for Norma in Jordan, based on information she had written in the book and given in interviews. We couldn't find her.'

Amal had serious reservations about the veracity of the book, and wrote to both the US and the Australian publishers, asking them to check the information. Around the same time, she contacted Malcolm Knox at the *Herald*, who was interested in what she told him, but said he needed more to make the story stand up before they could run it. 'I was frustrated,' she told me. 'I knew our story was right.'

The American publishers didn't respond, but at least the Australians were polite. 'They said they would look into it. A month later, they came back saying they had spoken to the author, and she had answered their questions, and they were standing by the book.'

That was the beginning of what Amal referred to as her 'internet nights'. Having been unable to find a skerrick about Norma Khouri the writer – there were three women of that name in Jordan at the time she was investigating – she trawled for long hours on a hunt for Norma's real name. Eventually she found it, published in a European interview. 'Baghian! Then, it became so easy.'

In December 2003, Amal emailed Knox and told him she had his Christmas present: Norma Khouri's real name and family background. She was Norma Majid Khouri Michael Al-Baghian Toliopoulos, married to John Toliopoulos, an American of Greek heritage. For the next six months, Knox determinedly set about trying to prove who Norma Khouri really was. He eventually went to the United States and door-knocked to flush out the truth.

Far from planning a hairdressing salon in Amman in her twenties, when she was three, Norma had left Jordan for America with her family. From 1973 to 2000, she lived in Chicago, where she and her husband had a daughter, Zoe, and a son, Christopher. Then, in November 2000, Norma spent a week in Jordan, to get her identity papers sorted out (she had become a US citizen in 1996) and possibly to find some local colour to inject into the book she was writing about the mythical Dalia.

Exposed as a literary con artist, Khouri continued to defend her book, but things got worse for her. The *Sydney Morning Herald* reported that she had defrauded friends and family of nearly one million dollars over ten years, had been eluding the Chicago Police Department for five years, and was, according to the CPD, one of the best con women they had ever seen.

'That girl is disturbed,' Amal said. 'She has challenged me to a debate about this book. But I don't care about Norma Khouri. What I care about is that her book set women's rights in Jordan back about ten years.'

Khouri's book underlined a problem for Jordan. In the Western mind, the country is Honour Killings Central, linked inextricably with the brutal crime. The truth is a little less explosive. 'The numbers are in decline,' Amal explained. 'In the late 1980s, the numbers were around twenty to twenty-five women a year murdered in what were called honour killings. So far this year [late September 2004], there have been thirteen.'

Other countries see their women murdered by husbands and lovers with possibly greater frequency. In the United States, between forty and sixty per cent of murdered women are killed by their husband or boyfriend. In Australia, the grim truth is that women are most likely to be murdered in their own homes, in their own bedrooms, by the men closest to them. How many of these would fall in the category of 'honour killing'?

The Khouri book made problems for the Jordanian National Commission for Women, which had to deal with Jordan's sensitive politics, the country's conservative politicians and a set of equally conservative laws. Part of the country's criminal code states: 'A husband or a close blood relative who kills a woman caught in a situation highly suspicious of adultery will be totally exempt from sentence.' The code also guarantees a lighter sentence for male killers of female relatives who have committed 'an act which is illicit in the eyes of the perpetrator'.

Jordan's current king, Abdullah II, is on the side of Jordan's women, and backed proposed legislation in February 2000 to change the penal code articles that were allowing men to literally get away with murder. Ten days after parliament refused to pass the draft law (in three minutes flat), five thousand people took to the streets of Amman in support of the rejected legislation. The protesters included some local heavy-hitters, among them the king's brother and personal guard, and the country's adviser for tribal affairs.

The support from the Jordanian royal palace also encouraged activist groups to speak out even more strongly against the practice. And six years later, by agreement between the government and the judiciary, the rejected draft amendment is now in operation in the courts; it just won't be on the statue books for a while.

Amal and I moved on from honour killings to other Western obsessions and their relevance to Jordanian women. First up was polygamy.

'It is a personal choice,' Amal told me, 'one I would not condone because I am a Christian. But it seems to be on the decline generally.'

And what about the veil?

'I fully support women who wear the veil on religious grounds, as long as they are not being forced to wear it. For some women, wearing the veil and the coat is not just a religious requirement, it is also better economically. These clothes are much cheaper than Western clothes.

'And for other women, wearing the veil is a political choice. I know women from solid, middle-class families who, since the start of the first Palestinian uprising, began to wear the headscarf. It is about solidarity for them with other Muslims.'

In fact, the issues that were consuming the Jordanian National Commission for Women and Amal Al-Sabbagh were the laws pertaining to divorce in Jordan, and personal status laws for women.

'Women need to be able to seek a divorce and get one quickly,' she said, and added that women also needed to be able to take part more fully in Jordan's political and public spheres. 'The king is helping with that. He has allocated seats for women in parliament, with three in the cabinet and seven in the senate.'

It's a slow road for Jordan, which is among the poorer countries of the world, and in a difficult position geographically between

Israel and Iraq. But the Noor Al Hussein Foundation is at the forefront of women's health and safety in the country. That would be my next stop.

The Noor Al Hussein Foundation is presided over by Queen Noor of Jordan, and its particular bailiwicks are micro-financing and community income-generation projects. On a hot Sunday, I went to the foundation to talk to the executive director, Hana Mitri Shahin, about its work.

'When Queen Noor married King Hussein in 1978, she decided she wanted to do something to help Jordanian women economically and socially,' Hana explained. 'From 1985, the foundation which she set up has been promoting projects to help women in remote areas.'

The foundation, which operates under the umbrella of the King Hussein Foundation, seeks to foster peace, sustainable development and cross-cultural understanding through programs that promote education and leadership, poverty eradication, women's empowerment, and democracy. One of the ways it helps with poverty, for example, is through micro-financing, aiding the revival of traditional Jordanian arts and crafts. Hana told me that Queen Noor, a statuesque blonde, was often seen at formal events, dressed in the richly embroidered gowns that women in remote Jordanian villages were famous for making. By helping women learn, relearn or transmit those skills, by giving them small loans to buy their own looms, the foundation is laying the basis for an economic revival in the countryside.

'Women are learning to be self-reliant. And they are learning how to use money,' said Hana. 'Some of them do not tell their husbands how much they have been loaned, or how much they are making.'

That could shift the balance of power in a marriage, I suggested.

'Yes, it could.'

The foundation treads carefully among the villages and tribes. 'We don't go into places and tell them what we will do for them. We ask them what they need, how we can help.'

With women in Jordan learning to be more entrepreneurial, were there any objections from more conservative men?

'There will always be some,' she said, smiling. 'But I asked one woman how her husband felt when we financed her into a little business. At first, she said, he was negative and he screamed at her about what she was doing. Now that he sees the work she does, and understands the income is for the family, he makes the children stay away so they won't disturb her when she works.' On the other hand, Hana told me, if some of those women hide their money from their husbands, as insurance against the day they are divorced, or seek a divorce themselves, that's a private matter and not the business of the foundation at all.

There is still a lot for Jordanian women to do. And fortunately there are Jordanian women of energy and intelligence who are getting on with it. They don't need women like Norma Khouri lying about their lives and making blood money to set back their efforts.

Chapter 16

Lady and the Dame

> I want to live . . . I want a wild roving vagabond life . . . I wish I were a man. If I were I would be Richard Burton; but, being only a woman, I would be Richard Burton's wife . . . I would at this moment sacrifice and leave all to follow his fortunes, even if you all cast me out – if the world tabooed me.[1]

Imagine how Isabel Arundell's mother reacted when she received that letter from her romantic daughter in 1859. Though perhaps she would have been used to her flights of passion; Isabel after all had been waiting for a man just like Richard Francis Burton ever since a gypsy fortune-teller had told her to expect him. 'You will cross the sea,' wrote Hagar Burton, who claimed to be a Romany princess. 'And be in the same town as your Destiny and know it not. You will bear the name of our tribe, and be right proud of it. Your life is all wanderings, changes and adventure. One soul in two bodies in life or death, never long apart.'[2] Isabel learned the text by heart, and it became the template of her life. Odd, considering her solid, aristocratic beginnings, the way things worked out for her.

She was born in 1831 in London, into one of the oldest and most important Catholic families in England. They weren't rich, but their noble connections meant that her wine-merchant father and his family could live in part of Wardour Castle, the seat of Isabel's godfather, Lord Arundell. Her childhood and adolescence were unremarkable – like most teenagers, she went through a stage of being headstrong, lumpy and secretive. Isabel was a solitary child who preferred her own company and was content to while away the time at home in her den. She confided in her journal that she longed for gypsies, Bedouin Arabs, and 'everything Eastern and mystic; and especially a wild and lawless life'.[3] These were hardly the sorts of things that usually ran through the well-behaved brains of girls about to be presented at court, but Isabel Arundell was an original.

She made a brilliant entrance into society at Almack's Assembly Rooms in St James, and her first London season was a triumph. She had developed into something of a catch: a beauty who bore the aristocratic name and blood of the Arundells, a combination that was enough to counterbalance the lack of a dowry. But Isabel would have none of the suitors trailed in front of her by her mother and aunts.

As she was facing a second season, and her father the attendant costs, the family withdrew to the Continent to husband their resources until Isabel's next foray into the marriage market. They lived in Boulogne for two years. There, Isabel lived a life of blameless boredom, the only high point being that she and her sisters learned to thieve and smoke their father's cigars. A walk along the seafront, a bit of needlework, some shopping, a little reading and writing – it's hard to imagine now how confined and chafing that existence would have been to the girl who yearned for a vagabond life. So she passed the time imagining her ideal husband:

> Six feet in height; he has not an ounce of fat on him; he has broad and muscular shoulders, a powerful, deep chest; he is a Hercules of manly strength. He has black hair, a brown complexion, a clever forehead, sagacious eyebrows, large, black wondrous eyes – those strange eyes you dare not take yours from.[4]

Isabel was warming to her subject, and it's easy to understand why, but the paragon was an impossible dream. 'His religion is like my own, free, liberal and generous minded,' the wish list continued. 'Such a man only will I wed. I love this myth of my girlhood – for myth it is – next to God.'[5] It seemed unlikely that Isabel, tucked away in the backwater of Boulogne, would have a chance of meeting her destiny. But *inshallah* . . .

One day, some two years after she said she'd compiled her list, Isabel was walking home with one of her sisters after their regular constitutional. Suddenly she was stopped in her tracks: a vision was coming towards her. This dreamboat, said by his friend the eminent Victorian poet AC Swinburne to have 'the brow of a god and the jaw of a devil', was perfect in almost every respect. He had but one flaw: he was an inch shy of the required height.

Richard Burton was thirty when he and Isabel met, and had already lived a full life. He'd studied at Trinity College, Oxford, joined the army and been posted to India. In Baroda, he began to learn Hindustani, and in Karachi, Persian. By 1845, when he was twenty-four, he had begun work as a surveyor – a perfect cover for his intelligence activities. The following year, ill with cholera, he went on two years' sick leave, and the year after that, he was in Goa, still convalescing. He remained too ill to work in 1848, but he returned to Sindh and kept studying languages, including Arabic, Sindi and Punjabi, as well as being indoctrinated in the mysteries of the Sufis.

It was Burton the Sufi master, linguist, explorer, spy and adventurer that Isabel saw that day in 1851. She might have been just twenty, but armed with Hagar's prophecy, she recognised her destiny when it hove into sight. 'I stole a look at him, and met his Gypsy eyes and saw something behind them,' she confirmed.[6] Even better, he seemed to recognise her, too.

Isabel was in a fever, describing her state as 'red and pale, hot and cold, dizzy and faint'.[7] Her parents sent for a doctor, but only Isabel could name her ailment.

She saw him again, at a *thé-dansant* given by her cousin: 'There was Richard like a star among the rushlights . . . he waltzed with me once, and spoke to me several times, and I kept my sash where he put his arm around my waist to waltz, and my gloves, which his hands had clasped. I never wore them again.'[8]

True love had to wait, however. Burton was off on a secret pilgrimage to Mecca and Medina, where discovery of his identity (as an infidel in the holy city) would have meant certain death. He then went with John Hanning Speke, an officer in the British Indian

Army, to discover the source of the Nile. During the expedition, Speke was captured, but escaped; Burton was speared through the jaw and left with a broken palate and heavy scarring. Then he went to the Crimea in 1855, to volunteer.

Isabel tried to join him there. She applied to Florence Nightingale to become a nurse, but was rejected: too young, too inexperienced. Once more she was thrust onto the marriage mart, refusing suitor after suitor, and amusing herself by reading accounts of the man she loved and his amazing adventures in Arabia. She might have been jealous of the women he visited in disguise as a doctor, envious of the time he spent with the falconers in the valley of the Indus, but she had to bite her tongue and bite hard.

One day, at home in England once more, Isabel's object of desire was suddenly less obscure. While out walking with her sister, there Burton was again. They saw each other every day for two weeks, and then he proposed. Perhaps he saw in Isabel a woman who would be an asset in a camel caravan, not a missish creature who would dissolve into tears at the least obstacle. She saw in him a marriage foretold, an inevitability of fate. 'I would be Richard Burton's wife,' as she had famously said.[9]

But before she could marry Burton, she had to wait a few more years, while he returned to Africa with Speke. This time, they found the source of the Nile. In 1859 Burton and Speke were on their way home to London, but Burton became too ill to travel. Speke went on alone, and grabbed the credit for the expedition.

Finally, in 1861, the gypsy's words came true. In the face of her parents' continuing opposition, Isabel and Richard eloped and wed on 22 January with a minimum of fuss and people, at the Bavarian Catholic Church in Warwick Street, London. The next day he confessed by post to his new father-in-law: 'I have committed a highway robbery by marrying your daughter Isabel.'[10] His mother-in-law remained unconvinced, declaring until she died that 'Dick Burton is no relative of mine.'[11]

Money was short, so Burton took up a minor diplomatic post on the Spanish island of Fernando Po (now called Bioko), off the coast of Cameroon in the Gulf of Biafra. Isabel wasn't allowed to stay with him in the region, which was known as 'the white man's grave', and farewelled him in Liverpool. She was distraught, and petitioned the Foreign Office – in tears – to send him home on leave. She became further unnerved when he travelled into Dahomey, where the king was reported to have a force of Amazon women, one of whom was functioning as Burton's aide. (And perhaps more than that, since Burton didn't seem to remain faithful to Isabel when she wasn't within reach.)

The second time he left England for Bioko, Isabel clung to him as far as Madeira, before being sent home. It was the first of their journeys together, and soon Isabel was scheming for a posting that she could go on as well. In 1865, they were together in Brazil, and in 1869, Isabel's dreams of 'everything Eastern and mystic' came true: Burton, with her help, was posted to Damascus.

Isabel was ecstatic; she would be living among the Bedouin Arabs and breathing in the desert air. She would also be her husband's 'companion, secretary and his *aide de camp*'.[12]

This was the period in her life when Isabel Burton flourished, despite some setbacks – including an ambush aimed at her husband. 'I was never more flattered in my life than to think that it would take three hundred men to kill me,' he wrote afterwards.[13] Isabel faced her own dangers. She went into the Turkish baths and harems of Constantinople, and in the Syrian Desert discovered how to shoo off of a pack of ravening jackals (waving a handkerchief was most effective, apparently). Adding to her version of living dangerously, Isabel kept a panther cub as a pet at home in Damascus.

Like Lady Mary Wortley Montagu and another English traveller, Lady Hester Stanhope, Isabel found that dressing like the male locals was a comfortable and practical way to traipse around the desert:

> My dress was very picturesque . . . It consisted of large yellow button boots and gaiters, and English riding-habit with the long ends of the skirt tucked in to look like their Eastern baggy trousers, an Eastern belt with revolver, dagger, and cartridges. My hair was all tucked up under the *tarbash*, and I wore one of the Bedawin veils to the waist, only showing a bit of face. The veil was of all colours, chiefly gold braid, bound by a chocolate and gold circlet near the forehead.

> Richard slung over my back and round my neck a whistle and compass, in case of my being lost.[14]

The British Foreign Office blamed Burton and his innate lack of diplomacy for the increasing problems in Syria, and recalled him – which resulted in the famous 'Pay, pack and follow' instruction to Isabel. Life in pedestrian Trieste followed, but it could never equal the power of the life they had shared in the desert, where they camped every night and galloped across the blazing sands during the day.

They went to India together, and Egypt, but the life of wild abandon Isabel had dreamed of as a child never returned. Still, they could write about it, and they did. When Burton, who had been knighted in 1886, died on the Continent, she took him home to England and entombed him in a stone Bedouin tent in the grounds of St Mary Magdalene Church in the London suburban of Mortlake. She wrote his biography, *The Life of Captain Sir Richard F. Burton* (published in 1892), and worked as his literary executor until she finally joined him in his tent in 1896.

Isabel Arundell Burton was an extraordinary woman, one who made her mark the way women did in those days: in conjunction with her husband. Dame Freya Stark, however, who was born in 1893, was a woman of the twentieth century. She made her mark completely on her own. In the annals of women writing about their travels, Freya's is one of the freshest and most perceptive voices. Her range was wide and long: she lived for almost one hundred years, and travelled often to the Orient, Turkey, Persia, the Arab countries and central Asia. A short marriage and two world wars might have slowed her a little, but nothing stopped her for long.

Isabel Burton would have understood the passionate attachment to the Middle East that Freya felt and expressed in the following words: 'I never imagined that my first sight of the desert would come with such a shock of beauty and enslave me right away.'[15] Freya wrote that, despite the fact that she was used to beauty in landscape and had been wandering from birth. She was born in France, where her parents, Robert and Flora, were painters. They were devoted to natural beauty and had been influenced by the writer and artist John Ruskin (the man said to be the greatest Victorian who wasn't Victoria), as well as the designer and craftsman William Morris. The family could hardly have been called settled: they summered in Devon, Robert's home, and went to Genoa, Flora's, for Christmas. They lived the rest of the time in Asolo, in the foothills of the Dolomites.

Like many children, Freya fell in love with the romance and the otherness of *The Arabian Nights*, and when she went to London in 1911, she carried some of those Oriental dreams with her. Attending Bedford College for Women, she studied English and history but, after World War I, she made an unusual decision: she studied Arabic, first in Italy, and then at the London School of Oriental Studies. In December 1927, she left Europe for Lebanon, ostensibly to restore her fragile health, but also to work on her Arabic, she said. While she was boarding in Broumana, the summer resort town in the mountains to the east of Beirut, the tranquil countryside of the Levant (modern-day Lebanon and Syria) was within her reach, and Baalbek, with its magnificent Ancient Roman ruins, was close by. In 1928, when she relocated to Damascus, she played the tourist thoroughly in Syria, then travelled to Palestine to see Acre and Jerusalem, and then on to Jordan, where she tramped down the narrow passage to Petra before moving off to explore Egypt.

The journey foreshadowed a restless life. In 1929, she was working as a journalist based in Baghdad, where she gathered material for *Baghdad Sketches*, a travel book published in 1937. She was becoming more adventurous, visiting the abandoned castles of Islam's radical sect, the Assassins. Her style of intrepid travelling, accompanied by photographs she took, was established. Difficulty and fierce legend did not deter her: 'The lower parts of the castle are inaccessible without climbing shoes; there, legend says, seven black dogs guard Hasan-i-Sabbah's treasure; they breathe fire, but fly when challengers approach.'[16]

Freya kept travelling. She was in Arabia in 1935, and wrote two books of memoirs about that trip. During World War II, she worked as an expert on southern Arabia at the Ministry of Information in London, then later moved to Aden, Cairo and again Baghdad. When she was in Aden, working at the British Secretariat, she met her future husband, the Arabist and historian Stewart Perowne. Married in 1947, they stayed together for only five years, during which Freya travelled to the Caribbean, North Africa and Paris. In 1952, the year her marriage ended, she discovered Turkey. That love affair lasted until her death in 1993.

Fearless and indefatigable, Freya Stark adventured and wrote throughout her long life. She produced more than twenty books, and eight volumes of her letters have been published. When she was in her seventies, she went to China for the first time; at seventy-six, she jeeped across Afghanistan. At the age of seventy-four, she went on a pony trek in Nepal, and made a final trip to the Middle East, where she rafted down the Euphrates with a film crew.

That's what happens: you start off reading *The Arabian Nights* and end up living and telling some stories of your own.

Chapter 17

My First Gigolo

Every journey has a chance to become a forced march, commanded by the primacy of next meal and next bed.
John Krich

THE AIR WAS HOT and close as we wound our way through desolate streets on the city's fringe. A hypnotic soundtrack of Lebanese pop music was providing the insistent background noise for our pell-mell drive from the airport. Stopped at a set of traffic lights, I saw a clock tick over to midnight. At that instant, all the neon signs switched off and the streets sank into semi-darkness. Even the trees, similar to those of my subtropical home town, looked alien and threatening. So this was Beirut.

In spite of its recent turbulent history, the city has retained an aura of glamour, with its hypnotic blend of Levantine languor and French chic. In 2004, Lebannon was being talked up by its tourism operators: things were back to normal, the country was safer than it had been for years. I wanted to believe the hype, which is why I found myself in downtown Beirut in the middle of the night, ready to see the miracle of 'the Land of Cedars' for myself.

Lebanon has been in recovery mode since the devastating civil war between the Muslims and Christians ended, in 1990. The conflict, which had smouldered for generations, ignited in 1975, after four Christians were murdered in an attempt on the life of Pierre Jumayyil, founder of the Phalangists, one of the Christian parties. The next day, Phalangists retaliated by attacking a busload of

Palestinians in a Christian neighbourhood of Beirut, killing nearly thirty people. Street warfare broke out and some took the opportunity to settle personal rather than political scores.

Lebanon had been the Paris of the East until then, but overnight it turned into a quagmire. The old city centre of Beirut was devastated; everywhere, bullet holes in walls signalled a society in crisis.

From the south, Israel grabbed for advantage, while from the north and the east, Syria threatened. The fighting spread to the countryside and sectarian violence saw divisions within the ranks of both sides: Palestinian Muslims fought Druze militiamen, Maronite Christian groups disputed with Phalangists. Sectarians retreated to their strongholds, the Lebanese Army divided into factions and an effective power vacuum developed.

The civil conflict continued for fifteen years, exacting a terrible toll. In the first two years, an estimated 44,000 people died, about 180,000 were wounded, while countless others were displaced or emigrated. In total, an estimated 150,000 people were killed during the war.[1] The centre of Beirut, once the glamorous portal of the Levant, was destroyed.

With those dark days now long gone, the process of rebuilding is starting to bear fruit. A Syrian-backed government, propped up by Syrian troops stationed in Lebanon, kept an uneasy peace while Rafik Hariri, a self-made billionaire and occasional prime minister, was busy leading the charge of urban renewal in downtown Beirut. Billions of dollars have been spent restoring the city to its former glory – little wonder then that some of the Lebanese I encountered liked to boast that the real estate here was now more expensive than in Manhattan. Hariri wanted Lebanon to be the Switzerland of the Middle East again. 'People still mourn the Gold Age which ended when Israel invaded in 1982,' he said, noting that a million tourists had visited Lebanon in 2003, most of them coming from other Arab states.[2]

The project to revive the heart of Beirut has been extraordinary. This area had been the worst damaged during the civil war, and was now coming to life again thanks to Hariri's vision and ability to talk the talk. The old souk was gone, replaced by expensive designer-label boutiques and rafts of coffee shops, but it's not as if the past has been lost completely to the future. While the work was going on, the excavations peeled back the layers of history here: Canaanite, Phoenician, Persian, Hellenistic, Roman, Byzantine, the times of the caliphs of Baghdad, Crusader, Mamluk, Ottoman and the most recent occupiers, the French.

Hariri has not been without his critics, however. Some people have criticised his vision and the result, claiming the renovation was devoid of soul and there were too few inhabitants. When I caught a glimpse of the cream-stoned, expensive heart of the city from my taxi window, I saw what he meant. It looked like a film set: hollow and soulless.

My taxi slipped out of the city and pressed on through the night, twenty-one kilometres north, along a multi-lane highway edged to the left by the blankness of the Med. I had missed the water since leaving Istanbul and the Bosphorus, which had filled my vision and nose morning and night – and Nebi, who had filled my hours. Here, traffic fumes overcame the fresh smell of the sea, but I was pleased to see that it was within reach.

'There!' said the driver, pointing slightly to the right up ahead. 'This is Jounieh.'

What was once a sleepy village had developed recently into a strip mall of high-rise, high-price buildings full of nightclubs and glitzy shops. Backed by the mountains, it's stopped from falling into the sea by an apron of wasteland.

'Look! Your hotel. Very nice.' In the middle of the darkness, the hotel rose out of the top of a hill. It was lit up like a Christmas tree, complete with illuminated palm trees and terraces. Fairy lights traced its distinctive silhouette. It looked like a step-pyramid, an architectural throwback to even more remote places and times. Welcome to the ziggurat.

Inside was a foyer that combined the Holy Dooley school of architecture (walk in, look around, be stunned, mutter 'Holy Dooley' under your breath) with a naval theme. It looked as though it was at sea. Past the endless reception lounge, through wide, deep windows sat the view: Beirut by night down the coast to the left; the Mediterranean straight ahead.

But as I opened the French windows onto the balcony of my

room in the tower, I saw that the sea was hundreds of metres away, across the freeway and a desolate no-man's-land. So much for thinking I might go for a run on the beach before breakfast. I looked down the coast towards Beirut and felt uneasy. I couldn't put my finger on the reason why, but I had a sense of foreboding that the best thing about the city might well be my room high on the hill overlooking the coast of the Phoenicians.

Those ancient traders, the Phoenicians, had been in the news recently. Spencer Wells, a *National Geographic* explorer, and Pierre Zalloua, from the American University of Beirut, were busy doing a series of DNA tests to examine the connections between the modern Lebanese and other people in the region. There was some concern that the results of these tests would find a difference between Christians and Muslims, proving that Christians had been there longer and therefore had more right to the land. The results, published in *National Geographic* magazine in October 2004, showed no difference in the DNA between Muslims and Christians.[3] All the same people. Perhaps they could stop fighting now.

I turned on the television news for company, but it offered cold comfort: four dead in a car bombing in Mosul; Israel and Syria rattling their sabres at each other again; Lebanon – with me in it – stuck in the middle. My foreboding meter climbed into the red zone.

By daylight, the sense of ill omen remained and made me inert. Every time I thought about going out, I found a reason not to. There was something about this bright, troubled city, with its deep bank of slate-grey smog out to sea that was intimidating, bringing on a sudden attack of agoraphobia. I had wanted to go to Sidon; and to Tyre, 'the Queen of the Seas', which lay eighty kilometres south of Beirut; to Baalbeck; to the Crusader castles along the coast at Byblos; to the cedars at Bcharré . . . But I could hardly move. I went for a swim in the hotel's indoor pool instead, then ordered room service for dinner, soaked in the tub, and climbed between the Frette sheets, promising to try harder the next day.

When it dawned, I started with baby-steps to the nearest mall in Jounieh. But I felt odd there too, and it wasn't just because it was full of expensive tat. In comparison with the fashion retailers, the Mothercare wasn't too bad, but the mall was an experience of limited thrills, so I bought a pair of hot-pink slides and a CD by the popular Beirut-born singer Fairouz.

'She is the soul of this region,' the CD salesman told me. 'You will not know us until you know her.'

I bought a second to make doubly sure I would get the message, then scurried back to the hotel as quickly as I could.

I couldn't shake the feeling that something was terribly wrong in the state of Lebanon, and decided that a little water therapy might be the answer. Fortunately, at the back of the hotel, there was one of the most extraordinary water parks I'd ever seen – named, without any apparent irony, Watergate. The complex took up more than twenty thousand square metres, and included a dazzling variety of ways to get wet and stay that way.

I was being shown around by a tall, blond man with green eyes and curly hair, who seemed to be the manager. 'When the park closes next month, I will become a night-duty manager at the hotel,' he said with some pride. 'Where do you live?' he breathed.

Sydney.

He looked interested. 'Beautiful, Sydney. Are you married? Do you have any children?'

Bored enough, I made up a story. Suddenly, I'd acquired a husband. And a child. 'We have one daughter. She is twenty-three and at university.' I felt a bit guilty for this deception, but couldn't stand to explain yet again to a horrified Arab how I had managed to avoid my destiny as a wife and mother so thoroughly.

'Is she pretty like her mother?' he asked.

'Oh, no. She's beautiful.'

'Why isn't she here with you?'

'She's at home, studying. She is finishing her master's degree in linguistics.' I was warming to this. If you have a fantasy, it might as well be a good one.

He walked me to the front gates of the aqua park. 'If only you were staying longer, I could show you around,' he said.

Now this was turning odd.

'Would you like a drink tonight?'

Very odd.

'Would your daughter call me?'

'How old are you?' I asked.

'Thirty-seven.'

'That's a bit old for twenty-three.'

'Not if we like each other.'

'You might not like her.'

'I can tell I would. To know about a daughter, you should look at the mother.'

I began to feel as though I should disappear in a puff of smoke, to match my purely fictional, brilliant, beautiful child.

'I am a Christian,' he said, perhaps to reassure me. 'My name is Michael.' Then my future son-in-law began to tell me about his world. 'Life is terrible here. There is no future. It is hard to tell when the Israelis will invade, or when the Syrians will. The only sure thing is that something terrible will happen here. I must get out. I have to leave. We have nothing.' His father had died three years earlier, aged eighty-two, Michael told me. He'd been in real estate. Michael's mother was much younger than his father. He now lived with his brother and mother in a block his father had bought for them. His mother did all the work around the house for her sons. Michael had been married once, in America, but just for the green card. He didn't have the card anymore.

And suddenly it all became clear.

At that very instant, my new friend ducked behind a pillar. 'Come over here,' he hissed. 'I am under surveillance.'

What? I was getting the impression that this character was in the habit of handing his card to single women. Could he possibly be a gigolo?

'Call me tonight, we can go out,' he said, eliminating any doubt about his night job. 'We can have a drink. We could go to dinner.'

As if, I thought, as I made my farewells.

'This is my address,' he said as he handed me his card. 'Your daughter. She can write to me. You call me tonight!'

I retreated to the hotel's indoor pool again, and eased into its warmth. Sunlight filtered through the floor-to-ceiling windows, bending in the water, and was reflected blue, green, gold by the mosaics on the pool floor. I floated in the water, looking out over the sea ruled by the Phoenicians. I was completely alone.

A couple of days afterwards I left Beirut, the danger I'd felt there became a reality. A former economy minister, Marwane Hamadeh, was the target of a bomb blast, after he and other members of the government resigned over a plan to keep the Syrian-backed government and its president, Emile Lahoud, in office. His driver was killed. It was a blow to Rafik Hariri's plan to revitalise tourism in his country.

There was more, worse, still to come. Hariri, also an opponent of Lahoud, was known to have aroused the enmity of the Syrian president, Bashar Al-Assad. On Valentine's Day 2005, Hariri himself was assassinated. As his motorcade drove past the St George Hotel on the waterfront, a car bomb loaded with a thousand kilograms of explosives was detonated. Sixteen people died, including Hariri, and one hundred others were injured. It was the beginning of the end for Syrian control of the country, as the Cedar Revolution gathered momentum.

Chapter 18

Belles of the Desert

ALTHOUGH I HAD CHOSEN a fairly cushy route, my journey through the Middle East and North Africa was part of a continuum. Women travellers have been crossing these lands for thousands of years. Some, like Balqis, the Queen of Sheba, went on affairs of state; others, like Helena Augusta, the mother of the first Christian Roman emperor, Constantine, who lived around 248 to 328, went on pilgrimage to Holy Land sites including Bethlehem, Jerusalem and Mount Sinai, had churches built and gave to the poor of the region.

In around 381, a Spanish nun, Egeria, followed in Helena Augusta's footsteps, and wrote the first known travel book by a woman. She recorded her voyage, which would have had none of the comforts afforded to the mother of an emperor, in letters she sent home to her fellow sisters. Extracts that have survived seem to have been transcribed by a monk called Valerius, in the seventh century, and can be found in a manuscript called *The Pilgrimage of St Silvia of Aquitania to the Holy Places*, which was found in a monastery in Arezzo in the late nineteenth century. Of Egeria, Valerius wrote: 'Nothing could hold her back, whether it was the labour of travelling the whole world, sea or rivers, crags and mountains.'[1]

Using the Bible as a map and reference, she travelled the wilderness described in the book of *Exodus*; climbed Mount Sinai and the mountain above Jericho; went to the traditional sites of the Burning Bush, where God spoke to Moses, and of Lot's wife's transmutation; celebrated communion on the most sacred sites of the Holy Land;

and recorded the Jerusalem liturgy and services for Epiphany and Easter.

Egeria's intrepid spirit meant she was among the first to study and record the differences in the rites of the early Christian church, from Europe to Asia Minor and Africa. She was a woman who recounted the mysteries of her faith as she discovered them with real joy.

The First Crusade (1095–99) saw another woman take up her pen, to record its history and, in doing so, become one of the world's first female historians. Anna Comnena, daughter of the Byzantine emperor Alexius I, was well educated in her youth, and in a pole position to experience and write about daily life at her father's court, the exploits of her family, and contact between the Western Crusaders and the Byzantines.

By the time of the Second Crusade (1147–49), women took their place among the men, and Queen Eleanor of Aquitaine took up the cross alongside her first husband, Louis VII of France. She travelled with three hundred of her women, all dressed as Amazons, and one thousand knights from Aquitaine. She said she and her women were there as nurses, but she still took part in strategy meetings. When she sided with her uncle, Raymond of Antioch, against her husband on the question of whether to attack Jerusalem, their marriage was effectively at an end.

By the time Eleanor's son Richard, 'the Lionheart', embarked on the Third Crusade (1189–92), women were banned from the endeavour – all except the elderly, who could be no temptation to the Crusaders of the Church Militant. These were welcomed as washerwomen, to keep down the populations of lice in the soldiers' clothes. Despite a Papal veto, there were women at the Siege of Acre in 1189–91. The highest ranked of them on the galleys of reinforcements that Richard brought with him was Berengaria of Navarre, his new bride and so queen of England. In the absence of Richard's mother, Berengaria was accompanied by his sister, Joanna, the recently widowed queen of Sicily, who briefly looked as though she might have come in handy as a diplomatic pawn. At one stage, a union was proposed between her and Al-Adil, brother of Salah Al-Din (better known in the West as Saladin), the Saracen commander.

The proposal was that Joanna and her new lord should settle in Jerusalem and there rule together. Apparently the idea failed when it became clear that Joanna did not care for the match.

But women were not just diplomatic pawns at Acre. According to the writer Imad Al-Din, Western noblewomen also fought there. One, he noted, a queen, was 'accompanied by five hundred knights with their horses and money, pages and valets'; she paid all their expenses, treated them well, and when she rode into battle, they 'charged when she charged, flung themselves into the fray at her side'.[2]

There were other women, less elevated and less celebrated. Among the Frankish troops, women warriors, dressed in cuirasses and helmets, fought in the thick of the action. They were not recognised by the enemy as women until they were captured and stripped. Some of them were executed by Saladin, others sold as slaves.

Eastern women were in the fight as well, continuing the long tradition of Islamic women on the battlefield. At Acre, they carried water to the men, and stones to fill the moat of the castle that sat on the promontory at the northern end of Haifa Bay.

There were also, of course, the women who followed the camps of the Crusaders, and their more upmarket sisters-in-the-field. Imad Al-Din noticed them, but then it would've been hard to miss 'three hundred lovely Frankish women, full of youth and beauty, assembled from beyond the sea and offering themselves for sin'.[3] Many of these were, he said, 'expatriates come to help expatriates, ready to cheer the fallen and sustained in turn to give support and assistance, and they glowed with ardour for carnal intercourse. They were all licentious harlots.'[4] In his reports, he implied there were no such harlots in his own camps, although he did admit that 'a few foolish mamluks and ignorant wretches slipped away, under the fierce goad of lust, and followed the people of error.'[5]

The Levant (Lebanon and Syria) was the stamping ground and eventual graveyard of two of the most formidable English women travellers in history.

Lady Hester Stanhope, the self-styled 'Queen of the Desert', was born in 1776 into the upper reaches of the English aristocracy, the eldest child of Charles, third Earl of Stanhope, and his first wife, Lady Hester Pitt. The young Hester spent her early years comfortably at her father's ancestral seat, the great house of Chevening in Kent, but she obviously had a childish inclination for adventure. When she developed an early interest in France, she acted on it, and was discovered one fine day in an appropriated dinghy, rowing out into the English Channel. Fortunately she was only about ten metres from shore when she was collared and beached.

After her father's death, she was taken in by her uncle, William Pitt the Younger. At the age of twenty-seven, she became head of his household at Walmer Castle and began a celebrated career as a political hostess. She entertained Pitt's guests, became renowned for her wit (although sometimes her sharp-tongued remarks wounded and made her keen enemies), created a salon, ordered his life, and ran his staff. In 1804, Pitt became prime minister and her life reached its glittering zenith.

In 1810, after two unsatisfactory love affairs and Pitt's death, and armed with a pension from the British government of twelve hundred pounds a year, Hester set off for the Mediterranean on the great adventure of her life.[6] Naturally, she was not alone. Hester was accompanied by her private physician, Dr Charles Meryon, and, by the time the party left Gibraltar, a certain young man named Michael Bruce. The twenty-year-old Englishman soon became Hester's lover. Dr Meryon was somewhat displeased, since he considered that to be his role.

By Corinth, she had nine people in her retinue and, most importantly if implausibly, she had a plan that involved travelling to Constantinople, ingratiating herself with the French ambassador to the Ottoman Empire and thus obtaining a passport to France, then journeying through Hungary and Germany to Paris. There she planned to become the confidante of Napoleon himself, discover how his brain worked and, armed with that knowledge, advise the British government how best to overthrow him. When Whitehall learned of her scheme, it was scotched. Hester, with not much else to do, pressed on from Corinth to Cairo.

It was a trip which generally took a week by ship, but thanks to a storm and a shipwreck, the party was forced to take refuge on Rhodes and wait in a shabby windmill for another ship to rescue them. While they were there, Hester began to wear male attire – something she did for the rest of her life. This was not an affectation necessarily taken seriously by the locals. Hester fondly imagined she was wearing authentic Oriental costume, but the residents of Rhodes barely swallowed giggles when she appeared decked out, as one writer noted, in a rig closer to 'Regent Street Tunisian'.[7]

In February 1812, two years after Hester and her group had left England, and two months after they had cast off from Corinth, they arrived in Alexandria. The Anglophones in the group immediately set about learning Arabic and Turkish. 'The East was in her blood,' noted the writer Daniel Da Cruz of Hester, 'its combination of mystery, romance, mysticism, hardship, fatalism and fanaticism having captured her English soul as it was to capture so many of her countrymen in future decades.'[8]

Used to dealing with the highest levels of government, she called in on the Egyptian ruler, Muhammad Ali Pasha. To her, it was a meeting between equals. Soon, though, she'd had enough of the difficulties of Cairo – the humidity of the Nile Delta, the fleas – and planned her next move. She decided to go to Palestine, which was something easier said than done, as there were bandits between the port of Jaffa and the Holy City of Jerusalem. Hester needed a safe passage, and that was at the disposal of the local sheikh, Abu Ghosh. She got it by the simple expedient of marching up to his camp, chatting him up, paying him off and threatening him with dire consequences should her caravan not arrive safely. The sheikh did as he was bid and kept the local bandits under control and away from her while she made a grand tour of the holy sites from Jerusalem to Nazareth, Acre and beyond.

Lady Hester, the English noblewoman, had largely been subsumed into the mannish figure her new life required. She constantly cross-dressed, smoked a water pipe and – the joy of travel! – was able to curse her caravan drivers roundly and fluently in English, Arabic and Turkish.

The Arabs were noted for their hospitality and kindness to

visitors. Their deference to people who seem to them 'afflicted of Allah' – in other words, mad, and therefore under the protection of God – was well established. To the locals, Hester was certainly a visitor, and she seemed to be mad. Consequently, she was well received, but her reception appeared to her to be simply part of the homage she was due, thanks to her blood line and connections. She thought she was being acclaimed and admired for her inherent superiority, and to the end of her life, no one disabused her of the idea.

In Sidon, Hester was asked to call on the overlord of the Druze sect, Emir Bashir, at his castle at Deir-el-Kamar in the Lebanese mountains. Of course she went – who could refuse such an invitation? The relatively unknown sect had split from Orthodox Islam in the eleventh century and controlled a series of mountain strongholds. Its leader seemed to Hester a truly romantic figure.

Dr Meryon, Hester's long-suffering travel companion, had another view. In a letter home, he wrote, with supreme irony: 'They say he is a very good man. It is true he blinded his three nephews and had his prime minister strangled . . . but these things go for nothing in Turkey.'[9] Hester was not to be deterred. The party travelled light (only twenty-two camels, twenty-five mules and eight horses) and the excursion was a huge success. Emir Bashir told her she could visit his domain for as long as she wanted.

One last challenge remained in the region: the 'forbidden city' of Palmyra. Close to the Tadmor Oasis, east of Damascus, Palmyra had been the seat of the desert kingdom of Queen Zenobia in the third century AD. From there Zenobia had defied the power of the Roman Empire until she was defeated, captured and taken to Rome as the star in the triumph of the emperor, Lucius Domitius Aurelianus.

Hester's approach to the despot who ruled Palmyra was typically direct: 'I know you are a robber and that I am now in your power. But I fear you not. I have left behind all those who were offered me as a safeguard . . . to show you that it is *you* whom I have chosen as such.'[10] The emir could not resist and invited Hester to visit. She turned up alone except for two guides, and stayed for a week.

During that time, she inspected the Roman ruins and allowed her fantasies to take flight: with a retinue of local ranking Bedouin and some less elevated tribesmen, she proceeded down the colonnaded avenue that led to the great temple in the centre of the city; beside each column she passed was a young woman, and as Hester rode by, each girl fell in beside her, as escort.

Word of Hester's adventures in Palmyra had reached England, and she began to receive letters asking for advice from people planning similar trips. To one, she earnestly advised taking a chamber pot: 'Imagine Madam, a plain which never seems to end, and consider what you are to do when you are eight or nine hours together. It will be in vain to see a bush or a tree for any *little purpose*.'[11]

Hester was happy then. The rest of her life would not be so. Everything after this was pallid by comparison, and lonely. Michael Bruce, her lover, had gone back to England in 1813. In 1821, Hester finally took up permanent residence in a large and odd old house guarded by Albanians, in Djoun, a small village among the olive groves of southern Lebanon. From there, she dominated the surrounding districts, though not always her admirer, Dr Meryon. He was tired of life in the Levant and planned to leave. In fact, he made two false starts, and at the third attempt, was gone forever.

By this time, Hester truly was 'touched of Allah'. Convinced she possessed the gift of divination, she studied alchemy and astrology, half-poisoned guests with potions she brewed up, and made her black house-slaves treat her like royalty.

Occasionally she could still seem like the Hester of old. She encouraged a local chieftain to begin a war against a northern sect, the Ansaries of Latakia. She had been horrified and outraged when they had broken the law of hospitality by murdering a French consul. She wanted them to pay, and pay they did. Some three hundred innocents died at Hester's behest. When Ibrahim Paşa, an Egyptian general, was about to invade Syria in 1832, he first sought Hester's neutrality.

She even managed to persuade the Ottoman government to fund an excavation, which she said would reveal a buried treasure in Ascalon, the Saracen stronghold demolished at the end of the Third Crusade. Unsurprisingly, the dig degenerated into complete farce with not a single coin or jewel discovered. Later she became convinced that the Mahdi, the holy warrior of Islam, was about to appear in the East. Naturally, she saw herself as his bride.

Hester's eccentricities became still more extreme – for example, she kept an Arab mare that she had fed with sherbets and sweetmeats. Her debts increased, her friends melted away and her enemies bayed for money or blood. Finally, the British government cut off her pension to placate one of her creditors.

After this, Hester began to commit slow suicide. She dismissed all her servants and had the gateway to her house in Djoun walled up. Thus immured, she died poverty-stricken and in shocking squalor in June 1839. Lady Hester Stanhope, aged sixty-three, perished alone in a world where she was what she had always been: an alien. After her death, the thirty servants she had bullied mercilessly for so long ransacked her house.

Gertrude Bell was another restless adventuress and, like Hester, developed a passion for the East. If her friend TE Lawrence ('Dear Boy' to her) was Lawrence of Arabia, Gertrude deserves to be Bell of Mesopotamia.

For better or worse, she effectively carved modern Iraq out of the earth and defined it on a map for the first time. According to some of her biographers, she was the unaccredited driving force behind the Arab Revolt against the Ottoman rule (1916–18) that Lawrence was hailed for assisting. She also convinced British prime minister Winston Churchill to appoint King Faisal, just deposed as the king of Syria, as the first king of Iraq, and she became the most senior female civil servant in the British Empire.

Born in 1868, Gertrude Margaret Lowthian Bell had the good sense to land in a family of means, an industrial northern clan. As a child growing up in Washington Hall in County Durham, she showed a precocious intellect. That early promise was fulfilled when she went up to Oxford, completing her degree within two years rather than the usual three. Although she was the first woman to complete a first-class degree in modern history, she was not permitted to graduate; women might have been admitted to Oxford since 1879, but they were not awarded a degree.

What to do next? 'Few such moments of exhilaration can come as that which stands at the threshold of wild travel,' she wrote, and travel she did.[12] She took off around the world, climbing in Switzerland and digging in Turkey, where she discovered a natural love and affinity for archaeology and language.

Gertrude became one of England's great explorers, travelling through the deserts of Arabia, where she travelled happily as the only woman among men (though she later would not walk unchaperoned in London's Piccadilly and helped to found the Anti-Suffrage League). During her travels, she cultivated friendships with Arab chieftains, princes and sheikhs – to them, she was a 'daughter of the desert'.[13]

The open plains and the deserts had become her spiritual home, and she wrote of the adventurer's yearning for what Vita Sackville-West had called 'this question of horizon' in her first book, *Persian Pictures*: 'the boundless plains stretching before him, the nights when the dome of the sky was his ceiling, and he was awakened by the cold kisses of the wind'.[14]

Kisses of any other kind were not often in the equation. Gertrude never married, though she had two love affairs, the most durable with Dick Doughty-Wylie (nephew of the Charles Doughty whose *Arabia Deserta* had travelled with her in Arabia).

By the beginning of World War I, Gertrude was in Baghdad. She was well positioned to advise the British government on the size, placement and temper of Arab forces who might join Britain and her allies against the Turks. She was drafted into the Arab Bureau in Cairo (its only woman member) and in 1919 she argued the Arab case at the Paris Peace Conference.

Her knowledge and understanding of Mesopotamia – the countries of Iraq and Persia – and Arab culture and temperament were of continued use to Britain in these post-war years. In 1920, she co-wrote the white paper 'Review of the Civil Administration of Mesopotamia', in which she outlined a plan for the future Iraq.[15] It was the first paper ever written by a woman for the British government.

As colonial secretary, Winston Churchill called a conference in Cairo in 1921 to determine the future of the Middle East, and summoned forty experts. Naturally, Gertrude was there, and again she was the only woman. She had achieved her ambition in life: to be taken seriously, and treated like a Person.

The conference paid attention to the recommendations in Gertrude's paper, and she not only took part of the determination of the borders of the new nation of Iraq, but its first ruler, Prince Faisal ibn Hussein, the deposed king of Syria, was her candidate. She had known him through the war, and was not only his sponsor, but also his closest personal and political adviser. Because of her closeness to the king, she became known as the uncrowned queen of Iraq.

Those days were the high point of her public career, but TE Lawrence garnered all the public attention and kudos that should have been hers. It created a bitterness in her from which she never recovered.

Gertrude didn't care much for London; she liked Iraq, and its capital Baghdad. She was galvanised by its energy as much as its romance, and her soul warmed in the sun. Years before, she had written of the freedom of her Oriental life: 'you feel the bands break that were riveted about your heart.'[16]

Gertrude became the first director of the Baghdad Archaeological Museum, the same museum that was looted during the fall of Saddam Hussein's regime in April 2003. She died in 1926, in the city she loved so much. According to some, she had overdosed.

The Barbary Coast

Chapter 19

❀

Night Flight from Beirut

Curiosity is the one invincible thing in Nature.
Freya Stark

THERE MUST HAVE BEEN a quicker way from Beirut to Marrakesh, but I wasn't on it. My journey took the long way, round the Mediterranean, and almost a day to fly from Beirut to Milan, Milan to Casablanca, Casablanca to Marrakesh. With every passing moment I edged closer to the legendary kingdom of Maghreb.

For much of the flight, I looked out the window. My neck became cricked but eventually my attention was rewarded. Thousands of metres below lay the edge of Europe, defined, just as it was in Turkey, by a narrow, blue thread. The Strait of Gibraltar links the waters of the Atlantic Ocean and the Mediterranean Sea by forty-three kilometres of fast-running current, while it separates the continents – and populations – of Europe from Africa.

Down there, too, was the rocky outcrop of Gibraltar, formerly known as one of the Pillars of Hercules, the northern sentinel that guards the western end of the Med. Gibraltar means 'Tariq's mountain' and was named after the military commander Tariq ibn Zayd, who in 711 led seven thousand Berbers across the strait to the rock. When he landed, he promptly destroyed any exit plan the cowardly might have made, by incinerating the ships that had transported them there.

Tariq's bonfire was a real *auto de fé*; he reasoned that his army had nowhere to go but onwards, and he was right. Reinforced by another five thousand Berbers, Tariq and his men met the 60,000-strong army of the Visigoth king Rodrigo, and put it to flight. The following year, the gates of the Visigoth capital, Toledo, were opened to the invaders, and the Moorish kingdom in Spain, Al-Andalus, was born. Given its history and proximity, it's little wonder that illegal immigrants from the countries of Morocco, Algeria and Libya, as well as others of sub-Saharan origin, still see that sliver of water – only thirteen kilometres wide at its narrowest point – as a minor impediment to a journey to a better life in Europe.

On the southern side of the strait lies Morocco, fabled 'Land of the Furthest West', a hypnotic blend of Arab and Berber, sea and mountain, ancient and modern. It has been seducing Western travellers for generations, with one notable exception: the English diarist Samuel Pepys remained immune to its charms. Pepys was stationed in Morocco in the seventeenth century, as secretary of the Admiralty. Britain briefly held Tangier during this period; it had been handed over as part of the dowry of Catherine of Braganza on her marriage to the British king Charles II. It was a place, Pepys wrote, where there was 'nothing but vice in the whole place of all sorts, forswearing, cursing, drinking and whoring'.[1] He forgot to mention the marijuana. Those elements are exactly what many people still come to Morocco for.

I'd been planning to visit ever since I saw a photograph taken in the 1960s of Talitha Pol Getty, the Balinese-born model, and her husband, John Paul Getty II, on the rooftop of their palace in Marrakesh. Artfully arranged on a tiled terrace, they were the essence of cool, so chilled out they looked as though they could barely be bothered to breathe. In the background of the photo was one of the most insistent landmarks of Marrakesh, the Koutoubia Mosque. This gem of Moorish–Andalusian architecture was built in the twelfth century by the Almohad sultans, to commemorate their triumph over the Almoravids, the founders of Marrakesh. The Almohads, like their predecessors, were builders, and furnished Marrakesh with beautiful gardens, immense palaces, and mosques like Koutoubia, with its seventy-metre-high minaret.

But the mosque was just a backdrop for the Gettys, the most beautiful and insouciant of the hippies who swarmed over Morocco for the drugs and free sex in the 1960s. At the epicentre of the social scene of Marrakesh, they entertained on a monumental scale, their 'One Thousand and One Nights' parties famous for continuing, not for three years, but at least for days. The Gettys' 1968 New Year's Eve party saw the cream of international rock enjoying the couple's hospitality at their palace in the old part of town; both Paul McCartney and John Lennon were there, unable to walk or talk, according to writer John Hopkins.[2]

Within three years, Talitha had died from a heroin overdose in Rome. John Paul became a drug-addicted recluse and eventually moved to Britain, where he gave more than one hundred and twenty million pounds to worthy charities and the Conservative Party. So much for *la dolce vita*, Moroccan-style.

Marrakesh remains a haven and refuge for misfits and malcontents, as it has been for centuries. Some of its more colourful denizens have included rapper Puff Daddy, the band Blur (who launched an album here) and Andrea Bocelli, but over the years Morocco has hosted the great and the greatly overrated equally. Woolworths heiress Barbara Hutton lived here; Charlie Chaplin, Rita Hayworth, Gary Cooper and Omar Sharif visited; literary figures such as Edith Wharton, Jack Kerouac, Paul Bowles and William Burroughs came; in the 1960s, Rolling Stone Brian Jones visited with his girlfriend, and the next year came back with Mick and Keith.

My plane landed at Casablanca, where I discovered that half of my luggage was missing, so when I eventually stepped out of the baggage hall, I was one Louis Vuitton grip short of total happiness. The plane had been on the ground for more than an hour by this time, and the terminal was as empty as a state school playground on Sunday afternoon. I fully expected the driver I'd booked to have given up and made his lonely way back to Marrakesh by then, but this driver was not the sort of man to lose patience or buckle under pressure.

Mustafa clucked in sympathy and tucked me into the back seat of his aging navy-blue Mercedes-Benz, poured some water in the radiator, and we set off for Marrakesh. Mustafa was tall, neat and well made, with green eyes that I could see in the rear-view mirror. As we jolted over the ruts in the road, I was lulled to sleep, but came around half an hour later when the car suddenly stopped at a garage in the middle of nowhere. The muezzin was calling and there was a prayer room here, Mustafa explained. He shot off to join his Muslim brothers for the ten minutes or so that the prayers took, and then loped back through the garage shop. He was a gatherer – and a sharer – who returned armed with water. He gave me a bottle and half of his luncheon croissant as we hit the road again.

Mustafa navigated the stately vehicle down the road from Settat to Marrakesh, across the gorge gouged by the Oued Oum as it flows towards the North Atlantic, and up to a plain of the wide, arid, red lands known in these parts as the *bled*.

Mustafa, a man closing in on forty, was a lively conversationalist and his English was muscular and graceful. One of eleven children, he had four sisters, three of whom wore the veil. His wife wore the veil as a mark of faith, a decision he had nothing to do with, he said. 'It is not up to me to ask such a thing of her,' he explained.

As the road sliced through the countryside, it crossed farms, their fields defined by hedges of prickly pear. Some of the farmhouses were fortified, a testament to the days when life along this remote way was not so peaceful. It seemed that things might still be a little dicey from time to time: at intervals in the fences along the sides of the road stood what looked like surveillance posts.

Great fat drops of rain began to fall, not enough to cool the afternoon, but sufficient to streak the red dust into mud across the windscreen, and to send a herdsman scurrying home. On the misted horizon, the purple bruise of the the range guarding Marrakesh's northern flank lay low. Local legend has it that the nountains are haunted by invisible spirits, which, according the Qur'an (15:27), are created from the fire of hot wind. The spirits are also said to protect the city to the south.

This was the road by which Morocco's first English-speaking travel writer, the venerable Edith Wharton, descended on Marrakesh in 1917, before the November rains set in. The spirits were certainly on her mind then. 'There are countless Arab tales,' she wrote in *In Morocco*, 'of evil *djinn* [spirits] who take the form of sandstorms and hot winds to overwhelm exhausted travellers.'[3]

As a guest of General Louis-Hubert Lyautey, the first French resident-general of the Protectorate of Morocco, and his wife, Edith was bewitched by Arab North Africa. The sights and the smells of it sucked her straight into a vortex of Orientalism that would have made the staunch anti-Orientalist scholar Edward Said tut furiously. In Salé, the whitewashed city across the estuary of the Oued Bou Regreg, which had provided the corsairs of Morocco with their bolthole, Edith was dazzled by the street life and wrote of 'the stalls with fruit, olives, tunny-fish, vague syrupy sweets, candles for saints' tombs, Mantegnesque garlands of red and green peppers, griddle cakes sizzling on red hot pans'.[4]

But as Edith travelled further south, towards the High Atlas Mountains, she became pressed for time. World War I, still raging in Europe, had rather inconveniently cut her visit in Morocco to only one month. Even if she'd had a spirit's magic carpet, 'precise observation' would have been difficult, she declared.[5] Fortunately, she had a rather more practical form of transport, as General Lyautey put a military car at her disposal. And, better than that, the road she travelled along had been made by French sappers, which added to her comfort.

> Presently we crossed the Oued Tensif on an old bridge built by Moroccan engineers. Beyond the river were more palms, then olive orchards, then the vague sketch of the new European settlement, with a few shops and cafés on avenues ending suddenly in clay pits, and at last Marrakesh itself appeared to us, in the form of a red wall across a red wilderness. We passed through a gate and were confronted by other ramparts . . . suddenly we were in the palace of the Bahia, among flowers and shadows and falling water.[6]

When Mustafa and I arrived in Marrakesh, I needed a pharmacy, not a palace. My missing bag held all my toiletries, and I was carrying an injury that needed sticking plasters. All that walking across Turkey and Jordan.

Not a problem, Mustafa indicated, and dropped me at the doors of a cavernous supermarket on the outskirts of the *medina*, or old town. Had I needed white goods, dozens of bottles of mineral water, sides of beef, gigantic packet of crisps or a flat-screen TV, this would have been the perfect place. It had nearly everything, including a swoop of swallows who lived in its remote rafters and who, to brighten up their rainy afternoon, were making long and noisy bombing runs among the customers. No plasters though, so I asked again for a pharmacy, and Mustafa eventually delivered me to one.

My Arabic not being up to much past making small children shriek with laughter, I essayed the purchase in French. When that didn't work, I resorted to mime, taking off my shoe, pointing at the offending digit and hopping in mock pain. The assistant called for the chemist, and I was made to do the whole performance again, to wild applause, but they had no plasters either. I gave up on the pharmacy idea, and so did Mustafa. He took me to a palace instead.

Chapter 20

The Magic Kingdom

THE LEGENDARY LA MAMOUNIA Hotel is situated just inside the pale-ochre twelfth-century rampart gates of the *medina*'s New Gate. According to the British wartime prime minister Winston Churchill, it was 'the most lovely spot in the world', one that soothed him and recharged his batteries as no other place could.[1]

Churchill even convinced the American president Franklin D Roosevelt to spend a few days' holiday there after the Casablanca Conference in 1943, at the height of World War II. Churchill went up to the roof and painted; Roosevelt relaxed in the splendour of the hotel and the parks, which were established in the eighteenth century when Sultan Mohamed Ben Abdellah gave them to his fourth son, Prince Moulay Mamoun, as a wedding present.

General Charles De Gaulle, the leader of the Free French, also stayed there after the conference. The hotel even had a special bed made to accommodate the general's great height.

Their names are in the hotel's guest book, along with many other notables. Erich Von Stroheim filmed *Alerte au Sud* here in 1953. Marlene Dietrich slept here, as did Charlie Chaplin (though not with her) – and Omar Sharif, Joan Collins, Whoopi Goldberg, Tom Cruise and Nicole Kidman, and Elton John. Ronald and Nancy Reagan, Princess Caroline of Monaco, Prince Naruhito of Japan and former South African president Nelson Mandela have all wandered through the gardens that gave the hotel its name.

Opened in 1923, La Mamounia, a blend of Moorish design and Art Deco, had an air of indulgent glamour which started at its front steps, where fezzed and uniformed staff relieved me of my baggage.

Its fountained halls were redolent of roses – there were thousands of them in the public spaces. For a woman looking for the glamour and sensuality promised by *The Arabian Nights*, this was not a bad place to be.

I felt a bit like I was cutting school: I should have been in Rabat, interviewing activist women and politicians as part of my research. But since the Moroccans had refused to answer even a single fax, I had changed my plans and decided to have a couple of days off instead. Of all the places in North Africa to take a holiday, Marrakesh was one of the most appealing.

The hotel provided me with a perfect refuge from the modern world, but the Arab world was insistent, and wouldn't allow me to be there for long without a reminder of where I was. Just before dawn, the sound of muezzins woke me. In the half-gloom, I stepped out through the French doors of my room to the wide balcony. Below, some of the eleven hectares of gardens stretched towards a creamy-pink minaret and on towards the peaks of the Atlas Mountains in the distance.

By half past ten I was on my way to Marrakesh's legendary souk, the place that made this city so fascinating to writers such as Paul Bowles. It was a pleasant, flat stroll past the Katoubia Mosque and the local tourism office, closed firmly against pesky visitors who might want some information on one of Morocco's imperial cities.

Eventually Djemma El-Fna, the huge square at the heart of the *medina*, opened up. At dusk, the walls around the square turn blood red and the square becomes a site of medieval misrule: snake charmers, open-air dentists, pickpockets, adventurers, acrobats, musicians and gigolos throng there. During the day, it was a rather more sedate affair, with dozens of juice sellers hustling for business, and German tourists parked on their backpacks around the edges. I walked across the square, turned right up an alley and was suddenly back in the Dark Ages.

Sunshine filtered through the slatted roofs of the souk that I had discovered, and dappled its alleys with patterns of light and intriguing dark. An old man with his donkey and cart navigated the press of half-dressed tourists and veiled local women as they shopped. There were clothes markets, shops that sold tassels, squares that used to be home to the slave market, and Berber boys who spoke six languages and looked as though they would have the fillings out of your back teeth just for fun. Five hundred dirhams, said one, for three pairs of slippers. Too much, I said. Fierce haggling broke out. Time passed. These people are tough: I saw some following tourists trying to make a sale, stalking them across the piazza, haggling, disputing, fighting to close the deal.

It was a game to me, and I eventually got to a price my salesman found acceptable.

'Are you a Berber?' he asked. I must have looked shocked. 'No, no, *madame* . . . it is a compliment. Most Westerners don't seem to enjoy bargaining as much as you.'

In confusion, I slipped into a shop called Boutique Rais Abbes. That's when the young Elvis fell upon me. Ali was a charming flirt, and I bought two pairs of silly shoes from him, too. He finished the job his earlier colleague had started; I had no cash left at all.

Further into the labyrinth of the souk, I came upon an apothecary's shop, which had cages of chameleons and all sorts of wildly exotic wildlife – tortoises being the least of them – hanging up outside. There were baby falcons standing on the dead heads of chickens, tearing their sightless eyes out with razor beaks.

The apothecary, Abdu, grabbed hold of me. 'Would you like a skin?' he asked, pointing to the wall, where numerous species had given up their coats. He had leopard and cheetah, but I quickly looked away.

'We're not allowed to have those things in Australia,' I stammered.

Abdu, with his Asiatic look and pale, wild eyes, drew me into his shop. It was packed with jars of fragrant powders and dried leaves, like star anise and dried roses; things that cost a bomb, like saffron; and still more 'eye of newt'-style products that smelled disgusting.

'This used to be the slave market,' he said, indicating the crowded square outside, at that moment full of women and a scene of tranquil harmony. 'Today it is the ladies' market. They bring second-hand clothes to sell, others come to buy.'

In the early eighteenth century, this scene would have been quite different. Millions of slaves passed through the markets of North

Africa – an estimated one million of them European. Here in Morocco, conditions were terrible: the sultan Moulay Ismael was determined to build a palace to rival that of Louis XIV's Versailles, a structure that would stretch for hundreds of kilometres. He needed slaves for this enterprise; thousands of them died trying to build it, and were buried where they collapsed. Some fell prey to Moulay Ismael himself. He was a man who had to answer to no one on Earth, and behaved like a despot on drugs. He had been known to decapitate the slave holding the head of the horse he had just mounted, or behead members of his own Black Guard as he reviewed them.

The terror of new slaves at auction, stripped of freedom, dignity and clothes, facing this life, was unimaginable.

Abdu gave me his card.

'Are you on email?' I asked.

'We are Berbers, not Arabs! They go with the modern things, not us. We obey the old traditions.'

Then this old-fashioned Berber asked me if I wanted to get the best view of the souk and the square, and the next thing I knew, I was following him through the market maze wondering, as we went further and further into it, if I should be leaving a trail of breadcrumbs. In my mind were two voices: one was saying that I didn't have to accept every invitation just for another experience to write about, and the other was that of Sharon Garrett, whom I had met in Dubai. She had been shopping in Cairo, alone, and when a merchant asked her up some stairs to look at more stock, she followed him. As he stood at the top and advanced on her with intent, she realised she would have only one shot at getting away, so when he was close enough, she kicked him solidly in the balls and bolted.

Abdu abruptly turned right and stepped up to the doorway of what looked like an empty building. As he pushed open the door, a couple of men appeared behind us, just within the frame of my peripheral vision. They seemed about to follow us into the building. Abdu started up a flight of stairs.

At the foot of the stairs, I panicked. The door to the street was closing behind me. What if, what if, what if? I feigned a fainting fit and shot back out of the door, almost bowling over the two men who were about to come through it.

Not knowing or thinking about where I was going, I ran through the souk, almost scuttling someone's donkey along the way, back towards the light. And then suddenly I was at Boutique Rais Abbes. Ali, the flirtatious shoe-seller, was sitting outside the shop, on one of those white plastic garden chairs that are found everywhere in the world, eating an apple.

'Did you miss me already?' he asked as I smiled, pleased to see a familiar face. Like some transgendered Eve, he obligingly offered me some apple and drew me back into the shop.

'Coke or apple tea?' Ali didn't seem put out when I declined both. 'Where are you staying?'

I told him, knowing he would have no chance of getting across the front foyer.

'Oh, I like that hotel,' he said. 'Very much. I would like to visit there. I could visit *you* there. Do you want something?'

But he had to be satisfied with having a photograph taken with me, as I had planned an afternoon back at the hotel's *hammam*. It was a custom, like mint tea, that I had readily adopted. Even though I was on holiday, having strangers I picked up in a market come back to my hotel with me seemed a custom that it would be best not to develop.

Chapter 21

❀

A Brief Life

MY DECISION TO LEAVE Ali chewing his apple at the shoe shop in the *medina* was one that would have mystified one of the most extraordinary women who ever arrived in North Africa. An adventurer who spent much of her short adult life in the region – and quite often picked up strangers in souks for sex – she still makes people shake their heads when they come across her story for the first time.

Isabelle-Wilhelmina Marie Eberhardt was born in 1877 in Switzerland, into an irregular union. Her mother, the beautiful Nathalie de Moërder, and her husband, a Russian general, had three children, Nicholas, Nathalie and Vladimir. But then Madame de Moërder's eye was caught by her children's tutor, Alexander Trophimowsky, a handsome Armenian ex-priest who was also married with children. Ignoring those considerable impediments, the pair eloped to Geneva, followed shortly by the general. He wanted his wife back, even though another son, Augustin, had been born to her during her relationship with Trophimowsky. The obliging general recognised Augustin as his own, and then proved even more obliging by dying and leaving his estate to his widow.

Madame de Moërder promptly bought a house, the Villa Tropicale, which she renamed the Villa Neuve, in Geneva, and installed her brood in it. Five years after Augustin had joined the throng, another child was born: Isabelle-Wilhelmina Marie Eberhardt.

Family life could not have been easy, as the general's children were at war with their mother's lover. They had some cause. Trophimowsky was a difficult man – an intellectual, an atheist, a Utopist, friend of revolutionaries, enemy of the prosaic and the mundane, a follower of Tolstoy, and a man with a passion for cacti. Still, he did teach the children. Isabelle learned languages, including Greek, Latin and Arabic, and philosophy, chemistry and metaphysics. She seemed an apt pupil, because in her later life she was praised by native Arab speakers not only for her control of classical Arabic, but also for her knowledge of North African dialects.

At the same time as the teenage Isabelle became the pen pal of a French army officer stationed in the Sahara, her father began to fill the house with more and more Muslim visitors. Isabelle's mind and soul turned towards Islam and the desert. So when it was suggested she and her mother should move to North Africa, it seemed a perfectly logical step: Isabelle's brother, Augustin, was in Algeria; they had Arab friends; and Isabelle's pen pal, Eugène Letord, could assist them in the settling process.

Madame de Moërder and Isabelle arrived at Bône, now called Annaba, on the Barbary Coast halfway between Algiers and Tunis, in May 1897. Isabelle began her career as a writer, and worked on stories, her journal and a novel. The local newspaper published one of her short stories, she converted to Islam, and she started to make forays into the *bled*, the bright desert, which became the spiritual sustenance of her life.

However, the rosy future Isabelle and her mother had planned under the North African sun came to an abrupt end when Madame de Moërder died of an unexpected heart attack. Isabelle remained in Bône long enough to put a stone over her mother's grave, and then, dressed as an Arab boy and using the name Si Mohammad, she bought a horse and at full gallop left the sadness of the city behind. It was the beginning of her nomadic desert life, and she discovered she was made for it. But she had no money, so she was forced to leave the glories of the desert and the glamour of the Mediterranean coast of North Africa for the mouldering, overgrown and dank Villa Neuve in Geneva, where her father was still living.

There, for one shining moment, it looked as though Isabelle would be freed by marriage. And even better – a marriage to a Muslim, a Turkish diplomat, was in the offing. Rehid Bey, whom she had known for some years, offered for her. He was expecting a posting in an Oriental location. Isabelle was devastated when, instead of the mysterious East, gloomy Sweden was nominated. Having previously accepted his proposal, she now refused.

Augustin came home, and the two of them nursed their dying father. Trophimowsky had cancer of the throat, and was suffering enormously. One night, Augustin and Isabelle mixed him a draught of the depressant chloral hydrate, to ease him into sleep. By the morning he was dead, and their economic situation was even worse. Trophimowsky's wife, long ago abandoned in Russia, claimed her revenge: his property, bought with the money of his mistress's husband.

Everything changed. Augustin married a woman whom Isabelle always referred to as 'Jenny the worker', and the triangle proved an unhappy one. Isabelle decided to go back to North Africa, but first she set off to Paris to line up some writing work.

Isabelle would have cut a fascinating figure in the salons of Paris, dressed as an Arab boy – a custom that she continued after leaving North Africa. There are studio portraits dating from 1895 that show Isabelle cross-dressing. In one, she is a sailor, the name of the ship *Vengeance* embroidered onto her cap; in another, she is dressed in zouave trousers, burnous and waistcoat – the whole North African fantasy.[1] It is difficult to work out what was going on with Isabelle–Si Mohammad. Did she think of herself as a man or a woman? Was she running away from her gender, or had she discovered a way to make herself even more fascinating to the men whose casual sexual attentions she craved?

When author Lesley Blanch was researching Isabelle's story, she found a woman who had known Isabelle in those heady days, and how she had lived. The woman provided the following insight into this complex character:

> At one time, she used to spend whole days in the *souqs*; when she saw a man she wanted, she took him. She'd beckon him over and off they'd go. She never made any pretences; she never hid her character. Why should she? They were only one side of her character. She had her deep religious ecstasies, I believe, and those she did hide. She was very strict in her

> observance of ritual. Five prayers a day, in the mosque, in the street, or the desert. Wherever she was, she prayed.[2]

Isabelle was not only deeply observant, she tended towards a Sufi's passion for the mysteries of her adopted faith.

Although she was no beauty in the classic sense, Isabelle was interesting-looking and had a compelling personality. Her Slavic genes gave her high cheekbones and almond-shaped eyes set into a round face. She was tall and lean, with an athlete's frame, and almost completely flat-chested, which would have come in handy when she disguised herself as a beardless youth. But on this body, clothes were practical aspects: they were always comfortable and cheap. They also gave her anonymity in the souks and the hostels that she haunted in North Africa.

Isabelle was back in Algeria by July 1900, and had taken up residence in El-Oued, the city of one thousand domes that is the biggest town in the oasis area of Souf, in the east of the country. There, she fell in love with a young Arab who was the quartermaster of the French regiment stationed in the area. Slimène Ehni was a rather commonplace young man, but he spoke French and was a French citizen. They dreamed of a life together, perhaps setting up a little shop, or a Moorish café, which they could leave in the care of his relatives while they took off across the desert.

But Isabelle was never one to travel the careful road. She had become involved with an Islamic sect and its dangerous, dazzling leader, Sri Lachmi. He was as likely to play the Sufi mystic as he was to grab his gun and jump on his horse to lead a *fantasia* – a traditional Arabic event involving crazed clashes between men and animals, shouts and shots, and one of the most savage and intoxicating celebrations in the desert.

In January 1901, Isabelle was taking part in a pilgrimage led by Sri Lachmi when a follower of a rival sect decided to eliminate her. He struck her on the head with his sword. The blade glanced off, but the blow almost severed her wrist. As she lay bleeding, she forgave the man who had just tried to kill her; he prayed and pretended to be mad. Isabelle survived and saw her attacker charged and sentenced to twelve years' hard labour. But there was a sting:

because of her increasingly erratic behaviour, Isabelle had become a persona non grata and was expelled from North Africa by the exasperated French colonial power.

She went to Marseilles, where, in a fog of depression, she attempted suicide. Isabelle missed the desert, the Arabs and Slimène. She began to obsess about death and her projected marriage. Eventually, in October, Slimène turned up in Marseilles, and the two were married. As the wife of a French citizen, she was free to go back to North Africa – 'the open and splendid Maghreb', she called it – and she did.

Slimène, who had left the French Army, found a job in Ténès, close to the coast between, Oran and Ech Cheliff. They set up house in a single room, with only an inkpot, straw mats for bedding, Isabelle's books, some bookshelves, and a pot to cook in.

Those who met her at this time saw a woman dressed in an immaculate white burnous, the high red boots of the Spahis (the elite, mounted soldiers of the Ottomans) and a turban. She swore vigorously, had a nasal voice and little sex appeal.

Isabelle and Slimène were not at ease in Ténès. The expat community disliked them; Isabelle was profligate and they were accused of electoral fraud. So it was a relief to all when, cleared of the charges, they left. By autumn 1903, Isabelle was writing from Algeria's Sud-Oranais for a news journal based in Algiers.

She was not well. There was a yellowish cast to her complexion, and she suffered from malaria. She was almost certainly an alcoholic, according to Lesley Blanch's eye-witness's account of her reckless life. 'That was the only thing out of key with her profound acceptance of Moslem faith,' Blanch reported decades later.[3]

It has been speculated that Isabelle's sexual proclivities exposed her to a host of sexually transmitted diseases. But even though she sought excitement outside marriage, she was devoted to her husband, constantly thanking God for the beauty and goodness of his soul. When he could get away from his work, he would travel hundreds of kilometres to go home to her.

Isabelle wrote about what she knew: the markets and the merchants, the crooks and the children, the isolated forts and the equally isolated people, the serenity of the desert at night and the pitilessness of it at noon. North Africa was like a drug for her: she had wanted to possess the country and it had possessed her.

In the end, it took her utterly. In October 1904, suffering from malaria, she was admitted to a hospital at Ain Sefra, a town on the edge of the Sahara. One morning, Isabelle ignored her doctor's orders to stay some days longer and checked herself out. She had a rendezvous planned with her husband that day, so she left the hospital at around 9 am and went to the tumbledown mud hut where she was staying.

There had been rain in the neighbouring mountains that morning, and the rivers were rising. By eleven o'clock, a torrent poured through the dry wadi bed and into Ain Sefra, bearing with it people, animals, trees and houses. The water demolished everything in its path and carried away Isabelle. Two days later, French soldiers found her body lodged underneath a fallen beam of her house. She was only twenty-eight, but she had lived ten lifetimes measured in Geneva experience.

This was the ultimate paradox for a woman who was a jumble of them: she drowned in a desert. Raised in grey Geneva, she died in the sunny Sahara. She was a woman who dressed like a man; a European who became a Berber; a girl who used men for sex; the child of an atheist father who became a Sufi; a nomad who longed for the settled life of a shopkeeper. She was Isabelle Eberhardt, the woman who could navigate the salons of Paris with ease, and Si Mohammad, accepted as a man in the hostels of North Africa; a hashish-smoking alcoholic who was a devout Muslim. She had become a legend.

Chapter 22

❀

Impossible Queens

ONE MORNING, MUSTAFA AND I headed for the Ourika Valley in the High Atlas Mountains, about sixty kilometres from Marrakesh. There, he promised, it was eternal spring.

But it was also Friday, the Muslim holy day, so should he be away from his family?

He didn't seem too worried – Morocco works on French time, he said, so it wasn't a day off at all.

Along the way, we saw kids going to school, which was par for the course, and middle-aged women going to school, which was not. Adult literacy is a big challenge for the Berbers, so classes have started to help women in their forties and fifties receive some education. A problem, though, has been deciding which language the Berbers should be literate in; there are three distinct Berber languages in Morocco, and not one of them is written.

As he drove, Mustafa talked about race relations, his family, his wife and his daughter. His family had thought they might have Arab origins, but Mustafa's green eyes gave the game away – he has Berber blood, as does his wife. But as for their little girl, Oumaima, who is about six, who could tell about her ancestry? After years of trying, Mustafa and his wife were not able to have a child of their own; they were lucky enough to adopt.

We pressed on, across the flat countryside, with its undergrowth penetrated only by the domes of mosques, along a road that wound through a red gorge cut deep into the Atlas. The mud houses nestled close to the road all had something in common: on top of the distinctly primitive architecture were totally modern satellite dishes.

'For the soccer. We are football mad in Morocco,' Mustafa explained.

'Is there a local team?'

'Yes. Manchester United. Though since Beckham went to Real Madrid, some of the people here are less keen.'

Mustafa took me to a kasbah, which wasn't nearly as exciting as I had hoped. I wasn't in the market for rugs, but the rug sellers didn't seem to have anything else to do, so I submitted to a lesson in the colour of Berber carpets: red from henna, green from mint flower, blue from indigo, yellow from saffron, black from naturally occurring kohl. Pomegranate seeds are useful, as red is obtained from the flowers and also from the rind of unripened fruits.

We went further up the valley to visit a traditional Berber house. The river provided the lifeblood to it: income, hygiene and a primitive dishwasher. It ran a flour mill operated by the father of the family living in the house. Mohammed, a fourth-generation miller, showed us over his home, even while lunch was being prepared. Some thirteen adults and children lived in the house, with its hard dirt floors and whitewashed walls. There was a *hammam* and a central courtyard, which had the kitchen area to one side. A diverted stream flowed through a scullery corner – the luxury of running water was remarkable here – which was also used as a rubbish sluice. There was a pantry, a storeroom (where the good silver was kept), a sitting–dining room and a room that also doubled as a bedroom at night.

Outside was a shop selling trinkets. The kids of the household operated their own impromptu tipping school, hanging around and begging for money.

During our conversations, it became obvious that my guide Mustafa was a thoughtful man, alive to changes in his country and its culture. 'Did you know that when the king, Mohammed VI, married, his wife was photographed without her veil?' he asked.

That was a hugely important moment in Morocco's history, and one I had hoped to discuss with women in the Moroccan government. But my requests for interviews with government members or civil servants had not been acknowledged. It was a boon in some ways. Had I managed to get government appointments, I would have been stuck in Rabat, the capital, and would never have seen Marrakesh or the High Atlas.

Despite its marked lack of openness to foreign writers, Morocco is undergoing a series of subtle changes regarding the status of women. The most public face literally and figuratively of the changes is Princess Salma, the wife of Mohammed VI. The couple married in March 2002, when he was thirty-eight and she was twenty-four; and, unusually, details of the bride (described on a royal website as a 'pearl, radiant in her chastity') and her life before she joined the ruling family were disseminated prior to the wedding. 'Normality suits me,' the king said. 'So we are going to celebrate our marriage like any other couple, in joy and happiness.'[1]

The beautiful (naturally), red-haired Salma Bennani had gone to a private primary school in Rabat, qualified for an honours program from the Ministry of National Education and took her international Baccalauréat in 1995. She then graduated from l'Ecole Nationale Supérieure d'Informatique et d'Analyse des Systèmes, where she majored in computer science, and afterwards joined Omnium Nord-Africain, Morocco's largest private business – the president of which was Fouad ibn Abdellatif Filali, who happened to be the Mohammed VI's sister brother-in-law. Salma entered the company as an intern for six months. They liked her so much, they hired her. So did the playboy prince, who became the king known as 'M6' after the death of his father, Hassan II.

In Morocco, women were given the vote in 1963, and one generation later, there are marked differences in the education of women and the handling of royal brides. Few outside royal circles in Morocco even knew that the late king, Hassan, had married until Mohammed was born, at which point the king's wife was revealed as Lalla Latifa, a commoner who was officially referred to – when required – as 'the Mother of the Royal Children'. Few knew what she looked like; Lalla Latifa had joined the enclosed life of the royal harem.

In Mohammed VI's reign, for the first time, the wife of a Moroccan king would assume an official title – Miss Salma Bennani became HRH Princess Lalla Salma. That made her, according to one columnist clearly unused to the frankness of celebrity couples such as Posh and Becks about every detail of their private lives, 'a truly public personality'.[2]

Mohammed VI's decision to bestow the title of 'royal highness' on his bride was cause for comment in the Moroccan daily, *Al-Ayam*. It was 'a message from the king which reinforces the will of women to participate in public life', according to one of the country's leading feminists, Latifa Jbabdi. '[Lalla Salma] will truly neither be a hidden person . . . nor a human being denied her dignity.'[3]

To some university students, M6's break with tradition regarding his wedding was an indication that he was going to shape Morocco into a real democracy. He ascended the throne in 1999, and began to loosen what commentators had referred to as Morocco's political straightjacket. Late in 2003, he set up a commission to examine possible human rights infractions in the country; early in 2004, he pardoned thirty-three people deemed to have been subversive.

Although the king was a radical in regards to giving his wife a title, he didn't give her the one we could have expected – and he claimed historical precedence for denying Lalla Salma the title of 'queen'. 'There is no queen in Islam, so the question doesn't arise, at least not in Morocco,' Mohammed said.[4]

A common refrain among some Muslim fundamentalists is that countries ruled by women will not prosper. This opinion was raised against Benazir Bhutto, who, aged thirty-five, in 1988 became the youngest person and first woman to lead a Muslim country in modern times (Pakistan, in her case). The subsequent failure of her government was held as proof of the argument's veracity.

No queen in Islam? Tell that to Queen Noor, widow of King Hussein of Jordan; the Empress Farah Diba, widow of the last shah of Iran; and the exquisite Queen Rania, consort of the current Jordanian king, Abdullah. If he needed any further examples, Mohammed VI could call on his countrywoman the academic Fatima Mernissi, who lists a whole slew of Islamic queens in *The Forgotten Queens of Islam*, including the queens of Sheba, and Yemeni rulers such as Asma Bint Shihab Al-Sulayhiyya, who reigned with her husband until he died in 1066.[5] Like the Valide Sultans, she was a builder, expanding Sana'a's main mosque and building others.

And then there were the two queens in the Golden Age of Baghdad, both belonging to the time of the caliph Harun Al-Rashid (786–809), the hero of many of the stories in *The Arabian Nights*. First his mother, Khaizuran, and then his wife, Zubaidah, emerged from behind the veils of the harem to take centre stage during this period of history. Khaizuran was a slave girl from Arabia, taken to the court of the caliph Mansur, who had her sent to his son, Mahdi. Khaizuran had two sons, Musa and Harun. This was a family advanced for their time: women had real value, evidenced by the reaction of Mahdi and Khaizuran to the next arrival, their daughter, called Banuqah ('Little Lady'). She was adored by her father, and when he travelled, she went with him, disguised as a page to stop gossip. She died young and her father was grief-stricken.

Khaizuran's half-sister caught the attention of Mahdi's half-brother, Jafar, and they had two children: Ibrahim, and a girl, Sukainah. Her grandfather, taken with the child, renamed her Zubaidah, or 'Little Butter Ball'. It was this child, a year of so younger that Harun, who would grow up to be the second of the two queens of Baghdad. She became famous for her charitable acts, including building a series of reservoirs, wells and aqueducts to water the thirsty pilgrims in Mecca.

There were dozens of other Islamic queens, in Delhi, in Cairo, in Yemen, at least two among the Mongols, and some in Indonesia. Mohammed VI's aversion to women in power is based on Islamic tradition.[6] But the Qur'an teaches that God treats men and women as spiritual equals; at *Sura* 3:195, for instance: 'I will deny no man or woman among you the reward of your labours. You are the offspring of one another.'

The king would be horrified to hear that there were yet more women who wielded power in Islamic history – and in their own right, not through the weakness of their sons in the way of the Valide Sultans. To traditionalists, women like the exquisitely named Taj al-Alam, 'the Crown of the World', and Nur al-Alam, 'the Light of the World', who ruled for two decades in Indonesia, were aberrations. But it has never been in the nature of ruling elites to yield power, or even to share it, just because that might be the right thing to do.

As I travelled through these countries, I was struck more and more by the link between poverty, literacy levels and women's position in society. As the women of a country became literate, the GDP of their country would rise, and so would their position; while, in the poorest countries, one found the most oppressed women. A country like Yemen, on the heel of the Arabian peninsula, could do with another queen like the eleventh-century Orpha, who had total political authority and planned and executed wars. There seems little chance that Mohammed VI will make Salma a queen anytime soon, but, for the sake of Morocco's economic health, it could be a smart idea if he did.

Chapter 23

Industrial Tourism

TRYING TO EXPLAIN CLEARLY the Australian immigration system, with its quotas and points and programs, from family reunion to skilled workers, is difficult at the best of times. Indeed, the task sometimes fails both the relevant minister and the department, and they're supposed to have all the information. (Although, when you consider that they sometimes manage to deport Australian citizens and lock others up as illegals, and yet allow in people who seem to be plotting to kill the prime minister, you might be permitted a small moment of doubt.)

But as a simple citizen, try explaining the system's intricacies to an excited, French-speaking taxi driver on the trip from Tunis International Airport to the coast near the ruins of ancient Carthage. I had a go, but I don't think I made much headway with the anxious father of four who had an axe to grind with Australian immigration: his son wanted to travel to Australia and was experiencing resistance from the Australian government. Young, unmarried men of 'Middle Eastern appearance' were suddenly of reduced interest to Australian immigration authorities.

'Why is it so hard for him to go to your country?' he demanded, but he clearly didn't want to hear anything about skills or reunions. 'I have six in my family. I am the only one who works. My wife doesn't work. My eldest daughter is studying medicine. She doesn't work. The little ones are at school. They don't work. There is nothing here for my boy . . . he can't find work. Why won't your government let him in?'

The highway to Carthage and the sea to the north both slipped by unremarked upon as I listened to the increasingly frustrated father. 'And if he wants to go to your embassy, he has to go to Cairo. Cairo! You might as well tell him he has to go to the moon!'

A consular office, and then an embassy, were due to open soon in Libya, I reported. That would be much handier for him.

'Libya!' he almost spat. 'I hate Libya! They are all retarded there! Look at the way they make their women dress. Look at the way our women dress – however they please.' He pointed out two women dressed very however-they-pleased on the side of the road, but failed to observe that they were not good examples for his argument.

Our destination was just twenty minutes from the airport, but it felt longer, much longer, before we pulled into the driveway sweeping up to the front doors of my hotel. Here, the anger and resentment of the anxious dad were dissipated by gardens of manicured green, and obscured by the fragrance of flowers drooping out of Ali Baba pots, and then wiped out completely by the view of and from the foyer. There was a fountain, and a little river that flowed under the glass floor of the light, airy reception hall. Outside, there was a huge pool of sparkling aqua, and on the other side of it, a wide strand, peddlars, camel rides, and the Mediterranean. It was as though a Moorish palace had gone to the beach, and had managed to blend opulence, minimalism and opportunistic commerce.

I'd heard that women in Tunisia do well politically and economically compared with other women in North Africa, and I wanted to see if that was true, and how they managed their lives. The lack of assistance from the Tunisian government was a small hurdle. After lunch by the sparkling blue, I made a telephone call: the local politicians might not be willing to see me, but I was a woman with contacts. A cousin in South Africa was friendly with Anne Kabagambe, the head of partnership and co-operation for the African Development Bank, who lived in Tunisia, and had given me her number, so we made a date for lunch the following day.

Late that first night, I opened the French doors and lay in bed, watching the sea. The night wind from the Mediterranean ruffled the white gauze curtains on the stone floor and the sea sang me to sleep. A deep peace had settled over the coast of Carthage.

A few hours later, the TV news showed a contrary world: at Fallujah, an Iraqi had been decapitated as a collaborator. At Samara, ninety 'insurgents' had been killed; the two French reporters were still missing. An uneasy calm hung over Samara, giving the inhabitants some time to bury the dead. Ten Palestinians had been killed in Gaza, in retaliation for a missile attack on Israeli settlers that had killed two children.

It was barely dawn, and a fine chill thinned the air. Shards of light were struggling to part the thick banks of cloud that had rolled in overnight from the Med. Breakfast wasn't due for hours, so I turned to the daily newspaper, *La Presse de Tunisie*. Omar Sharif had been in town for a film festival and to promote his film *Monsieur Ibrahim et les Fleurs du Coran*. Explaining his attendance, the Egyptian-born movie star added that, to him, it was essential that he see ancient Carthage before he died, and that as a child his favourite line in French literature had been the first sentence in Gustave Flaubert's *Salammbô*.

The novel opens with the words 'It was at Megara, a suburb of Carthage, in the gardens of Hamilcar . . .' and is set just after the First Punic War (264–241 BC), when Carthage faced ruin and was unable to pay her mercenaries.[1] They were not slow to rebel. 'The soldiers of Carthage, whom he had commanded in Sicily, threw themselves a party to celebrate the anniversary of the battle of Eryx and since the master was absent, and there was a number of them, they ate and drank freely.'[2] In the middle of this disorder, Salammbô, the daughter of King Hamilcar, falls in love with Mâtho, the head of the rebels.

It is a doomed, romantic story, which I first encountered at university thirty years before, one that had made the city of the Phoenician queen, Dido, come alive. And here I was, on a balcony looking out to the Mediterranean and the horizon that had obscured Dido's lover, Aeneas, from her sight.

In honour of King Hamilcar, I decided to visit my hotel's version of his garden, attached to the *hammam* and spa. It had been five days since my last fix of water therapy, in Marrakesh, and I was in need of a little black soap, pummelling and scraping before my lunch appointment.

Desert squad, Sahara, October 2004. Hakim, Salah, Ali and Mohammed fill the back row, from left to right; while seated together in the front row, from far left, are Tariq, Masoud and Abu Bhakr. Jusef, the head driver, is on the extreme right of the shot; reclining in front of him is Ibrahim.

Norma's nemesis. Dr Amal Al-Sabbagh, secretary-general of the Jordanian National Commission for Women, at home in Amman, September 2004.

Sunday school. JoJo takes the class at the Jumeirah Mosque, Dubai, September 2004.

ABOVE AND OPPOSITE: Making camp on the edge of infinity. Note Skew, the ring-in from Niger, seated alone on the sand (above) … at just the right distance.

Office with a view. The author flat out working.

Nap-time, Ramadan. Feeling the pinch, the drivers flake out wherever shade and whenever time allow.

ABOVE: Lawrence and Florence of Libya. Salah and the author get into local garb to beat the dust.

OPPOSITE: The temptation of Christine. A boy, an apple … a twist on an old story.

Living treasure. Exterior of the men's *majlis* in Dubai.

Concentrate! The fine art of dominoes in the *majlis*.
PHOTO COURTESY MICHELLE SABTI

Odd shoe out. Among the sandals outside the men's *majlis* in Bastikya, the author's Dunlop Volley stands out. PHOTO COURTESY MICHELLE SABTI

Fertile then, desert now. Rock art in the Akakus, south-western Libya.

Ruined glory. Cyrenaica, north-eastern Libya, October 2004.

Byzantine brilliance. Mosaic at Qasr Libya's on-site museum, November 2004.

Ancient stones. Arcade in Leptis Magna, October 2004.

Modern Tripoli. Al-Jazeera Square, with mosque, October 2005.

Old Constantinople. Historic *hammam*, Istanbul.
PHOTO COURTESY ÇIRAĞAN PALACE KEMPINSKI HOTEL

Spice girl. Salah's niece Asma in the spice souk of Tripoli's old medina, October 2004.

Illustrated woman. Michelle has a henna treatment in Dubai, September 2004.

Sultan suite. Upmarket digs at the Çirağan Palace Kempinski Hotel, Istanbul.

Cairo – where you can see what you breathe, November 2004.

The mosque and me. The author outside the Turkish mosque in Tripoli's medina. PHOTO BY SALAH AMURA

Anne Kabagambe had chosen a restaurant not far from the hotel, that perched on top of rock pools and was lapped gently by the sea. A highly educated Ugandan, mother of two and wife of a doctor from Ivory Coast, Anne was in a position to assess the situation of women in Tunisia, and explained it over excellent grilled fish and white wine.

'Women here can do as they please, really,' she said. 'They have the freedom to be educated. They can be economically independent if they choose. Tunisian women are more liberated than other groups of women I have seen in Africa.'

Honour killings, female genital mutilation and polygamy were not features of life in Tunisia, Anne told me, but there were other social problems facing local women like those she worked with at the bank. 'They are very conscious that they should not be more educated than their husbands. Some of them will leave university so that they don't compete with him in that regard. And it is very marked that all the young women think about getting married; they have to be married. There is no other path in life open to them,' she said.

Like women everywhere, Anne's colleagues talked about their two jobs – at home and in the paid work force. With the holy month of Ramadan approaching, some Tunisian women were asking for special work hours to recognise their commitments, which meant less time at work.

As the chair of the African Development Bank Group Women's Network, Anne was involved in efforts to persuade the bank to improve conditions for all female staff, and to make sure women were properly and equitably represented at all levels within the bank.

'In Tunisia, there has been an emphasis on Europeanisation, which has made a great difference to the position of women in Tunisian society,' she explained. 'The participation rate of women in the workforce is around forty per cent, and the government knows that women's rights are not just a social issue – they are an economic issue.'

Anne considered what she was saying, and then delivered a message that is valid for emerging Third World nations, and a reminder to those in the First: 'The only way for countries to develop is to increase the participation rates of women in the work-force.'

Women's participation goes up, poverty and corruption decrease, and literacy rates and general wellbeing of the population increase. Tell that to regimes that routinely repress women and see the reactionaries react, she said, as we left the restaurant and I headed away from that part of the coast to another.

As Carthage is a dormitory suburb for Tunis, a well-heeled and well-mannered place, Hammamet, my next stop, is a resort town two hours south along a highway edged with through groves of olives and almonds, grape vines, and orchards of oranges and lemons. More typical of the Tunisia visitors see, it's the part of the country's booming tourism industry, where package holidayers move in for a week, spend their time next to the pool, miss most of the highlights of the country and its history, and then head home sunburned to a doughy red. Some eight million people visited Tunisia in 2003; by contrast, in Libya the number was around a hundred thousand.

When it comes to industrial tourism, Tunisia, and particularly Hammamet, take some beating. After I'd checked into my hotel, I went for a walk towards the town, to get my bearings. It was a soft, gentle evening, and canes of bougainvillea in magenta, orange and white fluttered in the breeze. The men of the town were in the Tunisian versions of their *majlis* – the terraces of the coffee shops – and the local women, except for one in a shop, were nowhere to be seen.

On the beach, where the cabana boys were packing up for the day, I sat on a rock with my feet dangling in the chilly water. A huge man, with a hand of Fatima on a silver chain around his neck (for luck), approached and began to speak to me. Wary after my encounter with Abdu in Marrakesh, it seemed unwise to sit on a lonely beach with a strange man as the light faded. I excused myself and went to dress for dinner.

Until recently, I had felt too self-conscious to eat alone in public when I travelled, so I generally ordered room service. But I didn't want to waste an *Arabian Nights* fantasy, so I took a book and presented myself at the hotel's restaurant. The maitre d' attempted to put me in the centre of the room but I clung to the sides, trying not to be noticed. During dinner, it transpired that the edge of the dining room was the safest place to be. A belly dancer appeared, all shimmy and shake, but without a single sheikh there to look at her. She worked hard for the money, and was kind enough not to come in my direction.

That night, the wind was offshore so I couldn't hear the sea, and without my lullaby I slept fitfully, only to wake up to a grim international news day: oil had risen to more than fifty-two US dollars a barrel; Iraq had owned no weapons of mass destruction before the US invasion after all; and the death toll had mounted in Afghanistan, Iraq and central Pakistan.

I decided to spend the rest of my time in Tunisia on a bus tour, which began the following morning. There were nearly thirty of us on the bus – English, Australian, French, Italians who looked like Arabs, Dutch, Slovenians and Germans. Clearly these people had not had the benefit of a high-SPF suncream.

Lamjed, our tour guide, spoke all the required languages, as well as his native Arabic, and translated sequentially. He switched with enviable ease between languages. 'If I don't do it, they will find someone else who can,' said Lamjed, with a shrug when I commented on it. He could have been speaking for the Berber boys in the souk in Marrakesh, or the Bedouin child at Petra. It was survival of the polyglot; the more languages these kids spoke, the more chances they had of getting someone's money out of them.

We headed for Kerouan, fourth holiest city in Islam, and after the obligatory visit to the carpet shop there, we moved on to the pretty port of Sousse, then Monastir, with its mausoleum of the first Tunisian president, Habib Bourgiba. We whizzed past the palazzo that Mussolini built at Bou Argoube between the wars, when he was planning to found his modern Roman Empire in North Africa. The following day, Sidi Bou Said, La Goulette (birthplace of screen siren Claudia Cardinale) and the souk in the *medina* in Tunis were on the agenda.

The last time Lamjed had been in the old slave market of the Tunis souk, he had bought a ring for his fiancée, Iman. 'It costs me money when I come here,' he joked. And the wedding would cost even more, he explained. There was a dowry for her, and a house for them to be finished.

Iman was teaching in the United States, Lamjed told me as we walked through the distinctive blue-and-white streets of Sidi Bou Said, known in some quarters as Bab Al-Jannah ('the Gate of Heaven'). 'She wants to come home for the holidays, but the time is too short and the money would be wasted. I wouldn't see much of her, anyway, because her family is from the south, and she would be there with them.'

Lamjed was twenty-eight, and Iman twenty-five. They had met seven years earlier when he was at university, studying to be a teacher. 'We will marry when I finish the house for her,' he explained. 'I have bought part of a family property but need another twenty thousand dinar. I will never get it if I keep phoning her!'

The village of Sidi Bou Said is situated at the top of the jutting promontory overlooking the Bay of Tunis. Legend has it that Saint Louis, here to fight a war, saw his troops die of cholera on the beaches of Carthage. Then he fell in love with a Berber princess, changed his name to Bou Said, settled down to married life at the Gate of Heaven, and then became the patron saint of the place.

It has been a haven for artists for centuries. In 1579, Miguel Cervantes, the author of *Don Quixote*, was here, and Flaubert's visit in 1860 inspired him to write *Salammbô*. In the early part of the twentieth century, the French writer André Gide and painter Paul Klee were among the artistic tourists.

The whole village is now a historical site, a coherent entity of white walls, blue windows and doors, cobbled streets, green cypresses, flaming bougainvilleas, stark cacti and throngs of people. The latter's prime focus is the courtyard house of a former mufti that now houses a wedding museum.

'There are Berber, Arab, Turkish and Adalousian costumes,' said Lamjed, whose bride would be decked out in the Berber style for their wedding, in a garment that would cost thousands of dinars. And she would have the traditional six henna nights before her wedding, all of which would require new clothes. The cash registers would be ringing merrily away.

'The depth of the colour of henna on the hands indicates the fertility of the bride,' Lamjed told me, standing with his forearms bent to demonstrate the way Berber brides in the region have shown their readiness for breeding for generations. His palms were exposed, as Iman's would be during her henna ceremonies, in exactly the same position that the chief goddess of Carthage, Tanit, or Ishtar, is sometimes depicted in these parts.

Walking through the leafy lanes of Sidi Bou Said, we paused at the shop of a friend of Lamjed's, where he bought us some *beignets*. We munched the doughnut-like snacks in companionable silence as we wandered towards the expensive, shining marina. There are two hundred and thirty-two steps down from the lighthouse to the beach, eighteen fewer than when the Roman writer Virgil counted them in 19 BC.[3] Now, as then, they are edged with palms, flowerbeds and young figs. It occurred to me as I bit into my doughnut that Iman was a very lucky woman, even though she was stuck in America for the moment, and even if she had to wait another eight months for an official engagement, and a further two years for her wedding.

Chapter 24

❀

Toasts of the Coast

MODERN CARTHAGE IS A real estate agent's dream. Conveniently located not far from the bustle of Tunis, this is the dress circle of the former French colony. Tunisian president Ben Ali lives here, in a huge compound on a bluff overlooking the ruins of the ancient city. It's the home of the rich and the well connected, of ambassadors and businessmen, drawn by the lush gardens, large, well-tended houses, and air of peace, gentility – and security.

It took the Ancient Romans three days' sailing to get to Carthage; I got there in a couple of hours from Hammamet by bus, with Lamjed leading in six different languages once again. It was clear that morning, but the sun was working up to a relentless noon as we stood at one of the marvels of ancient Carthage: its military harbour. Here, the bones of Hannibal's war machine are just visible, despite the fact that it's now edged with some highly desirable residences.

This was the second of Carthage's harbours, and linked to the rectangular commercial port. Both of them were engineering marvels (some 235,000 cubic metres of earth were excavated to build them) and were linked to the sea by canals that could be closed off with iron chains. The military harbour, lined with shipyards, could take two hundred and twenty vessels at a time. The docks each had two columns at their entrances, which gave the port a sweeping portico around its circumference.

In the middle was an island, where the admiral of the fleet lived. From its height, he could survey what was happening out to sea as well as in port. The island is overgrown now, and vacant. The water lapping around the foundations of one of the modern houses was limpid, its translucence slowly swirling over the sludge of history.

Carthage is a place of myth and memory where, in 146 BC, the Romans finally defeated Dido and Hannibal, gaining domination of the Mediterranean. The conquerors, sick of the constant threat to their empire and jealous of Carthage's prosperity, decided to destroy any chance the city might have to rise against them again. When the consul Cornelius Scipio Aemilianus took command of the third and final Punic war, he forced the Carthaginians behind their city walls. Then he blockaded the harbour to stop supplies reaching the besieged citadel, and laid waste the surrounding countryside. By spring, the city itself was under attack and six days of hand-to-hand street-fighting followed. Before the final surrender, the city which had been home to around half a million people was reduced to fifty thousand defenders. Scipio was ordered to raze Carthage; the captives were sold into slavery. The Roman troops plundered the city, destroyed the harbour, and then burned it to the ground in a ten-day bonfire.

Another fire marked the end of the life of the woman who, according to legend, founded ancient Carthage. Dido, known also as Elissa, the Princess of Tyre (and the niece of another Princess of Tyre, the infamous Jezebel), had been married to an influential Phoenician, Sychaeus, high priest of Melqart. Dido's brother, the tyrant Pygmalion, had Sychaeus murdered for his money. Subsequently, the ghost of her dead husband appeared to Dido, told her what had happened and where to find his treasure, and encouraged her to flee. Dido did as she was told, organised her escape – and that of others oppressed by the evil Pygmalion – and they all sailed off in ships laden with gold and silver.

Dido and her fleet sailed first to Cyprus, where they provisioned for a longer voyage. While they were there, twenty virgins who had served at the temple of Ashtarte (Venus to the later Romans) abandoned their vocations, and married some of Dido's entourage. The group sailed on until they reached the shore of modern Tunisia.

In around 814 BC, Dido is said to have begun negotiations with the local king, Japon, to buy an ideal piece of real estate – a promontory, easily fortified and impregnable, that had previously been a Phoenician trading post. Legend has it that Dido was guided to this site by Tanit, the Mother Goddess and the symbol of love and fertility. She promised Japon good rent for many years for any piece of land that she could cover with the skin of one ox. Japon, who thought he was going diddle Dido, was scammed himself. Dido had an ox hide cut into slivers, which were then sewed together into one continuous strip. Using the sea as one of the boundaries, a semicircle was then described with the ox hide from a focal point on the coast. There is a trace of that deal still obvious today – the hilltop overlooking Carthage is called the Byrsa, or Oxhide.

Japon was impressed with Dido's mathematical skills, and asked her to marry him. But she refused, and busied herself with her followers, building Carthage, whose name comes from the Phoenician for 'new land'. Every year, in recognition of their origins, the people of Carthage paid tribute to the temple of Melqart in Tyre, and were closely linked to that city until 332 BC, when they became independent.

The Carthaginians, first a colony, became colonisers themselves in the western Mediterranean, eventually founding or occupying three hundred city states and territories.

While Dido, the widowed queen, presided over the civilised and burgeoning city right on the trade routes of the Mediterranean, news of her spread quickly. Dido's encounter with Aeneas, the legendary hero of the Trojan War and founder of Rome, is recounted in *The Aeneid* – an epic tale written in the first century BC by the Roman poet Virgil. According to the legend, one day, the currents of the Mediterranean washed some refugees from the Trojan War onto the shores of Carthage. Their leader was Aeneas, the son of the Anchises and the goddess Venus. Aeneas and his followers had been wandering ever since they'd escaped from Troy during its sack by the Greeks, seven years before. The Trojans, exhausted by their journey, begged Dido to allow them to stay in Carthage. 'Gentlemen, do not hesitate to come under my roof,' said Dido.[1]

A banquet was prepared for the Trojans in a room hung with richly embroidered tapestries in the purple that the Phoenicians crushed from local murex shellfish, and for which they were famed. The plate was solid silver, the ewers and the drinking vessels gold.

Aeneas thought it might be wise to give Dido something as a gift in return. One of his officers went back to the ships, and fetched a golden robe and veil which Helen of Troy had been given by her mother. Aeneas also gave Dido a pearl necklace and the sceptre of a Trojan princess.

Not surprisingly, Dido fell in love with Aeneas. He stayed in Carthage as her lover and superintendent of her public works. Zeus, the father of the gods, was not pleased, and sent his messenger, Hermes, to tell Aeneas that this Carthaginian sojourn was not part of the program.

'So now you are laying foundations for Carthage, building a beautiful city to please a woman, lost to the interests of your own realm?' Hermes said to Aeneas.[2] The Trojan, stung, remembered his destiny – he was due in Italy to found Rome. He had to leave Dido and her city.

Aeneas had his men prepare the fleet in secret on the beach, and get ready to fight their way out. But Dido discovered his plans, and challenged his perfidy.

'In Italy lies my heart, my homeland. You, a Phoenician, are held by these Carthaginian towers, by the charm of your Libyan city,' he told her.[3] When she protested, he was obdurate: 'No more reproaches . . . they only torture us both. God's will, not mine, says "Italy".'[4]

Dido felt aggrieved: she had rescued Aeneas and his fleet when they were lost, saved him and his friends from death. He had been a refugee when the sea tossed him onto her sands, and she had shared her kingdom with him. 'I implore you, and by our union of hearts, by our marriage hardly begun, if I have ever helped you at all, if anything about me pleased you, be sad for our broken home, forgo your purpose, I beg you, unless it is too late for prayers of mine!' she said.[5]

Still he was firm, and she became vengeful: 'When cold death has parted my soul from my body, my spectre will be wherever you are. You shall pay for the evil you have done me.'[6]

She asked him to delay his leaving a little, so she could grow accustomed to the loss, but he sailed anyway. Dido went a little mad: she saw holy water turn black, wine turn to blood, and her dead husband came once more to speak to her. As Aeneas's ship sailed away, she had her sister build a pyre which included their conjugal bed, then hurled herself first on Aeneas's sword and then on her own funeral bonfire. On her tomb, according to Ovid in his *Heroides*, was the epitaph 'Aeneas caused her death and lent the blade, Dido by her own hand in dust was laid.'[7]

It seems an ignominious end for such a valiant warrior queen, but that sort of unrequited love makes legends.

Another queen from this part of the world was 'the Kahina', also known as Dihya or Kahya. She was a Berber who lived in the late 600s in the Aurès Mountains, in what is now Algeria. According to some sources, the Kahina and her tribe were Jewish, and that is possible given that during the period many Jews sought refuge from Byzantine persecution in the Aurès, which mark the northern edge of the Sahara and the eastern limit of the Atlas range.

The Kahina was, by all accounts, worthy of the title 'warrior-queen'. In her youth, she freed her people from a tyrannical ruler by first agreeing to marry him, and then murdering him on their wedding night. The mother of three sons by father or fathers unknown, she was also said to have the gift of second sight and to have adopted a captured Arab officer, but nothing further is known of her private life.

During the second half of the seventh century, Arab armies marched into North Africa as conquerors, ready to convert their new subjects to Islam. Within ten years of the death of Mohammad, they had taken territory in Syria, Palestine, Egypt and then Persia. By 680 they had swamped North Africa from Egypt to the Maghreb. One leader, Oqba ibn Nafi, apparently stood in the waters of the Atlantic off the coast of Morocco and slashed the waves with his sword in frustration, because he had run out of land to take.

The Berbers, of the nations now called Libya, Tunisia, Algeria and Morocco, resisted the Arab invasion, and decades of war followed. The Arabs provided these disparate groups of Christians, Jews and pagans with a new enemy. For five years, the Kahina bound the tribes in their common cause against the invaders.

It seems that the Berbers defeated the Arab conqueror of Carthage, the General Hassan ibn Al-Numan, after he had taken the city from the Byzantines. When Hassan retreated, the Berbers took Carthage, and from that time, the Kahina ruled most of Berber North Africa.

She was an unforgiving enemy and ruthless leader. She told her people that the Arabs wanted Africa only for its riches, so she ordered the nomadic Berbers to destroy the cities, livestock and farms of the sedentary Berbers. She wanted to make North Africa a desert that the Arabs would no longer covet. Her scorched-earth policy split her people, pitting the nomads against the town Berbers.

In 702, Hassan was back. His forces quickly overran those of the Kahina. According to one source, historian Charles-André Julien, 'on the eve of the final battle, the Kahina ordered her sons to go over to the enemy.'[8] The Kahina seems not to have survived the battle, though it is uncertain whether she went down with her sword in hand, was captured and executed, or committed suicide.

Would Dido or the Kahina have related to the position of women in the region now? Tunisia prised her independence from France in 1956, after a four-year guerrilla war led by the country's first president, Habib Bourguiba. In 1959, the women of Tunisia were given the vote, and the principle of equality between men and women is enshrined in Tunisian laws.

In the same year as he took power, President Bourguiba oversaw the introduction of the Code of Personal Status. Its provisions included the abolition of polygamy; the establishment of divorce courts and ensuring that both men and women had equal right to seek a divorce; a minimum age of marriage for girls (seventeen) and the requirement that they agreed; and the custody of children being granted to the surviving parent if a father died. Amendments to the laws in 1992 further strengthened the rights of women by eliminating from the statutes all ambiguous provisions regarding the equality of men and women that could be read as discriminatory or sexist.

The amendments declared that husband and wife 'must treat each other with kindness and consideration, and assist each other in the management of the household and the affairs of their children', deleting a previous clause that said a wife must obey her husband.[9] A mother's consent was now required for the marriage of a minor child, and she was allowed to participate in the lives of her children and the management of their affairs, 'particularly in the case of a divorced mother who has custody of her children'.[10]

Most interestingly, a fund was created to guarantee child support and maintenance to divorced women and their children. This fund 'ensures the payment of pension and annuity decided by the court, which remain unpaid to divorced women and their children because of the obstinacy of the condemned party'.[11]

The improvements to the Tunisian laws continued: judges had to be educated in women's rights; in the Penal Code, sanctions for marital violence were toughened; the preamble to the Labour Code included an article explicitly stating that there was to be no discrimination between men and women in any aspect of labour; the Child's Protection Code ensured 'the socialisation of children to a free and responsible life . . . where the values of equity, tolerance and moderation should prevail'.[12]

Women are making their marks politically. In 2004, for instance, Salwa Mohsni was named as the country's first woman governor. She is part of a growing number of women participating in Tunisian public life. They make up 11 per cent of the Chamber of Deputies, 25 per cent of judges, 26 per cent of lawyers, and 55 per cent of the student bodies at Tunisia's universities.[13]

Occasional problems arise. The Tunisian government's tight controls on society don't suit everyone. In October 2003, Reuters newsagency reported that one of Tunisia's leading human rights activists, Radhia Nasraoui, was 'willing to give her life to stop the practices that she says mark her country out as a police state'; the price of national stability was too high, according to the 49-year-old lawyer, who went on a hunger strike to protest against what she called 'systematic government harassment, beatings and police surveillance'.[14] And torture: 'As a lawyer, I have to denounce the use of torture . . . I can't be party to such practices. Never. I'd rather die,' she told Reuters.[15] Some of her grievances seemed to spring from the hard line of President Ben Ali, who has crushed radical Islamic opposition and is credited with fostering increasing economic prosperity in Tunisia.

While Nasraoui was objecting to torture, other women were protesting about the government's position on the veil. Officially it is 'discouraged' in Tunisia (theirs being a secular government), and wasn't generally seen, until recently, except on quite elderly and traditional women.

However, according to Arabicnews.com, the headscarf was back in force on the streets of Tunisia, due in part to the second Palestinian uprising in 2000, the September 11 bombings in the United States in 2001 and the invasion of Iraq in 2003, and also to the banning of the headscarf in French schools.[16] Certainly the women I spoke to – none of whom wore the hijab – said that they had noticed an increased number of veiled women. But that might just be relative: five years ago, there were virtually none.

I wondered, as I looked at some older women doing their shopping in the airless souk, covered from head to foot, what Dido and Kahina would have made of these veiled figures; how they would have received the obscuring of the feminine from the public spaces of government and power. I decided they would have found the thought not at all to their taste.

Sand, Sun and Stars

Chapter 25

❀

Salah Redux

If only you could awake in the dawning Sahara
And set forth on this carpet of pearls,
Where flowers of all colours shower delight
And perfume us on our way.
Emir Abdel Kader

THE SKY WAS FULL of steely-grey, puffed clouds and the sun just beginning to gild the horizon on the morning I left Tunis for Tripoli. I was nervous, wondering if anything could live up to my memories of my first trip to the desert. Would this turn out to be a giant let-down?

Salah would be waiting to collect me at the airport. Was he the gentle, kind man I remembered from my trip to Libya twelve months before, or had my imagination embroidered him in the meantime into an impossible paragon of virtue? The closer the plane got to Tripoli, the more my palms pricked with alarm.

Then suddenly, there it was: the blue-edged coast of Libya, the brown plain between the escarpment and the sea, the airport itself. As I went through immigration, down the stairs to the final X-ray position, I wondered if Tripoli was the only place in the world where they X-ray your luggage in front of you as you enter the country, rather than behind the scenes before it arrives on a baggage carousel. Struggling with my Matterhorn of bags, I could see Salah, wearing a red polo shirt, out in the arrivals hall on the other side of the doors. I dropped my bundles and everything fell off the trolley.

He laughed when he saw the state I was in and asked permission to come though the barriers to help.

'How many kilos you got here?' he asked me, as one of the customs agents spoke to him in Arabic. 'They want you to open this one.'

Uh-oh. 'Why?'

'They say there's something pulsing inside.'

Pulsing? Like what?

'Timers for bombs can pulse,' he said. 'And electronic clocks.'

Bugger! Betrayed by the travel clock! I busied myself opening the suitcase and finally produced the pulsing clock; any other contraband that might have been in there remained unseen.

As we drove towards the city, I took a look at Salah. He hadn't changed a scrap since the last time I had seen him, over those endless cups of tea in the Sahara. He was tanned, still very fit. My contemplation was interrupted by a motorcade speeding in the opposite direction towards the airport. That's the way famous and important people get around in Tripoli – in a screech of black limos. This one belonged to Silvio Berlusconi, the Italian prime minister, who had been in town signing a huge gas deal. Since I had been here last, various heads of government had beaten a path to the tent of the Libyan leader, Colonel Gaddafi. It had been a busy few months for the country: just after I left in October 2003, British prime minister Tony Blair had visited Libya, as had Australian foreign minister Alexander Downer, on a trade mission and to talk about setting up an embassy in Tripoli. By the following April, Colonel Gaddafi was in Europe for the first time in fifteen years, seeking full normalisation of relations and entry into European Union programs; the United States resumed full diplomatic ties and ended sanctions; the EU lifted its arms embargo on Libya.

When I had visited before, official visits from the heads of only relatively obscure Eastern European countries were on the leader's agenda. On my return in October 2004, he had just farewelled Berlusconi and within days he would welcome the German chancellor, Gerhard Schroeder. President Jacques Chirac of France was booked in for a visit the following month – the first ever by a French head of state. Chirac would declare the acrimony over the bombing of the French jet over Libya in the 1980s as past, and that a 'new chapter' in relations between France and Libya was opening up.

On Berlusconi's agenda for his visit had been an overture to Gaddafi to enlist his help in stemming the tide of sub-Saharans who had been using Libya as a thoroughfare on their way to illegal status and an uncertain future in the European Union. The perils of international people-trafficking would have been fresh in the minds of both the Italian PM and the Libyan leader, since, over the first weekend in October, some seventeen people had drowned and forty-seven gone missing when a boatload of illegal immigrants sank off the coast of Tunisia. That boat, carrying seventy-five people in all, was believed to have set sail from Libya, and Berlusconi's government was discussing a raft of ideas with Libyan authorities, including have Italian soldiers patrolling Libyan ports and borders, and Italian ships patrolling Libyan waters.

Italian businesses had begun to invest heavily in the Libyan tourism sector: the country had embarked on a five-year, US$7 billion plan to attract three million visitors a year – up from the 100,000 who were there in 2003 – and much-needed infrastructure. The government had signed an agreement with an Italian company for the creation of a huge tourism complex near the Ancient Roman site of Leptis Magna. It would be the biggest contingent of Italians to arrive in Libya since Italy was shoved out of the country at the end of World War II.

Salah pulled in to the driveway of the same hotel that I had stayed at the previous year, and it was as though I'd never left. The fountain was still not working. Men were still littering up the front. Check-in still took an age. Most importantly, on its north-eastern side, it still had a view of the sea and revelled in on-shore breezes.

Salah left me for the King Idris Mosque just up the road, then collected me again after Friday morning prayers. As we walked through the Italian quarter, along the cool, colonnaded streets, it seemed impossible to believe that a year had passed since we had last seen each other. He was very familiar to me, and dear.

Over lunch with Béchir Trebelsi, again my host in Libya, we also rediscovered the ease and comfort of old friends meeting after a time apart. I was reunited with Libyan food and remembered as it came to the table (soup, chicken, salad, fruit salad for pudding, accompanied by pink bitter soda and tea to drink) that *Lonely Planet* warned that Libyan cooking was nothing out of the box.[1]

Later that afternoon, Salah came again to collect me for our constitutional to the *medina* and, as we ambled through the back streets, the sound of the muezzin filled the air.

Like the souk in Marrakesh at dusk, the *medina* in Tripoli looked lost in time. In the gathering twilight in the old Jewish quarter, kids played in the street while their parents watched from doorways.

'Illegals,' said Salah. 'You could almost be in Africa.'

I shot him a look. He was serious. 'I've got news for you, mate. Africa? We're standing in it!'

He laughed but then explained how the illegal trafficking into Europe happens. 'A local buys a Zodiac for around twelve thousand dinar – that's around twelve thousand Australian dollars. He sells places in it for twenty-four thousand dinar. Gives them a map and waves them goodbye as they set off at night.'

I looked at the kids playing and wondered how parents could take such terrible risks with their children's lives.

'They all trust in God and hope that they will make it,' Salah explained. 'And they all know that if they don't, there is nothing for them in their home countries except death and despair anyway.'

Near the big old *hammam* in the Turkish part of the *medina*, he suddenly turned up some steps, across a stoop and through a doorway. I followed. I could hear the low, melodic voices of men from inside. This was one of the *medina*'s oldest Qur'anic schools. The students, the *taliban*, were behind closed doors, and unseen, but their praise of Allah floated out of the courtyard of the *madrasah* and across the old city like a banner of belief.

Salah kept going, heading up into the night markets. Despite the fact that it was a holiday, the place was alive with people. The stalls of knick-knacks, underwear, toys, make-up, sweets, spices, shoes and linens were all trading. Across the road from the souk stood a row of inexpensive hotels. Here, young women – Moroccan and Algerian, mostly – had taken up residence and were working the area as prostitutes.

The town was in an odd mood and it was all about football. That night, the Libyan national team was at home to Egypt. Everywhere in the narrow streets of the town, the flickering lights of television sets tuned in to what was a grudge match punctuated the dark. Then disaster struck. The power failed, and some of the *medina* faded to black. A collective groan of despair flew up to Heaven to join the Qur'anic verses from the *madrasah*.

We wandered through Green Square, which was, as usual, busy mid-evening. The touts were out in force, baby gazelles in tow, waiting to take the snaps of children and the shivering animals that are as much a rite of passage here as having one's photo taken with a koala was when I was growing up.

As we walked up September Street, past Ferigani's bookshop, to al-Shahed, my favourite coffee shop, on Kuwait Street, I noticed that the lights here in the Italian quarter were still on. Inside the café, the clientele were glued to the screen in the corner, cheering on the home team.

Salah turned his back. 'I can't watch. I can't stand the tension,' he said. 'If I watch, Libya will lose!'

We put away two of the best coffees in the world. In Libya they learned from experts, namely the Italians, who were here from 1911 until midway through World War II. Mussolini's dream of the new Roman Empire came to nothing, but he left Libya with some benefits: great coffee (at this shop, they added their own twist to the cappuccinos – grated nuts on top instead of chocolate), a taste for pasta and gelato, and graceful, colonnaded streets and cool piazzas in Tripoli's Italian quarter.

Next stop was a five-star Turkish restaurant. We could have fed a family of five for about twenty dinar and still have carried the next morning's breakfast home in a doggy bag. We had settled in for dinner when it became clear that a couple of the young women in the restaurant with older men, impossible to believe as husbands or boyfriends, were from the group of prostitutes we'd seen earlier. In conservative Tripoli, they stood out like bruises in too much make-up. The men were probably Turkish businessmen, Salah hazarded, but they had the look of baddies out of a 1960s film noir.

I felt sorry for the women. Not only did they have to sleep with those men, but they had to be seen out in public with them. Who knows? Maybe it was a treat for them to get out of their wretched hotel rooms, have a meal in public and feel like a normal girl on a date.

I ordered a lamb kebab and a Diet Pepsi and considered Salah. He was as proper as ever, and as neat, never seen with a hair out of place. His expression was thoughtful as he looked at the Moroccan women and their 'dates'.

Our talk drifted to the coming tour and the arrival of the Sydney University group the following morning.

'I am going to miss having you all to myself like this,' I teased him.

'Don't worry. I will be with you to the end,' he promised.

I fell asleep back at the hotel that night with the doors overlooking the sea open. The sound of noisy car klaxons on the street below marked a Libyan victory in the soccer.

Chapter 26

A Passage to Libya

WE WERE IN HELL. And it had a name: Al-Hammadah Al-Hamrah, or 'red stony plateau'. We'd spent our first night in the Sahara on a bit of it, a place so ghastly that I'd crawled into my coffin-tent snuffling with disappointment.

I knew what camping in the Sahara was like – soft, silky sand and cool, clear evenings – and it certainly wasn't this waking nightmare. This was hot and lumpy and hard. Finally I gave up trying to sleep and rummaged around under the foam mattress that was keeping my three-season, polyester-filled sleeping bag out of the dirt and grit. There I discovered a rock the size of a house brick, which had been trying to bury itself in my left haunch.

We were here on the horrible plateau between Ghadames, close to the Tunisian–Algerian border, and Ghat, the Touareg capital further south, for a couple of days. It had an evil reputation and was considered dangerous enough for Yusef, the head driver, to hand over pathfinder duties to someone who appeared to have superior local knowledge, despite our being accompanied by a mixed band of Berbers, Africans and Touareg who were renowned for their ability to navigate by the stars and the shifting sands.

That was how Skew came to be leading our convoy of ten four-wheel drives towards Al-Aweinat, gateway to the Jebel Akakus, the mountains of Libya's south. Skew had made quite an impression when he'd turned up in Ghadames looking for a lift, and he'd had no trouble attaching himself to our party. Hospitality is part of the tradition of the desert, as is sharing and taking people along for the ride. That generosity can make the difference in some cases between life and death, and it's non-negotiable. Skew took up residence in the lead car with Yusef and behaved with such authority that some of the Australian adventurers assumed he was a permanent fixture. Very tall, with a cloudy complexion and deep furrows on his cheeks, he might have been in his forties, perhaps older, and appeared to be in need of some emergency dental work. He was the exception to Muslim men for me; generally, they were kind, chivalric and respectful, but somehow Skew made my flesh crawl. It seemed that wherever I was, he was in my line of sight. I learned to become aware of where he was and made sure I moved in the opposite direction whenever I saw him.

The addition of Skew took the number of our Sydney University tour party to thirty-eight. The locals consisted of our Libyan leader, Salah; two tourist policemen, Massoud and Hakim; Tariq, the cook; team leader Yusef; ten other drivers; their cook and a general hand. Then there were twenty of us from Australia.

After a difficult, long, hot drive across the red plateau, we were finally in the desert. A pearly-pink dawn greeted us as Massoud and Skew organised a group photo of the tourists before we set off. There was something worrying about Skew that morning, and I felt as though I was under surveillance. I asked Salah why this particular Touareg was in charge of the program.

'He is not,' said Salah, surprised. He ran through the hierarchy for me: Yusef was in charge of the support team; he, Salah, was in charge of the tour itself, and Brian, one of the Australians, was Sydney University's point man. 'Skew is not in charge,' he repeated. 'And he is not Touareg. He's from Niger. He is just someone who asked for a lift from Ghadames to Al-Aweinat, and Yusef agreed to bring him along.'

That settled, we joined the others and started to walk across a salt pan for a bit of a constitutional. Someone quipped that the drivers were planning to make us walk to Ghat, but they took mercy on us after half an hour, and picked us up to drive through the dunes and the morning, towards lunch. In the back of Ali's four-wheel drive, Pauline (my truck-mate for the tour) and I disagreed about Skew.

'I quite like him,' she said in her gentle, Irish way.

'He freaks me right out. Whenever I come around the back of a truck, there he is. It's creepy.'

'Yes, there is that, I suppose.'

When we were travelling in convoy, the drivers used a system of keeping all the trucks in sight at all times; when one fell back out of sight, all the others would stop and wait for it. The system snapped into operation later that morning when our truck, driven by Ali at the head of the convoy, lost sight of all the following vehicles. We sat in Ali's truck for a good while; Ali kept watch, Hakim folded himself up and slept, and Pauline and I continued our ad hoc Arabic class. That day, because the other four-wheel drives were missing, I decided to put some of our lessons into context. I got out the dictionary and looked up the word for 'problem'.

'*Yaa*, Ali,' I said. Hey, Ali.

'*Aiwa*, Christine.' Yes.

'*Fie mushkila?*' Is there a problem?

Ali and Hakim laughed. '*Mish mushkila*,' they said. No problem.

We sat and waited a little more. I looked up the words for 'lost', 'starvation' and 'dehydration' and tossed them over the front seat. More laughter.

After about half an hour, another truck suddenly appeared and we shot off after it. '*Mish mushkila*,' said Hakim with emphasis, as Ali rejoined the caravan. These stops and starts are part of the desert caravaning experience, and it is always amazing to see how the men are able to fix their cars time and time again.

At lunch, I was next to Andrée, a friend from Brisbane whose husband, Joe, was also on the tour. I was talking to her about the camel driver's pants I'd found in Ghat the previous year. What did they look like? she asked. Seeing Skew close by (naturally), I beckoned him over and indicated for him to show Andrée the embroidery on the bottom of his trousers. He started to bend down, and I could hear him speaking to me in Arabic.

I didn't understand what he was saying, but I certainly understood the tone, and the look on his face. My heart fell and the hairs on the back of my neck rose. He was standing right over me. The next thing I knew, Skew's mouth was on my right breast and I'd completely forgotten *Lonely Planet*'s instructions on the subject: 'If you are harassed, tell your unwanted friend firmly, but politely, to desist and try to enlist the support of other Libyans, most of whom will be appalled enough to shame the man responsible. If you scream blue murder, the situation could get out of hand.'[1] I screamed blue murder, shouting for Salah. Skew beat a hasty retreat.

'What's wrong?' asked Salah, worried by the look on my face as much as by the tone of my voice.

When I told him what had happened, he was shocked. That might have been because I ended with the promise 'If that creep ever touches me again, I'll punch him.'

'You don't need to punch him. We have two policemen here who can take care of that for you.' He looked concerned. 'What would you like us to do? We could put him in jail.'

Educated in the ways of politically correct, human resources practice, I suggested that Skew could use some counselling.

'He will be spoken to, Christine,' Salah assured me. 'You must not worry. He will not come near you again.'

It transpired that counselling was more than Skew's ego could stand. Massoud did speak to him, but tempers started to flair; by the time I was back in Ali's truck and ready to go, things had reached a head.

Skew denied everything, calling me a liar. When it was pointed out to him that he assaulted me in front of witnesses, he indicated that the witnesses were only women, and non-Muslims at that. I could see Hakim squaring up to Skew. Ali looked back at me sympathetically. '*Fie mish mushkila,*' he asserted. But it certainly looked like there was a problem. There was shouting, and that testosterone spike before men start to hit each other.

It turned out that Hakim was my champion. He declared firmly to Skew that he knew me, that I was not a liar, and anyway, why would I lie. Skew insisted on his innocence, and the local members of the team who knew him believed him. It put a division in the group, which would make the next couple of days very uncomfortable.

That afternoon, the trucks were on the move when suddenly the call of '*Muya!*' went up. Water . . . There was always more than enough bottled drinking water in the trucks, as well as warm soft drinks, but a spring meant we could fill our bush showers and wash ourselves properly, as well as do the laundry.

As Ali started to slow, Hakim and I were out of the truck, running to the source. I had the bush shower in my hand, ready to fill it. Some of the other trucks had already arrived, and their passengers were busy filling up bottles and jerry cans. As I headed towards the source, I saw Salah emerge from the bull-rushes wearing a towel around his waist. He was damp-soft, as though he had just come out of a *hammam*. And it turned out he had. In the middle of the desert, Jusef, one of the drivers, had found a well, which fed a pool slightly larger than a jacuzzi.

All the men went in first, and when they were finished, the women were allowed to take their turn. That was a bit of a shock to women accustomed if not to the Ladies' Line, then the idea of ladies first. (We mercilessly teased the men in the party about it afterwards, and Brian came up with the regionally correct response: 'If I had suggested the women go first, my reputation among the drivers would never have recovered!') I looked at the green pond and sniffed sulphur. I filled up the bush shower with the fresh water, and asked Ali to move the truck so that I could shower in private.

Most of the other women stripped off and slipped into what would immediately be renamed 'the Pond of the Virgins', though. Andrée and Marianne, a paediatric neurosurgeon, considered this desert delight, declared it a potential pool of bacterial meningitis and walked away.

The afternoon passed quietly in our four-wheel drive, as though the problem at lunchtime had cast a pall over us all. It transpired that the argument between Hakim and Skew had gone further than previously reported. 'Hakim told Skew that although he (Skew) was an old man, and he (Hakim) was a young man, Skew was stupid, not wise,' Salah told me.

The tensions of a long day, in the heat, and observing Ramadan subdued the drivers and the crew. I gave Skew a very wide berth. When it was time to make camp that night, Hakim took my tent and pitched it between Joe and Andrée's, Marianne's and the one that Salah shared with Tariq. I noticed that Hakim and Massoud had also established their swags on either side of me. I went to sleep feeling safer than I had all day, and hoping that the problem of Skew would disappear with him when we arrived at Al-Aweinat.

Chapter 27

Desert Daze

DESPITE THE SITUATION WITH Skew, I was enraptured to be back in the desert again, an old Sahara hand, a veteran of the sand hills. From my customary position on top of one of the dunes at around three in the morning, I started each day in soul-penetrating stillness. I watched as the dark night dissolved into dawn and the dunes edged from black to grey to pale-pink to blood-orange to juicy-red. By noon, they were leeched pale by the sun and the heat haze.

From around three in the afternoon, when the sun started to slant below the roof of the truck, I spent my time twitching makeshift curtains around a flat, stick-on sunshade in an effort to block it out. It was effective, this improvised palanquin, but it did give a usually macho vehicle an oddly girly aspect, and all the style of a shabby, motorised litter. This window dressing worked against the image of intrepid nineteenth-century women adventurers like Lady Hester Stanhope that I was hoping to project.

Pauline and I started every morning with an essential ritual. She had the cuticle cream, I had the Vaseline Intensive Care hand-cream, and we were not afraid to be seen using them. Just because we were off on the adventure holiday of a lifetime, standards of personal grooming should not be allowed to slip, Pauline and I had agreed from day one in the truck.

However, despite the good intentions, our standards of grooming slipped so far that they became almost sub-sand level. Some fool I saw once on a Lonely Planet travel program said that the first thing to disappear in the desert is vanity. That's not right. The first thing to go is a decent mirror. Occasionally I glimpsed myself in a rear-view mirror or side mirror of a truck, and it was not pretty. My hair was thick with grit, its expensive blonde highlights invisible. Pulled back into a ponytail, it was wrapped under a tight turban the way Abu Bakr had taught me the year before. I was kidding myself that it was quite fetching, indeed almost mysterious when the long, loose end of the material was tucked in like a veil. But it was effective against most of the thicker grains of airborne sand.

Almost everyone in our travelling party had adopted this mode of dress from the locals – even Salah, who, just a year ago, wouldn't have been seen dead in a headdress. As soon as our caravan looked as though it was about to leave a sealed surface, the drivers and crew wrapped their heads in lengths of cloth draped around their necks for just that purpose, and we tourists followed suit.

My turban was supposed to be white, but had a slight magenta-pink cast to it; the light colour was a mistake. There's a reason why the Touareg and the Libyans do not wear the white turbans favoured by men in the Arabian Gulf countries and Saudi Arabia, and instead wear the browns and khakis of desert camouflage: they don't show the dirt. A couple of the drivers also sported very impressive black turbans, which made them look hot. And not in a bad way.

After just three days in the desert, our group had settled into camp life. Most of us were up before dawn to pack up, have breakfast and be ready to get in the four-wheel drives by nine. That's when the sun started to bite into fair, Anglo-Celtic skins. We would travel to a site of interest – a town, a market, an ancient *medina*, a rock gallery – have a look around and sometimes shop.

At lunchtime the drivers would find some shade in which they could set up camp. If there wasn't any, they would rig a bimini sail between three of the trucks to create an artificial shade. After lunch, we usually lay around, chatting and gathering strength for the next stop in our program. The drivers were smarter: they were all under the trucks, asleep.

The afternoons between three and five were the worst, when the day felt old and worn out and we were dusty and tired. The sun, slanting low, had a cruel bite and our skins would redden despite being in the trucks.

Towards six o'clock, the tempo of the day would change. We

would stop and set up camp; the drivers would settle around their camp fire and wait for the sun to set and mark the end of their Ramadan fast. Some of them would sleep, and others would talk quietly, while their cook, the one we called 'Beaky' (because of his wonderful nose set between a pair of chocolate-brown eyes), started the evening ritual. He would put out the long-life and now-warm milk and plates of dates, an instant rehydrator and sugar hit for systems deprived of food and water all day. When that was done, Beaky started to make the smoky, sweet black tea which Omar had taught me was a feature of desert life. Beaky had a tea ceremony that rivalled Omar's, and his long, languid limbs gave the ritual extra grace.

At the same time, the cook truck opened for the tour group, starting with tea around the long, refectory-style setting of red plastic tables. Some of our party would already be out exploring the surroundings. One of the more senior members of the group always immediately climbed to the top of the nearest, highest dune. Others wandered around, cameras at the ready, silenced by the beauty appearing in the gloom, while the rest took the opportunity to disappear into the distance for an ablutions stop.

One night, Andrée found one of the drivers up on top of a dune, having a quiet gasper, and after a fashion (she having no Arabic, and he knowing little English) they formally introduced themselves. Because it was Ramadan, and because the group was so big, some of the crew and tourists had little exposure to each other, Andrée was delighted to have made a new friend. She was confused, as she recounted the story over dinner: 'He said his name was Graham. But that's a very odd name for a Muslim. And he's from Toorak . . .' It was 'Ibrahim', but he was renamed for the rest of the journey; Ibrahim the Touareg had become 'Graham from Toorak'.

Life in the camp revolved around our ablutions. It was a chancy business during the day, as we all tried to work out where the thirty-seven other people were and then set off into the distance to build our own outdoor bathroom by scuffing up a bit of sand. At night, it was easier and less fraught.

As our days and nights rolled on, we discovered more about each other, and more of the treasures of the Sahara – the drama of the

Wadi Mekthandoush, with its twelve kilometres of petroglyphs; the unexpected gaiety of a gallery of rock painting under a massive, upheaved sandstone rock in the Ubari Sand Sea; the soothing sight of the drivers at their prayers; the familiar beauty of oases surrounded by dunes and palms and gums; the dusty, colourful Touareg capital, Ghat; the hypnotic sounds of a drum beaten next to a camp fire. The camp was succumbing to the Sahara, a place that had been stealing the souls of travellers for generation after generation. Me, I longed for the nights, when an ink-velvet peace would wrap me in serenity, and the stars would come.

Chapter 28

Undercover, Under Fire

ROSITA FORBES WAS ANOTHER person infected by the sands. For a woman who ended up travelling all over the world, her life started conventionally enough – she was born in the early 1890s, into a pretty normal family in the English county of Lincolnshire. In 1917 she married Colonel Ronald Foster Forbes, and then things started to get interesting. By 1919, she was divorced and off on a trip around the world.

At the end of that jaunt, she found herself in North Africa, where she discovered the Arab world for the first time and became entranced with it. For a beautiful young woman with a taste for adventure, she was in exactly the right place – in Cairo (her set included Gertrude Bell and TE Lawrence) – at the right time.

Cairo was also home to a most young fascinating man named Ahmed Hassanein Bey, a clerk in Egypt's Ministry of the Interior. An almost fairytale character who blended his Muslim identity with an Oxford education, Hassanein was busy planning an expedition to a particularly remote part of the desert, in Libya.

She decided to accompany him on the trip and disguised herself as a Muslim and a Bedouin. She took the name of the Prophet's first wife, Khadija, but because she was fair-skinned and her Arabic was not good, she had to invent a Circassian mother.

While she shuttled between Egypt and Italy getting the supplies organised, Rosita studied Arabic. She also learned how to navigate in the desert using a sextant and theodolite, and how to behave as though she had lived her entire adult life as a veiled woman. She received the necessary permission from Emir Idris, the head of the Sanusi tribe (and later king of Libya), to make the journey to Kufra Oasis, the religious headquarters of the Sufi Sanusis.

Rosita knew she hadn't been given permission for this trip just because she was an attractive woman. International geopolitics were at play. 'They liked Hassanein Bey, but they admired and believed in Britain,' she wrote. 'They wanted us to secure them from Italy. If a British alliance was impossible, they [the Emir and his supporters] hoped for an Egyptian one.'[1]

Rosita and Hassanein's journey across the Western Desert to Kufra had been made by only one other European, Gerhard Rohlfs, in 1878–79. He had given precise map coordinates of the Kufra Oasis to the Africa Society, but the Royal Geographical Society disagreed with him. If Rosita had paid attention to Rohlfs, she and Hassanein would have been better off. As it was, she went with the Royal Geographical reference and almost died because of it.

Rosita and Bey were heading into the unknown; as far as they knew, Kufra was a number of oases inhabited by a famously reclusive people who didn't care to be troubled by strangers. For more than a century, the Sanusi had guarded their strategic oasis, especially from the Europeans who were in the process of destroying or taking over all the other caravan routes of the desert.

Rosita's caravan set out in December 1920 and immediately found the going difficult: hostile villagers refused them assistance; there were sandstorms; their camels fell ill, and they had to walk. On top of that, Rosita and Hassanein were nervous of their men and feared for their own lives.

Rosita had trouble controlling the camel-teers, but found – as many have before and since – that her authority increased when she was holding a firearm with intent. One day in the desert, she countermanded an order given by her guide, Farraj, and the men hesitated while trying to work out whom to obey. Rosita drew her revolver and announced: 'The man who refuses to march with me goes on a long journey.' When Farraj raised his rifle as if to shoot, Rosita was quicker. 'He was a good target against the sunset,' she wrote. 'My first shot grazed his hand; my second sent his Martini flying.'[2] Her head driver was impressed: 'By Allah, your words are as straight as your bullets.'[3]

But as tough as managing the caravan was, the conditions in the desert were tougher. The goatskin canteens were dry after more than a week without sight of a well. 'When we could hardly see or speak and were dragging our feet automatically across the sand, leaving blood or pus behind us, we came to a depression full of bones,' she recorded. 'It was a ghastly place.'[4]

One of the men recognised it: Al-Atash, 'the Thirst'. The bones were what remained of entire, lost caravans. Rosita was dispassionate as she recounted her own near-death moment: 'I lay down. My throat was parched and so stiff that I could not swallow . . . Next morning, there was a damp mist. It saved our lives, for it relaxed our swollen throats and kept us from the last madness of thirst.'[5]

However, conditions did not improve. They were imprisoned at another oasis, they were robbed, and then found yet another dead caravan in the Great Sand Sea. After weeks of these horrors, they arrived at Kufra – which turned out to be just a small oasis, not a group at all – in January 1921. They stayed for ten days, recovering and preparing for the return journey to Egypt.

That was a disaster too, and nearly fatally so for Hassanein, when he fell off his camel and broke his shoulder. When infection set in, he was unable to travel. Rosita then took a huge risk: with just one Bedouin, food for four days and one canteen of water, she continued eastwards to Egypt.

Late one night, she heard strangers approaching. Her guide told her: 'Get out your revolver, Sitt [Lady] Khadija. No good people march at night.'[6] Then the tune of 'Rule Britannia' came whistling across the dunes, the whistler turned out to be a member of a British search party, sent by the British ambassador to look for them. They were saved, and the journey that Rosita would later call 'a preposterous adventure' was over. Reunited, Rosita, Hassanein and their caravan continued to the Siwa Oasis, fifty kilometres from Libya's eastern border.

Rosita clearly had a thing for men in uniform. She was married for a second time, to Colonel Arthur Thomas McGrath, in 1921. This was around the time of the publication of her book *The Secret of the Sahara: Kufara*, which reinforced her claim to be taken seriously as an explorer and earned her a fellowship in the Royal Geographical Society.

Rosita kept Forbes as her professional name and kept travelling. She had plans to go to southern Arabia with the father of the notorious spy Kim Philby, but it was too dangerous, so she trekked through Ethiopia with a photographer called Harold Jones. Together they made a film of their journey – *Red Sea to Blue Nile*, released in 1926.

She travelled often with her husband, too, and when they were in London she was the perfect hostess, entertaining extensively. During World War II, Rosita supported the war effort by lecturing across America. In old age, she settled with her husband in the Bahamas, where she died in 1967.

Another extraordinary English woman who made her name in the Libyan Desert was Susan Travers. Born in 1909 and daughter of a Royal Navy admiral, Susan served as an ambulance driver in Finland in the early days of World War II. By 1941, she was working as a driver for a medical officer in the Foreign Legion, in the Syrian campaign. She was eventually assigned to the Free French general Pierre Koenig, and became his mistress, working as his driver during the day and living with him in his house outside Beirut as his lover during the night.

On Valentine's Day 1942, Susan and Koenig arrived at Bir Hakeim – 'nothing but dust under Libya's molten skies', she wrote in her autobiography. 'The word *bir*, I'd been told, meant water in Arabic and I had wrongly assumed it to be some sort of oasis. But instead of swaying palms reflected in a lake, there was flat rock and a few tumble-down cement shacks . . . Bir Hakeim was the least important and the bleakest outpost of the Libyan campaign.'[7]

Bir Hakeim was the southern-most point of the Gazala Line, a barrier that the Allies had strung from there to Gazala, near Tobruk on the coast. It was, Susan wrote, 'a vast minefield laid four square by sappers, with secret routes through known only to them'.[8]

To the south of the French holding of Bir Hakeim lay the parched desert; to the east and north was the British Eighth Army, protected by five hundred thousand anti-tank mines. The German

Afrika Korps, lead by 'the Desert Fox' himself, Field Marshal Irwin Rommel, was trying to push the Allies out of Libya and march on to take Egypt.

When Susan and Koenig arrived in Bir Hakeim, Rommel was one hundred kilometres to the west and on the move towards the Gazala Line's most vulnerable and southerly point. 'The French brigade had clear orders – to hold on to our desert citadel at whatever cost to give the Allied Command further north time to regroup and mount a counter attack,' she wrote.[9]

She and the rest of the four thousand members of the brigade were in 'this dreadful oven of a place' until late May,[10] with only an occasional gale-force sandstorm – whipped up by the wind known as the *khamsin*, which could last up to five days – to relieve the deadening boredom. 'The storms bought unbearable heat and carried a mist of dust as fine as talcum powder, which turned every face grey, filled the eyes, lungs, nose and throat, and tainted the food and water.'[11]

But the Afrika Korps soon put an end to the boredom of the desert when they attacked Bir Hakeim on 26 May. On the second night of the onslaught, the women were ordered out of the town, an instruction Susan obeyed reluctantly. She made Koenig promise that she could go back when things quietened down. She took an ambulance, and with two women in another, struck out northwards for Tobruk. Behind her, Bir Hakeim was surrounded.

Susan was determined to get back; she picked up a new car destined for one of the colonels at Bir Hakeim and headed south. Before long she had rejoined Koenig.

By 2 June, the outpost had been bombarded for days and was encircled. Rommel showed no sign of going away. One morning at four o'clock, he sent three officers with surrender terms; the French sentries turned them away at the gate, saying their general was not being woken up at that time for them. Eight days more of the onslaught followed.

The toll was shocking. There were more than 1400 missions flown by the Germans over Bir Hakeim and 1500 tons of bombs dropped. The French responded with 40,000 shells; the Royal Air Force lost seventy planes.

By 10 June, the siege of Bir Hakeim was almost over, and they were down to the last of their ammunition and water. Rommel signalled his headquarters, telling them that he would take his prize the next morning.

Preparations for the extraordinary retreat from Bir Hakeim were under way. The officers used the last of the water to shave. Windscreens were knocked out of the vehicles. What couldn't be carried was destroyed so as not to offer any comfort to the enemy. General Koenig had decided to take all of his men, able-bodied and wounded, to break out of one of the gates and drive straight for the Italians and the Germans through the minefield, while they were sleeping.

The night of 10–11 June was bitterly cold and dark. There was no moon when the French sappers went out to defuse their own mines. And then the whole camp ran for it. The siege of Bir Hakeim ended not with surrender, but with a breakout. General Koenig ordered Susan to the head of the column. 'We have to get in front. If we go the rest will follow,' he said.[12]

By ten thirty on the morning of 11 June, Susan and General Koenig were safe behind British lines. The Ford she was driving had lost a shock absorber, been hit by a dozen bullets, and the brakes no longer worked. But it got there.

Susan Travers won the *Croix de Guerre* for this action, and after the war had the unusual distinction of being the only woman ever to serve in the French Foreign Legion with the rank of *adjutant chef*. She eventually married another legionnaire, Nicolas Schegelmilch (who was also at Bir Hakeim), and the two of them served in Indo-China. Schegelmilch died in 1995, and Susan, who lived in Paris at the end of her long and extraordinary life, died in 2003.

Chapter 29

Location, Location

'WHERE ARE WE?' IT was the chorus from the camp every night as we gathered for tea before dinner. Who could tell? The drivers might, but they weren't saying, so the question was always launched at Brian, leader of the university group. One night, he looked a little more owlish than usual.

'We're here,' said Brian, indicating the wide expanse of the desert that surrounded us.

His audience – which included Bruce, a man who was so keen on knowing his location at all times that his watch told him how far he was above sea level – was not impressed. These people wanted a physical answer, not a metaphysical one. 'How far have we travelled today?' someone else asked.

'Wouldn't have a clue,' replied Brian.

'Get the map,' said one of them, as if to solve the matter once and for all. The Michelin flat plan of Libya was duly unfolded on the red plastic dinner tables.

'We were here last night,' said the unfolder, pointing at a spot of nothingness on the map.

'Let's ask one of the drivers,' suggested another. By this stage, Brian was becoming slightly prickly.

'You'll be asking them to do the impossible,' he said. 'For a start, they don't read English or French. They don't read maps. They don't see landscapes in two dimensions like this. You have to be taught to read a map. They see the landscape differently.'

After a few days in the desert, it was amazing that Brian was only mildly short with us. The fault lines between our personalities were beginning to show, magnified by the heat and the dust, and just plain old proximity. 'These people are right outside their comfort zones,' said Margaret, a retired university administrator, and she might well have meant me.

It was Ramadan, the time in the Islamic calendar when Muslims celebrate the beginning of the revelation of the Qur'an to the Prophet Mohammad by fasting from dawn till dusk. That means no food, no fluids, no inhaled substances, no sexual activity or medicine during daylight hours. The drivers were deprived of their nicotine fixes, something that made even the sweetest-natured of them a little testy by the time the sun went down. Still, they stuck to the fast, and with good reason.

According to Muslims, Ramadan, the ninth month of their year, is the opportunity for forgiveness. It's the time when the gates of Paradise are open, the gates of Hell are shut, and the devils are chained. No fighting, swearing or arguing is allowed, and the emphasis is on charity, the study and recitation of the Qur'an (many of the drivers had their holy books with them, ready to open at any time), patience and humility. The prohibition on sexual activity made Skew's offence even greater therefore; and technically Hakim also broke the rules, by arguning with Skew, when he defended my honour.

It seemed mean to be eating and drinking in front of people who couldn't, so in a show of solidarity with my fifteen Muslim brothers on this expedition, I had decided to practise the fast and to have a go at the patience aspect. In the spirit of enquiry, I also wanted to see how fasting felt. It seemed useful to know just when Ali might start to suffer from low blood-sugar levels and accidentally kill all of us in his four-wheel drive, and to be prepared for any other looming disaster. As a consequence, I was taking virtually nil by mouth from dawn to dusk.

While I was on the Ramadan diet there were now entire days in which I didn't have to find a sheltered spot behind a rock or tree to serve as my desert toilet. Those spots were few and far between, and were usually quickly discovered by other members of our party.

But I made up for my personal drought as soon as the sun set each day. I couldn't get the fluids into me fast enough. One evening, in Ghat, as the sun sank behind the dunes, I sank two mango juices so cold they made my teeth ache (didn't stop me), a couple of Diet Pepsis and a large bottle of mineral water, and then backed them up at dinner with two non-alcoholic Beck's (they tasted like champagne to me), a couple of Sprites and then another litre of mineral water as I went to my tent. Consequently, my kidneys worked overtime through the night.

So how does observing the Ramadan fast in the middle of autumn in the Sahara feel if you are a woman and not used to it? Not great, actually. It's particularly bad around three in the afternoon. It starts to feel a little better around six, when, after the seemingly interminable, baking-hot afternoon, you know the end of the day is close. By that stage, though, my mouth was invariably the consistency of a dried-out camel chamois. I blamed Salah, who was acting as my Islam coach. He had neglected to tell me that I could rinse my mouth out – but only the front part of the mouth, as Muslims do when performing the traditional ablutions that precede the daily prayers – as long as I spat and didn't swallow.

My Ramadan fast had a couple of unhappy side-effects. My breath was terrible, thanks to the ketones that weren't being flushed out of my kidneys; but that wasn't so bad, since everyone else who was fasting was in a similar situation, and I had exempted my Tic Tacs from the Ramadan ban. But there was worse. Suddenly, long-life milk tasted really delicious (even when it was warmed after a day of jogging along in the heat in the back of the cook truck); and beer with not a skerrick of alcohol in it tasted incredible.

The tanker-load of fluids I imbibed after dusk every night was not enough to stop dehydration. My long muscles started to cramp for the first time on our sixth day in the desert, and by the eighth I needed Gastrolytes to fix that electrolyte shortage. (Finally, I had a use for the first-aid kit apart from curing headaches.)

After nearly two weeks' fasting out in the desert, the drivers were getting tired, too. On the last day, the plan was to make a 10 am departure, but they clearly weren't paying the slightest bit of attention. They were up at the crack of dawn and packing up. Hamid nicked my office – the mattress – and tied it to the top of a truck. I had to sit on my bag to finish my diary notes.

Our desert experience was rolled up and packed into the Land-cruisers. Everyone, even those of us who loved the desert, was looking forward to sealed roads, a town with plumbing, and the rooms that Salah had organised at the hotel for us. So we were not unhappy to be whipped onto the trucks, and away.

Sebha, the end of our journey, hove into view. Signs of town life appeared. Shops and kids became more frequent. A yellowish, sulphuric glow bathed the place.

We were at the airport at 9 pm, in good time for the eleven o'clock flight to Tripoli. Our bags were piled up, our passports collected, and we were corralled – the usual drill. Then things took a turn for the worse. There were not enough seats for the group, despite the fact that we had confirmed bookings. Salah, Masoud and Hakim tried to sort out what was unsortable. A local airport official had boarded his friends and family already, and that left only a dozen or so spare seats. The rest of us would have to go by road overnight.

'Who wants to go by car?' asked Salah.

Several hands shot up, including mine.

Two Mercedes minivans were produced, and we were put in them. There was a reckless sense that we were setting off on an adventure that the others were unlucky to be missing. Off we sped to the north, away from Sebha. In front of us, the road stretched out to Tripoli.

We all tried to get some sleep. A little after 3 am, we pulled out of the night and in to a truck stop, where we discovered a sight that would be familiar to anyone who remembers the film *Baghdad Cafe*. Along an alien strip of brightly lit highway sprawled at least half-a-dozen cafés, kebab and teashops. Touts were everywhere, trying to get customers into their shops.

It was hot inside the café we chose. Hakim, Tariq, Salah and the drivers had decided to stock up for the Ramadan day ahead, so I stayed outside and amused myself with a chat to one of the kebab-stand owners until it was time to climb into the vans and get back on the road.

By dawn we were at Gharyan, six hundred and ninety kilometres north of Sebha. Light was creeping across the coastal plain to Tripoli as we descended from the escarpment and rolled into the city. It was just before ten when we arrived at the hotel. I caught a glimpse of myself in the minivan's rear-view mirror: it wasn't good. But I was pleased to note that I hadn't lost all my marbles: I managed to ask for (and get) a room that faced the sea, so guaranteeing me a most welcome on-shore breeze every afternoon.

Chapter 30

❀

Tripoli Treats

WE ARRIVED AT DUSK in Leptis Magna, on the Mediterranean coast about one hundred and twenty kilometres, and two hours' drive, east from Tripoli. The tourist buses were long gone, and the site was empty except for our party and the guards, who clearly had better things to do than wait for us to wander around gawping at what mighty Rome had wrought nearly two thousand years before. These ruins were the main reason I had wanted to go to Libya in the first place, and also for my return.

Other Ancient Roman sites such as Ostia Antica, Pompeii and the Villa Adriana at Tivoli outside Rome are certainly impressive. I'd spent time fossicking about the footings of Roman Bath and a military town just shy of Hadrian's Wall in the UK, but I wanted more, bigger, better ruins. I thought those just might be in Leptis.

There was no time for lollygagging around the site that many consider the finest Ancient Roman ruins in the world. We were on a mission to see as much as possible of the imperial city built by Septimius Severus, the emperor known as 'the Grim African', before we lost the light.

Leptis Magna (the 'Magna' differentiates it from the lesser Leptis, Leptis Minor, in modern Tunisia) was one of the three cities of Tripolitania, the ancient region that compromised Leptis, Sabratha and Oea – the latter being the Phoenician trading post established in the seventh century BC now known as Tripoli. Leptis and Sabratha still boast astonishing ruins, while Oea lies, by and large, beneath Tripoli.

Once past the ticket booth to pay the photography fee (a

common thing in Libyan museums and sites), we set off at a good clip towards the amphitheatre, an elliptical crater embedded into a hill and overlooking the northern flank of the inky-blue Mediterranean. Two-thirds of the size of the Colosseum in Rome, the theatre, which dates from 56, boasted seating carved from the rock of the hill and faced with limestone. Much of it is still in place.

When Leptis served as an imperial city of the Roman Empire, the theatre could have seated most of its population – close to sixteen thousand people – for the gladiator contests and the games. (The 'sports' included rabbit and rodent hunts first and worked up the food chain for both predator and prey; at its apex, human beings were thrown to lions.) Those who tired of the blood-soaked sand in the amphitheatre could stroll across from the colonnade at the top of the circular building to the circus, which lies between the amphitheatre and the sea, where horse races were held from 162.

Golden sunlight bathed the eastern side of the amphitheatre, and I was aware of sharing sensations familiar to those of the city's citizens in those far-off days: the warmth of the setting sun on the skin; the expectant cry of a gull wheeling above a fishing smack as it pulled towards the beach; and the sharp salt tang in the air. There was not a single intrusion to this scene from the modern world apart from us, determinedly snooping about the city, looking for traces of its former denizens.

Time pressure kept us moving, down to the old port, past a shepherd and his mothy, motley flock grazing near the edge of a wadi; then we crossed the dry river bed and climbed up through the colonnaded street and into the basilica, or law courts.

The ruins of the basilica at Leptis are so substantial that they give a clear idea of the majesty and power of the city. An accused person would have felt very small among the towering columns, with their beautiful *bas*-reliefs, which climb towards Heaven.

In the forum of Septimius Severus, I clambered up the stones at the end furthest from the sea, near to where the main temple of the imperial cult used to be located. The key elements of ancient Leptis were laid out in front of me: the forum, the courts, the colonnade with its sculpted Gorgon heads, the sea and the sky. From this perch the year before, Brian had given me a lecture about the uses of the public space in the city. That's hardly remarkable, except that he was standing in the body of the forum, more than fifty metres away, and we were speaking in normal tones. The acoustics are amazing, but amazement was the currency of Leptis Magna.

The city was designed to show the power of the emperor who built it, and as a marketing tool for Ancient Rome, it's still highly effective. This is what Shelley meant in his poem 'Ozymandias of Egypt': 'Look on my works, ye mighty, and despair!'[1]

For Ozymandias, read Septimius Severus, because this was his city, a wonder celebrating his accession to the position of the most powerful man in the world – Emperor of Rome – in 193. It's impossible to look on what Septimius did to his birthplace and not marvel.

Leptis Magna had been under the rule of Carthage and Numidia before it fell to Rome in 111 BC. By AD 130 it was already an important city, with extensive Hadrianic baths, a forum built in the time of Augustus (27 BC–AD 14), an amphitheatre, a theatre begun in AD 1 on the site of a much earlier Punic necropolis, a hippodrome and a market that dates from 8 BC.

By the time Septimius was born there, in 145, the city had grown even further in importance and stature. Septimius Severus built relentlessly, stuffing Leptis full of luxury and engineering marvels: the Severan basilica and forum; a Nymphaeum, or fountain consecrated to nymphs, with its exquisite red-granite façade and cipolin columns; the colonnaded street; and the port. His engineers joined offshore reefs and small islands with groynes as part of a major land reclamation project, and the existing harbour basin was made more regular. At four hundred metres each way, it was three-fifths the size of Carthage's harbours and signalled Leptis's sea power. The old market, rebuilt during the reign of Septimius, is still spectacular. The space was enclosed by porticoes and shops, and contained two circular structures surrounded by octagonal porticoes. God is amid the detail here, like the carved marble dolphins, which would have been supports for the tables of the seafood sellers.

The archaeologists keep finding treasures at Leptis. A villa, thought to date from the second century and located near the amphitheatre and harbour, was uncovered only in 2004. It was built in the local African style, and black-and-white mosaics found inside are Ionic and Hellenistic, with no Roman influence at all.

To end with, we legged it up the main street, marvelling at the city's sewer, which could be seen under the paving, and the four-sided arch of Septimius Severus. In true modern Roman style, this was shrouded, obscured by scaffolding for restoration. But we could see its unusual shape, its broken pediments, its domed roof. Its original relief friezes are carefully preserved against the weather and theft in the Jamahiriya Museum in Tripoli, but it's possible to see, on site, Septimius's commemoration of the visit he paid here in 203 with his wife, Julia Domina (daughter of the Priest of the Sun at Emesa, in Syria) and his sons, the emperor Caracalla and Geta.

The fortunes of the imperial city of Septimius Severus echoed those of the dynasty he founded. Septimius died in 211; the last Severan emperor, Alexander Severus, was assassinated in 235. The Roman Empire, which had created Leptis, began its retreat from Rome in 330, when Emperor Constantine moved the capital to Constantinople.

From that time, Rome was under pressure from the tribes on her borders. In 410 the Visigoths took and sacked the city. The Germanic general Odoacer deposed the emperor Romulus Augustus in 476, a date that some historians consider the year the Roman Empire finally fell. The Byzantines, however, were already well established in their court in Constantinople, the city with a foot in two continents, Europe and Asia Minor.

Under Emperor Justinian, a period of Byzantine expansion reached its peak when Belisarius was appointed as a general in the imperial army. Fortunately for Justinian, Belisarius turned out to be the empire's greatest warrior. He had served first as one of Justinian's personal bodyguards and then became governor of Mesopotamia around 527. Belisarius led his Byzantine troops against the Persians from 529, then salvaged Justinian's rule when he fought a rebellion at home, crushing the Nika Revolt, in 532.

In 533, Belisarius was at the head of the expeditionary force that reconquered North Africa from the Vandals (a campaign that destroyed the Vandal kingdom), and then reoccupied Sicily in 535. Justinian had reclaimed Leptis Magna from the Vandals but, by the seventh century, Byzantium had lost ground. Tripolitania was conquered by the Arabs, and Leptis Magna never saw its former glory again.

Economic and political eclipse was bad business for Leptis; it gradually sank under the sand. But such obliteration was great news for archaeologists, who were able to excavate a relatively intact site in the 1920s.

We left just as the light faded, and darkness once more shrouded the city that Septimius Severus built to celebrate himself. It was eerily peaceful and quiet, a situation that might not last much longer: the Italian company that has been commissioned to build a series of tourist facilities on the coast close to Leptis will be contructing a 500-room hotel; then a five-star luxury resort; and, of course, a golf course. Libya's tourist numbers, in 2004 around 100,000 a year, are expected to reach 300,000 by 2011.

We hadn't finished with the wonders of the past. Back towards the capital, right on the water's edge, lies one of the most beautiful sites in Libya, the Villa Sileen.

There is some debate about the date of this villa: some scholars describe it as Byzantine, but others insist that it has some late Christian elements and a round design that is African. Whatever its exact date may be, it is an architectural jewel and a monument to money – what it could buy, what it could create. During the rule of Rome and then Constantinople in North Africa, many officials and merchants settled in Tripolitania. Much of what happened in the region then is obscure, but one thing is certain: someone rich and important built the Villa Sileen. You only have to look at the bath complex to understand exactly how rich and important.

The baths follow the usual formal Roman layout – the disrobing room, the hot bath and sauna room, the warm pool, and the cooling-off bath. These rooms were heated by hypocausts under the floors and by hot air piped through the walls. One of the rooms in the baths would have been the sweat room, something better known now as a Turkish bath, or *hammam*. There was also a larger swimming pool, which would have been used as a relaxing refuge after the ablutionary routine of rinse, hot, warm, cool, sweat and scrape had been accomplished. Everywhere in this bathhouse were signs of immense luxury: traces of wonderful mosaics and remnants of the marble that would have lined all of the walls.

Brian was impressed when he saw the dome attached to the back wall of the house. 'Wow! That would have been the equivalent then of owning your own Lear jet,' he declared. And he kept declaring throughout our tour. 'The first problem would have been the water,' he said when we were looking at the baths. 'There is none near here. It would have to have been piped in from cisterns in the hills which are some distance away. Then think about how much water you would need to fill all these pools.'

Like Leptis, the Villa Sileen disappeared beneath the sand over the centuries, which ensured its preservation. Rediscovered in the 1950s and excavated in the 1970s, it features some eight hundred square metres of extraordinary mosaics across its forty or so rooms, including its dining room, which looks straight out towards the Mediterranean.

Brian and I wandered through the rooms of the villa, some of which were gloomy and exotic. The electricity supply was a little unpredictable, so the light of the bare bulbs hanging from the ceilings fluctuated, adding to the atmosphere. Brian decoded the mosaic images on the floors (not a complicated task considering that his special area of expertise was ancient history).

'Those women are the seasons,' he said of a group of glamour pusses in different states of dress, ranging from nearly naked to quite rugged up – it could obviously get quit nippy along this coast. 'In the middle, that woman represents Africa.' Next to that beautiful creature was an older man, linked to her by a garland. 'That's Annus, the year, and the circle through the whole thing signifies the year.'

Depicted in lively detail, the subjects of the mosaics were the usual fodder for the mosaicists, who, experts guess, were all African. There were symmetrical patterns, figures from Greek mythology such as Bacchus and Triton abducting a saucy nymph, maenads and Muses, scenes from the Trojan War, shields, sports, hunting scenes, pygmies with flowers, crocodiles, birds, an image of the hippodrome just up the way at Leptis, chariots, horses and riders, a bull fight, dolphins in a pool. The villa was one of the most beautiful, intriguing places I have ever been to. It was like walking through living pages of *National Geographic*. And so we went through the rooms of the house while outside, the sky and the sea bled indigo, one into the other.

As the custodians were preparing to close the house for the night, we walked out onto the terrace, across more mosaics, and down to the sea wall. It was truly the blue hour – sky, sea, air. It was a remarkably romantic spot, but one with practical applications. Carved into the rocks beneath the retaining wall were orderly little pools. 'Fish ponds,' said Brian. 'The fish would be caught, kept alive, brought here, then put in the pools to keep fresh until they were needed.'

The glory and wonder of Leptis and the Villa Sileen did not last for long. The power of Byzantium declined while that of Islam and the Arabs rose out of the Arabian peninsula. By the middle of the seventh century, just years after the death of the Prophet Mohammad, the future arrived in the form of the third caliph, Uthman ibn Affan. Between 644 and 656, Constantinople lost Palestine, Syria, Persia, Egypt and most of the lands of North Africa from Egypt to Algeria. Leptis and the villa were buried under tonnes of sand and so preserved for rescue far in the future.

The wind whipped across the water. All the fishing boats had pulled into port for the night. It was time for us to leave Ancient Rome and the Byzantine Empire. We time-travelled back to Tripoli, along a road lined by shops that looked unchanged from the Middle Ages – shops in which fruits and vegetables gleamed by flickering (electric) light, shops where bits of goat and camel and lamb hung outside, and subdued animals stood waiting for slaughter in adjacent pens. We reached the outskirts of the city, and suddenly we were back in the twenty-first century. Almost.

The next day, Salah and I were off on a journey into another world, though one only two hours out of town, on the coast towards the border with Tunisia. Hakim had invited us to dinner. It was a compliment, but one not without its difficulties.

'He wanted to know if you would eat with the women, or the

men,' said Salah, as we headed towards Hakim's family farm. 'I told him you should eat with us, because it's easier. And then you will go to the women.'

Hakim's family lived in a traditional household: his father and uncle had farms side by side, and all of his unmarried brothers and sisters lived at home. His married sister lived close by, and when Hakim and his brothers married, they would live in a block of apartments the family was building next to the main house on the farm.

Hakim was waiting on the side of the highway to guide us to the house, up a long country lane bordered by cultivated fields and pastures. There were large, plush-looking cows, and, at the end of the lane, a double-storeyed structure with a veranda out the front. He was excited to have us over for dinner, almost like a little kid at Christmas. He pointed out a camel, which had been acquired for his upcoming marriage. Just as soon as the apartment was finished, and the large reception room as well, Hakim would marry a young woman found for him by his family. She was a teacher, a distant relative, but when I asked if she would be coming tonight, I was told she would not. It wasn't appropriate.

'When will the wedding be?' I asked.

After Ramadan, Salah translated. 'His father will decide.'

We were ushered into the men's *majlis* of the farm, and Hakim's brother Hisham was already there. On the floor sat a platter of dates and milk, for the men to break their Ramadan fasts. There were glasses, too, of excellent banana smoothies and cold, non-alcoholic Beck's.

A lithe, dark-haired girl without a headscarf appeared while Salah was saying his prayers. Seeing him, she wouldn't come into the room, but stood outside and I went to say hello. She pointed to Hakim, then to herself, and said '*Ismi* Hanan.' I'm Hanan –and she made the index fingers of her hands parallel to indicate that she and Hakim were brother and sister. Then, embarrassed to be about without her hijab, she disappeared around a corner.

The room we were in was the communal *majlis* for the four apartments being built for the brothers to bring their wives into, and Hakim proudly took me into the one that he was readying for his bride. There were pillars, wide hallways, a reception room, three bedrooms, a big kitchen and a bathroom. There was dust everywhere, but it was taking shape, and almost ready to receive its new mistress. He also showed me the salon being added to the house for the wedding reception. 'You are invited,' he said through Salah when he took me back to the *majlis*.

Hakim's father appeared to greet us. I had been drilled in how to address him – having made the *hajj* (pilgrimage) to Mecca, his father was to be called 'Hajji', as a sign of respect. Hakim's maternal grandfather, another Hajji, also appeared. His mother, Fatima, came in with them, a smiling, warm woman in traditional country dress – a sort of toga tied over a cotton-knit shirt. She made us feel very welcome.

Then we sat down to dinner, prepared for us by 22-year-old Hanan, a student just three days into her tertiary course of Arabic studies. It was a feast of family delicacies (Libyan soup seasoned with fresh limes, dolmades, bean salad, stuffed rolls, crumbed chicken, fish, a savory rice dish) and was the best food I had eaten in Libya. Afterwards, Hanan took me over to the main part of the house and settled me on a cushion on the back terrace.

Women and children, sisters and aunts and cousins and their kids appeared from the gloom all at once. The young women were in the hijab, the two older women in their traditional Berber costume, with their scarves ready to pull over their faces should a strange man or a camera appear.

The children were nursed mercilessly; little Ali and Ahmad, dark-eyed baby charmers, almost had their plump cheeks kissed off. One little girl, with earrings, and dark circles under her eyes, had been in the hospital with asthma the night before and was still not quite up to par.

Hakim arrived from the men's *majlis*, leaving Salah behind with Hisham, his brother. This far into the house was the harem, out of bounds to male non-family members. As Hakim played with the children, teasing them, telling them to clear off, then gathering one little crying girl for a cuddle, my breath caught in my throat. I had never seen a man as open and as natural with children in my life. The kids were subjected to more loving torture when they were made to kiss everyone, and did so without protest.

'Will you come to stay again, and sleep over?' Hanan asked me.

'*In'shallah!*' I answered – God willing!

I would like to have spent more time with the women, and seen inside the family quarters of the main house, but language was a problem, and I didn't want to trespass on Fatima's hospitality. After half an hour, Hanan took me back to the men's *majlis* and she stayed with us. The little girl who had been ill came too, and snuggled between us on the cushions. The older men came and went, but Hisham's young, unmarried friends stayed together, out in the garden, behind a fence.

As it came close to time to go, I sent Hakim to his mother with the chocolates I had bought earlier that day, and Hanan came back with an enormous box for me. It was a collection of Gharyan pottery and I was so moved by the sweetness of the present, I didn't have time to worry about the weight of it until days later.

Salah and I drove away from Hajji and Fatima, Hakim, Hanan and Hisham, and I knew they had given me a gift far beyond the pottery, though that was considerable. To take a stranger – a foreigner, a woman, a Christian – into your home, to show them how you live and who you are, was a gift of trust and faith, and it was one I will never forget.

Chapter 31

Taking the Veil

IN THE PRE-DAWN, AN electrical storm crackled over the sea off the Tripoli coast, a suitably grey way for our Sahara group to split up. The farewells were rushed and then, in a wave, they were gone, and it was time for the next stage of my adventure with Salah to begin. A couple of days in the east of Libya.

We had been to Germa, on the southern edge of the Ancient Roman world; it was time to go east to see what the Greeks had been able to achieve in their age of colonisation, in the sixth century BC, in the towns of Appollonia, Tocra, Tolmeita and Cyrene. The entry point for us was Benghazi, the main city of western Cyrenaica.

It's a region that has a particular pull for many Australians, as Tobruk, with its Commonwealth war graves cemetery, is located here. For me personally, I remember my grandfather's stories from his time fighting in the Western Desert during World War II. But there is more to Cyrenaica than graves. It was on a busy trading route between the eastern and western Mediterranean, and its ancient ruins, while not the equal of Leptis Magna, have been well excavated and maintained. Like Leptis, the ruins were also said to enoy the benefit of not being overwhelmed by tourists.

We arrived at Benghazi late in the afternoon, picked up the hire car and headed off towards our base at Susa, a couple of hours' drive away. Without the cushioning of the group, I was feeling awkward with Salah. But as the countryside rolled by, our old easiness was restored. The views relaxed as well, from the hot, scrubby landscapes of the coast around Benghazi up to the greener scenery and crisper air of the Jebel Akhdar, the Green Mountain.

When we arrived in Susa, we checked in to a modern hotel which had everything: hot water, toilet paper, a view of the ocean, as well as a television that worked. There was also a flea, I reported to Salah. 'Did you bring that with you?' he asked, and the easy teasing between us was back on an even keel.

The next day I was invited to join a group of Italians who were being shown around Appollonia by the hotel's guide, Dr Fadalallah Abdussalm. Because Fadalallah had taken me under his wing, Salah would spend the morning resting, after which, it being a Friday, he planned to go to midday prayers at the mosque in nearby Cyrene.

The Italians were happy for me to join their group, although some of them were worried that I wouldn't understand what was being said. They started to translate for me, but when I spoke to them in Italian, they were relieved – if a little astonished to discover that an Australian could speak their language. As Fadalallah pointed out the wonder of the ruined city, I stood on a wall and looked down towards a curve of breakwaters that defined an area which would have been a port. Appollonia is like a real version of the lost city of Atlantis; under the water, it is possible to see columns and architectural details drowned by the years and the encroaching sea.

After my tour of Appollonia, Salah and I headed for Cyrene, which is an enormous site up in the hills above Susa. Standing in the ruins of the ancient theatre, looking across to the coast and the sea, I could hear the noon prayers being called from the mosque. The lecture of the imam was also broadcast, and he sounded angry and upset – but I discovered from Salah that some imams use that hectoring tone for effect, to keep their listeners from falling asleep in the heavy warmth of the mosques.

The sprawling site at Cyrene also includes a magnificent gymnasium, which dates from the second century BC; an open space that was converted into a forum by later Roman rulers; a square, the heart of the ancient Greek city, edged by colonnades and the vestiges of grand public buildings; an extensive necropolis; and some beautiful mosaics still in place. Not far from Cyrene, though, is its real jewel: the Temple of Zeus. Bigger than Athens's Parthenon, this temple was erected in the fifth century BC and destroyed in an earthquake in 365. Italian archaeologists put the temple back together, more or less, into the structure that Salah and I visited that afternoon.

Towards the end of the day, as our blood sugars were plummeting, we found another of the Greek cities of Cyrenaica – Tocra. Some seventy kilometres from Benghazi, this would be our last stop in Cyrenaica. The new village is unremarkable, but the ancient town of Tocra has been there since around 510 BC. It was one of the first Ancient Greek ports of the region, and some tombs dating from the period can still be seen close to the entry gate. Salah and I headed up the steps of a fort that dates from Ottoman times, and was later expanded by the Italians; it was a rickety climb, but worth the risk for the view from the top.

As the sun sank towards the sea, we climbed to the top of a Turkish fort in the old *medina* in time to watch it disappear. As it did, I headed down the steps to the car, to break the Ramadan fast.

'Come on, it's over,' I urged Salah.

'But the muezzin hasn't called yet.'

'Salah! The evidence of your own eyes tells you that the sun just set. Let's go and *eat* something . . .'

At the gate of the Tocra site, the guardians offered us dinner, but Salah went to the mosque for evening prayers while I sat eating bananas and drinking 7-Up in the car. Eventually we headed back towards Benghazi, and the next day returned to Tripoli.

With the other Australians having gone, it felt a little odd being back in the Libyan capital. So, with Salah spending some time with his extended family, I took the opportunity to make the acquaintance of some of my fellow guests at the hotel.

One was a fifty-something Jordanian airline pilot who was in Libya to fly pilgrims to Jeddah during the holy month. I'd first met him in the lobby before I went to Cyrenaica, and had fallen into conversation with him several times. He held court on the banquettes in the hotel's reception area, and was always up for a chat. This time, with an image of Colonel Gadaffi hanging above us on the wall, we sat for three hours and discussed everything from polygamy, fidelity, the marriage of Dubai's Sheikh Mohammad to Princess Haya of Jordan, to (inevitably) suicide bombings and terrorism.

The pilot advanced an argument that I had heard several times in the Middle East and North Africa to answer the 'terrorist or freedom fighter?' question. 'If you come to my house and take over and I ask you to leave and you don't, then I have the right to resist,' he said. 'But me, I could not do it. I could not be a bomber.' In his voice, though, was a tone that indicated he admired the sacrifice some of his firebrand Muslim brothers were making for their religion.

Regional politics was a long way from my mind that afternoon. I had been invited to break the Ramadan fast with Salah's family. At five thirty, Salah picked me up and we set off for the family compound his father had built more than forty years before.

Salah's mother lived with his eldest brother, Abdelrrouf, his wife Nadia and their children in the apartment she herself had raised her family in. It was enormous, with ceilings that looked as though they were more than five metres high, and high-quality finishes. In the sitting room, the dining table was set for ten, and it looked like our Christmas table at home. There were even red poinsettias on the napkins.

Nadia had done a huge job, and came out of the kitchen to welcome the visitors. Dressed in a caftan and veiled, though with some of her hair showing at the front, she was with her sister, Nahema, who was married to another brother of Salah's. Nahema was also dressed in a caftan but not veiled, I noticed.

Among the many children present was a beautiful girl of about twelve or thirteen called Anissa. I found it interesting that she was not wearing a veil at all while Iman, Abdelrrouf and Nadia's fifteen-year-old daughter, was fully veiled. I asked Abdelrrouf about the differences in the veiling. 'Iman's veil is Islamic,' he explained. 'My wife's is not. My sister-in-law should be veiled in front of her brothers-in-law.'

Salah and Abdelrrouf's mother was also wearing a scarf; but, in the Turkish fashion, her hair was visible front and back, and she was wearing earrings. She wasn't Islamically veiled, but her eldest son did not refer to her headscarf. A frail lady, she was the essence of hospitality as she presided over the table and an enormous dinner.

'Eat, eat,' said Nadia and Nahema, as the two sisters piled delicious food onto my plate: cheese pockets, bread, fish, ratatouille, and flat bread filled with tuna.

That night, while looking for a little light relief among the Ramadan crowds of Tripoli, I lost my wallet, credit cards, cash and all. I spent the first part of the next day trying to find them, but eventually gave up.

As I was waiting in the hotel foyer for Salah and Hakim, the Jordanian pilot came in, on his way that afternoon to Jeddah again. There was a cheekiness to him that I found appealing. Captain Flash – married, with three grown children – and I talked of lighter things than terrorism and suicide bombers this time. He had progressed from asking my age to when I'd had my first boyfriend. I told him that was none of his business.

He had a range of agenda items, though, and moved through them. He stopped for just a minute when he worked out that he might just find himself appearing in my book.

'If you had a romance with someone, would that be in your book too?' he asked.

Perhaps, I told him.

'But my wife . . . You must not. I am well known in Jordan.'

I refrained from pointing out that we were having a conversation, not an affair. At that point, I was saved again by Hakim, who appeared just ahead of Salah. They were on Libyan time again and forty-five minutes late to take me to report my lost wallet.

Béchir, Ali and Mohammed from the Sahara tour were at the hotel when we got back. This time, I discovered, I had lost my camera and my umbrella. Salah then forbade me to open my handbag ever again.

As for Béchir, he was still angry about Skew and the desert incident, something I had put well into the past. 'Christine, this man cannot do what he has done and not be punished,' he said. 'You are one of us, and what he does to you, he will answer to us for. We will bring him to Tripoli.' I didn't like the sound of that.

It had been a stressful day, and after I'd farewelled Flash, I went to my room, did some packing, then collapsed on the bed.

Around five o'clock that evening, I awoke, alarmed. The sky had suddenly darkened. I went to the sliding doors and opened them to the sea. A hard rain was coursing past my balcony, clattering against the walls of the hotel. Then I realised it wasn't rain at all, but a storm of locusts, blown in from the south-west, where countries like Niger and Mauritania were enduring their worst plagues in fifteen years. The locusts were headed along the coast, towards Hajji's prosperous and green farm.

As I dressed for dinner, I hoped that his fields would be spared, but had to concentrate on more immediate, personal matters. Salah and Tariq the cook (who, it turned out, was also between trips into the desert) had taken me down to the street of the scarf sellers one night, and bought me a hijab as a present. Our final dinner in Tripoli seemed the right time to wear one.

I had wanted to wear the veil for some time – out of curiosity more than anything else – but since it was a sign of Muslim faith, it had seemed presumptuous of me to put one on. Then there was that dinner with Salah's family, which opened up a new world to me; wearing the veil was about faith for some women, modesty for others, and culture for the rest perhaps.

But I had never been shown how to put it on, so I was really on my own, and less skilled that any twelve-year-old Muslim girl. I tied my hair back in a bun and pulled on the knitted, white cotton skull cap that I'd bought in Jordan. Over the top, I put a matching cowl. To that I pinned a white scarf, and over that, the pretty blue-and-white one Salah had given me.

I looked at myself in the dressing-table mirror. And tried again. After four attempts, I resigned myself to the fact that I was never going to look anything but old and crone-like, not like JoJo at all.

When I went down into the foyer to meet Salah, the security boys were silenced by this new headgear, but Salah was kind enough to say I looked very nice. The Turks in the Turkish restaurant also seemed a little taken aback. That might have had something to do with their own country's doctrine of secularism, which banned the veil in some circumstances. Salah told me that the Turks had said they couldn't understand why a woman would wear if it she didn't have to.

Hot and self-conscious, I could hardly wait to get the hijab off when we arrived back at the hotel. Then I went with Salah and Mohammed on a farewell lap of Tripoli. I didn't make it back to the hotel until 2 am.

Two hours later, the phone rang. It was Flash, just in from Jeddah, about to go to sleep but wanting to say goodbye first. At five thirty, I was up to pack, and at seven Salah took me to the airport in companionable silence.

'I told you I would be with you to the end,' he said, as he put me on the flight to Cairo.

And he was.

Delta Blues

Chapter 32

Lessons on Islam in the City Victorious

By the light of our earliest readings we look upon that other world as upon a fairy region full of wild and magical possibilities.
Gertrude Bell

FIVE THOUSAND YEARS IN the making, Cairo is one of the greatest metropolises on Earth. To the Ancient Egyptians, it was the place of Creation, where the world began. The Arabs called the city simply 'the Victorious'. It has been the seat of pharaohs, the citadel of sultans and kings, and a prize for Alexander the Great as well as Napoleon I. A study in contrasts, Cairo is a city of unimaginable poverty and wanton wealth riven by the narrow, eternal Nile as it snakes its muddy way to delta and sea, past the tombs of the ancients and modern skyscrapers and remnants of a genteel colonial past.

The skyline of Sebha had been sulphuric, but that was nothing compared to Cairo. A historic mantle of yellow-grey haze was wrapped around it, giving a peculiar look to the air itself. It was as though I was seeing Cairo through the fine gauze of my personal hijab.

Intrigued by Egypt, pharaohs and Ancient Egyptian religion for years, I had always wanted to see Cairo, and when I'd come to plan this trip, I wanted to begin in the most modern Arab countries and end in an ancient place. You can't get much more ancient than Cairo. But, surprisingly perhaps, it also has a vital and active group of feminists working diligently to improve the status of women across the country.

Without my credit cards, and unable to cash any traveller's cheques (the duty manager of my hotel had taken them against payment of my account), I decided I couldn't afford the Cairo Museum and so took myself off to Giza, to gaze upon the wonders of the past. I was excited, but my guide and driver seemed bored to sobs by our mini-group: there was just me and a photographer from an American newspaper on a death watch. She was hanging around Cairo waiting for the nod from her office to go to Gaza in time for the obsequies of the Palestinian leader Yasser Arafat, who was said to be dying in Paris. It mustn't have looked too promising from the front of the van: two distracted women in the back who could not be counted on for a meaningful tip.

We headed towards the Western Desert, along the freeway overpasses that weave their way among bleak tower apartment blocks separated by skirts of emerald-green vegetable gardens, and through the yellow-grey again, to the site of the pyramids.

Our guide looked disturbed when both the photographer and I refused to go down into the burial chambers. Claustrophobia, we claimed. It was the truth.

As soon as we got out of the van, we went 'under' in a different way – set upon by desperate, hard-faced touts who seemed to have learned their lessons of seduction from the same primer as those I'd encountered in Marrakesh and Beirut. As the photographer shot down the hill to book a ride on a camel, she was beset. 'Hello, honey!' the drivers yelled.

The one she chose was looking for an American wife. 'There you are, honey,' he crooned as he got her onto the animal. There was not a single tone of warmth in his voice.

'I like nice US bride. You American?' one sad creature hissed at me.

'Sorry. Australian.'

Hoping for a green card and obviously having neither family to be reunited with in Australia nor skills easily explained to an immigration officer, he quickly moved on to the next group of tourists. The United States might be seen as the Great Satan in some quarters of the Middle East, but here, beside the Great Pyramid of Khufu, the land of the far, far West apparently beckoned like one of unfettered promise.

The pyramids, which have survived the millennia, now look as though they are in danger of being loved to the point of annihilation. Inside the structures, apparently, moisture exhaled by thousands upon thousands of visitors is damaging the frescoes; outside, the blocks are quietly crumbling and subsiding. From a distance, the pyramids are magnificent, set on the outskirts of Cairo, right on the edge of the desert. Up close though, I had a sense of danger that the tourist policemen, mounted picturesquely on camels, did little to dispel. My unease was heightened when I remembered the group of fifty tourists killed in Luxor by extremists in 1997.

Next stop was the Sphinx, where a young Egyptian woman, Islamically dressed right down to her gloves, was working at the entrance to the site. A vision of demure modesty, she was collecting tickets, and took one from the hand of a large blonde woman dressed in red. The tourist's shorts were incredibly tight; if any more gynaecological information was to be had about this woman, a speculum would have been needed.

I looked around at my fellow travellers and thought the dress of most of them was insensitive in a Muslim country. Many of the women were wearing shorts, no sleeves, their breasts hanging out of their tank tops. Clearly they hadn't been taking advice from the Egypt section of Lonely Planet's *Middle East* guide, which says to 'dress conservatively (i.e. no shorts, tank tops or above the knee skirts except at beach resorts)'.[1]

We were taken on our guide's usual route – the papyrus shop and the perfume shop – where we spent a little, but perhaps not enough for him to make any real money out of us for the day.

Back in the hotel, I found that my life was on hold. The death of the Emirati ruler Sheikh Zayed had closed the American Express offices in the Gulf for four days of official mourning, and meant that no replacement AmEx cards would be issued in the region. I would have to wait until I was in Milan to get a new credit card.

So I was confined to the hotel, by and large, trying to find a remedy to my financial predicament and line up meetings with women I wanted to interview. The only spare cash I had was set aside for taxi trips into the Cairo CBD to visit Western Union. I could've explored on foot, but the hotel was on an island, and some distance from the centre of the city, so the best I could do to combat the cabin fever was to window-shop in the mall adjacent to the hotel's lush gardens.

This resulted in one happy and unanticipated outcome: I made a new friend. I noticed Mone in the chemist's shop, primarily because her *abaya* looked as though it came from the Gulf.

'I have them sent from Saudi Arabia,' she confirmed, and she fluttered as she walked across the shop floor. As a girl, she had worn Western clothes and short skirts, and had gone bare-headed – 'but I didn't know my religion then,' she explained. 'When I read my book [the Qur'an], I became another woman. I knew that I had to dress more respectably.' She had been wearing the hijab since 1985, as an outer indicator of her inner faith.

Mone's hijab was more complicated than JoJo's in Dubai, and sat on top of one of those tennis-visor things. She also wore a couple of different scarves over the top.

She was happy to spend some time talking to me about her life and her religion. I had been worried when I first spoke to her that I would be disturbing her, because she was deep in reflection at her desk, reading the Qur'an. But she closed it carefully and put it to one side as she told me that this was the third time she had read it, and hoped to complete it once more during the current Ramadan.

Mone was in her early fifties, and a mother of two: a daughter of twenty-six and a son of twenty-four who was about to get married. There was no groom in sight for her daughter at that time. 'I will try to choose for her,' said Mone. 'But it is up to God. If you accept that, then you will not feel confined by life.'

She knew I was interested in Islam, and Islam in relation to women, and was generous enough to help me gain some valuable insight. During a lull in the pharmacy, Mone took me into the nearby ladies toilet and peeled off the layers of her hijab. As she did so, she revealed a thick head of hennaed hair which, when loosened, fell below her shoulders. The impact of that vision, on top of the prim *abaya*, was shockingly intimate.

Then, she began to rebuild her hijab. There was a close-fitting cap, then a grey-black scarf over the top of it, closely clipped under the chin. Another, larger and lighter scarf of grey was added next, pinned to the side of her head. When she put it on, it was as though the sun had gone out: her brilliant-red hair was eclipsed, and the moon of her sweetly proper face was all that was left.

She did not feel oppressed by her clothing, she told me, but rather released by it, free of the speculative looks of men and other strangers. 'You must protect your own body,' she said. 'The bosom must be covered. God doesn't want people to hurt you.' In Mone's case, it was at least four times covered – by her underwear, her *abaya*, and two scarves.

Make-up was not permitted, Mone said. 'I forbid myself mascara.' But I noticed she was wearing kohl around her eyes. 'Kohl is not *haram* [forbidden]. It is mentioned in the Sunna.'

My lessons continued. 'Do you know how to do the proper wash?' asked my new, advanced Islam teacher. 'The *wudu*?' She began to mime the ritual cleansing that Muslims carry out before they pray: she washed her mouth ('to rinse out the bad words'), then the right and left forearm, the face, the top of the head, the feet.

Mone spoke circumspectly about her own marriage. 'He was a jealous man, and lacked self-confidence.' She was divorced, and had no plans to remarry – even though she said it was required of her by the Qur'an.

Would she never marry again?

'No. I dislike men now. God says you have to be kind to your man, and that you have to marry again. But I have my children, I have my mother to take care of. I can't make a new relationship with another man. I have no time.' She looked guilty as she said that. Mone knew that she was disobeying one of God's rules, but she was resigned to doing the best she could. She appeared ready to take it up with God if necessary when the time came.

Mone had a lot of time, though, to speak to me about the importance of her religion in her life. 'I study the Qur'an all the time. Every time I read it, I find more treasures.'

Unsure of what to do to thank Mone for her time and her interest, I tried to give her some of the little money I had left. She wouldn't take it for herself, but we decided that if she gave it to her daughter to use to buy meat for their local mosque's communal dinners, that would be acceptable. Since it was Ramadan, it seemed appropriate that I was practising another of the pillars of Islam: alms giving.

The next day, as I was packing to catch the flight to Milan, Mone called me in my room in the hotel. Would I come down to see her? she asked.

When I went down, it became clear that she had a present for me in return. There were two large books of *hadith* – the two-volume *The Meadows of the Righteous Books* – and a couple of smaller books about Islam for women, and sandalwood incense. As Mone gave me the books, she urged me to read the Qur'an. 'If you read, you must know,' she said.

I went back upstairs to do a little Islamic study and opened *What Does She Expect Better?*, the book about women and Islam. It examined, albeit from a partisan perspective, misconceptions about Mone's religion. Some of it was just wrong: 'Islam gives women political rights such as voting or occupying a convenient public office. It is common knowledge that women in Western developed countries did not acquire these privileges until the twentieth century,' it stated.[2] I supposed that depended on your definition of 'Western' and 'developed'.

New Zealand was the first country in the world to give suffrage to women, in 1893; Australia followed in 1902. In the last thirty-five years, countries as diverse as Yemen (1970), Switzerland (1971), Jordan (1974), Iraq (1980), Lichtenstein (1984) and Kazakhstan (1993) have enfranchised their women. Kuwaiti women finally managed to get the vote in 2005, but women in Saudi Arabia still do not have it, and neither do Emiratis.

In other parts, the book made good sense, and presented arguments that could be made by any fundamentalist monotheist, even a Bridget Jones type looking for her Mr Right. Are men seen as superior to women in Islam? Mone's little book said no. 'Men are the protectors and maintainers of women, because Allah has given the one more than the other and because men support them from their means' (Qur'an 4:34). 'This verse implies it is a man's duty to support his wife, but this in no way makes him superior to her,' *What Does She Expect Better?* concludes.[3]

Equality was a notion that would never have occurred to women in Egypt during its thousands of years of civilisation. Since 3000 BC, women have ruled the country at various times, and it seems impossible to imagine that historical Egyptian women – queens Neithotep, Nefertari, Hatshepsut and Cleopatra – would have had much truck with men being seen as even one degree higher than women.

Another woman of influence who emerged in the late 900s was Sitt Al-Mulk, 'Lady of Power'. A princess of the Fatimid dynasty, she was acknowledged as a great beauty and intellect, and was a woman who fascinated the caliphs of the time.

She was the daughter of Imam Al-Aziz and a Byzantine Christian mother, and the elder sister of the remarkable Imam Hakim. Her father built two magnificent palaces in Cairo, the Golden Palace and the River Palace, where Sitt Al-Mulk grew up. Al-Aziz was renowned for his generosity and predisposition towards clemency.[4] Under his reign, the people of the Book – Christians and Jews – had unprecedented freedoms and rights.

Sitt Al-Mulk benefited from her father's tolerance and openness, and inherited his looks and courage. Even as a child, she observed and was later involved in making decisions that affected the country, and following Al-Aziz's death, after twenty-one years as caliph, she expected to have her opinions considered.

The death of her father brought her brother, Al-Hakim bi-Amr Allah, to the caliphate at the age of eleven. In some quarters an unpopular figure, he was occasionally called 'Hakim the Mad'. There is some evidence for the appropriateness of this appellation: at the age of fifteen he was said to have had his tutor murdered. He was not fond of women, and apparently forbade them to leave home, and made sure they couldn't, by outlawing the manufacture and sale of women's footwear. Apart from women, he didn't much care for dogs, and was annoyed by their barking. He ordered them all to be exterminated. Al-Hakim banned the sale of grapes, wine and beer, and ordered honey to be dumped into the Nile.

Despite these odd decrees, some commentators considered Hakim to be a 'wise and tactful' leader.[5] He founded the House of Wisdom to promulgate Shia and Fatimid Ismaili doctrine. But towards the end of his 25-year reign, Hakim was increasingly unpredictable, and would often wander on long walks around Cairo and its surrounding hills. In 1021, he went out one night and never came back.

Forty days of mourning passed, and Sitt Al-Mulk had Hakim's sixteen-year-old son, Al-Zahir, proclaimed imam and caliph. As regent, Sitt Al-Mulk organised a peaceful transition of power. A woman could never be caliph; that was a position reserved exclusively for men because of its messianic and religious aspects.

Sitt Al-Mulk was followed – eventually – by another woman, Shajarat Al-Dur, who ruled in Cairo two hundred years later. Shajarat was a military leader and de facto ruler of Egypt from 1250 to 1257. This was even more remarkable, though, because she was a slave of Turkoman origin.

When Al-Dur's husband, Sultan Al-Salih Ayyub, died of a fever in the middle of the Nile Delta during a campaign against Frankish crusaders, Al-Dur concealed his death and controlled Egypt long enough to recall Al-Salih's son, Turan Shah, from northern Syria. When word leaked out about Al-Salih's death, Turan Shah was already in control.

This was a period of enormous political uncertainty, which in some ways was why Shajarat Al-Dur was able to further make her mark. The Mamluks defeated the Frankish crusaders in 1250 and took the French king, Louis IX, hostage; then they murdered Turan Shah and gave Shajarat the title 'Mother of Khalil'.[6] She reigned alone for eighty days and behaved like the head of state and faith – coins were struck with her image on them, and the Friday sermons were given in her own name. She also negotiated the ransom of the humiliated king of the Franks.

The caliph of Baghdad was displeased with Shajarat's power grab and sent a stern rebuke to the Egyptian emirs: 'Since no *man* among you is worthy of being Sultan, I will bring you one.'[7] Shajarat stepped down, and married the chief Mamluk, Aibak, who was proclaimed sultan. Since he spent much of his reign on campaign against the Syrian Ayyubids, Shajarat ruled for a further seven years; although, his frequent absences aside, she is generally considered to have been the dominant one in the partnership. Shajarat had coins struck in both their names, signed Aibak's decrees, and was addressed as 'Sultana'.

Things came unstuck when Aibak, whom Shajarat had forced to divorce his first wife to marry her, decided to marry another new wife. In a jealous rage, she had him murdered in his bath after a game of polo. When she tried to hide her crime, her past caught up with her. Aibak's first wife and son spurred on the women of the harem to beat Shajarat to death with their wooden clogs. She died in 1257, just one in the long line of formidable women I had discovered in Islam.

Chapter 33

Rehab in Cairo

I HAD ARRANGED AN appointment with another formidable woman: Rehab Farouk El Mezeini, who worked for Egypt's peak non-government organisation for women, the Association for the Development and Enhancement of Women (ADEW).

Rehab, the donor co-ordinator of the association – on her books are bodies such as the European Commission's Delegation to Egypt, the Swiss Development Fund, the embassies of Japan, Finland and the Netherlands, the United Nations Development Fund, and the Australian Embassy – appeared backlit through the front doors of the hotel. I recognised her at once.

She was almost thirty and looked more Western than North African; her long blonde-streaked hair fell in tousled curls past her shoulders, and she was simply but stylishly dressed in jeans and a shirt. After Mone and her sober *abayas* and triple-layered hijabs, Rehab was a completely different Cairene. But she came from an upper-middle-class family, was educated at the American University in Cairo (where she had specialised in international politics) and was well travelled. She had even spent time in Sydney, on 'R and R' from working for an international refugee agency on Nauru.

ADEW works in the poorest areas of Egypt. 'Our mission is the empowerment of women, economically, socially and legally,' Rehab said as she lit up a cigarette and ordered coffee.

Legally?

One of the big questions for Egyptian women was personal status, she said.

After growing up in Australia, and seeing the development of the women's movement, I found it almost impossible to believe that an estimated 1,000,000-plus women in modern Egypt were struggling just for basic recognition of their legal status.

'Under Islam, women are not supposed to be the heads of households,' Rehab continued. 'They should be cared for by husbands, fathers, brothers or sons. But in Egypt, we estimate that twenty per cent of households are headed by a woman. Some forty per cent of homes in the squatter areas of Cairo have a female head of household.'

She paused. I needed it, to try to imagine the size of a problem that had never occurred to me.

'The reality is that these women are the breadwinners. Most are illiterate. And many of them have no official documentation at all. They go from being dependent on their fathers to being dependent on their husbands. Their births were not registered, so they have no birth certificates.

'If something happens to a husband, such as death, desertion or divorce, then the woman begins to have a problem. She can't enrol her kids in school, she cannot claim social benefits. Legally, she does not exist.' It had a huge impact on the self-confidence of women in this situation, Rehab said. 'They know they are not on anyone's priority list.'

In the last ten years, ADEW had established the legal identities of 25,000 women, 4000 of them in the previous twelve months. It was a long, slow process, which could take a month if the woman had a birth certificate and six if she didn't, but it was worth the effort for every individual.

'They get their papers, and you can see it in their eyes: finally, they exist.'

We moved briefly past domestic violence, which ADEW estimates runs at one in three women being the victim of abuse – similar to figures from around the world – to forced marriages and the education of girls. Finally we came to female genital mutilation, a practice that I had found no evidence of at all during my trip. 'Un-Islamic,' I was told from the Emirates to Morocco. 'Sub-Saharan.'

While it holds a particular gruesome interest in the modern world, the practice was also of some interest nearly a hundred and fifty years ago, when Florence Baker was travelling on an expedition with her husband, the English gentleman and explorer Samuel Baker. He had bought Florence out of a slave market in 1859, and the pair continued with his plan to go down the Nile. On this trip, Florence had a first-hand experience of female circumcision, which was later recorded in her husband's journal.

They were at Gozerajup in Nubia, near the junction of the Nile and Atbara rivers. The area was populated by Bishareen Arabs, the largest Arab tribe in the region. The river there was 'as thick as pea soup', Samuel wrote; and the water was not only undrinkable, but 'unwashable' as well.[1] Every drop of water and milk needed to be boiled before it was safe for human consumption. It was an odd, threatening place, where the couple discovered a very disturbing aspect of the culture.

A little girl of the town had begun to trail around after Florence, and Florence in turn had become attached to the sweet-faced child. One day, the girl's mother asked Florence to join them for a big ceremony. It was, explained the mother, a time of great danger for the child, and men were excluded. The ceremony was to take place in an isolated hut, which was crowded with other women from the village and heavy with the smell of burning herbs and unwashed bodies.

The little girl, who was about three or four, sat naked in the centre of the hut. Around her was ranged a circle of women. The child was happy and proud to be the centre of so much attention. Her mother had her lie down, and began to massage her head and shoulders. Other relatives massaged the girl's hands and feet. Then an old woman began the work they were there to do.

In that society, it was an essential rite of passage. All the tribes did it. A woman who was not circumcised, Florence was told, was unclean, and an uncircumcised wife could have many lovers without her husband ever knowing.

After it was over, Florence managed to overcome her nausea and got back to Samuel. What she told him of her experience he recorded in the name of scientific research:

> The operation upon the females to secure their chastity is performed from the ages of two to five – the parts being

> scarified or rather the edges being shaved off with a razor, the knees and the big toes are tied together and the child lying in this position for about fourteen days, everything heals together like a natural wound. Thus an orifice no larger than a quill is left for the demands of Nature and there is no more semblance of sex than upon a marble statue.[2]

As you can imagine, the pain of sexual penetration – if it were possible – would be horrendous. So when the marriage night approached, the women of the village would get busy again.

> The women operate on her by inserting a probe in the small orifice and pushing it upward in a direction towards the surface, the point of the instrument is soon felt near the skin. The probe acting as a guide, an incision is made with a razor from the entrance to the place defined by the point, but the aperture is not usually so large as originally intended by Nature.[3]

The problems with this form of genital surgery did not end with sex. When it came to childbirth, the woman needed to have the aperture enlarged again. Samuel Baker reported that the mother-to-be would be naked, kneeling on a pile of sand and clinging to a rope to keep herself upright, while her friends moved their hands forcefully down her back, as though squeezing the baby out of her. Meanwhile: 'another woman [inserted] the tube as formerly, enlarging the aperture to the greatest extent with a razor, and the infant at length enters his life turning a somersault upon the heap of sand.'[4]

After her accouchement, the new mother would be kept on her back for fourteen days once more, her knees and her toes tied together, so the wounds could heal. 'A piece of wood is inserted to ensure an aperture of the size desired and this is strapped around her to certain it in place until all is properly healed.'[5]

Samuel could not resist taking a final swipe at the locals who followed this custom: 'Thus do these beastly savages mutilate themselves to ensure chastity before marriage, but to increase their lustful desires afterward.'[6] He was referring to the fact that the vaginal opening was always tight, thanks to the procedure.

Female genital mutilation was also a form of social control – a woman who could suit herself when it came to choosing who to sleep with, and when, would put a question mark over the paternity of her children. And that would lead to extraordinary community disorder.

But the practice is not only historical; it exists in countries in East and West Africa, and in parts of the Middle East, India and Pakistan today. It is carried out on girls as young as three, and by people who often have no formal medical qualifications at all. Even though the most extreme form of female genital mutilation, infibulation, is illegal in Sudan, where medical practitioners are banned from carrying it out, a survey published in the *British Medical Journal* discovered that fifty-seven per cent of female university students were circumcised, and just under ten per cent thought it was required by their religion.[7]

But it is not a custom that appears in the Qur'an, which enabled ADEW to try to enlist Egypt's chief religious authority to stand against the practice. The problem, according to Rehab, was that it is mentioned in an unconfirmed, unauthenticated *hadith*, when Mohammad, informed that a girl was about to circumcised, told those involved that if they had to cut, not to cut too much. The chief mufti of Egypt, who is the supreme religious authority, does not recognise this *hadith* and himself stands against female genital mutilation.[8]

In many communities, it existed as a practice before Islam arrived, and became incorporated into local religious observance. At its heart, it is done in the best interests of the girl, since her community credits it with ensuring health, chastity, social cohesion (the same argument used within families for male circumcision), family honour, hygiene, fertility and successful childbirth. It is practised in countries where Christianity predominates, for example Kenya and Ethiopia, and in multi-faith countries such as Eritrea and Sierra Leone, where both Christian and Muslim communities carry it out. It is rare among Muslims in countries such as Iran, Turkey, Lebanon, Jordan and Syria, and is not done in Morocco, Algeria, Tunisia or Libya.

ADEW has recruited women who were circumcised themselves to go into the squatter areas of Cairo, to educate women about leaving their daughters intact, Rehab said. These women were among the staunchest opponents of the practice, having suffered from it all through their adult lives.

Among other traditional aspects of life which Rehab's organisation was busy trying to wipe out was the Oriental wedding night, when the honour of the family is attached to the virginity of the bride, and requires the ostentatious display of bloodied sheets the morning after the wedding to attest to her purity. Concerned mothers and midwives were sometimes called in to deflower the brides properly, and for those women approaching the marriage bed without their hymens, vials of pigeon blood were smuggled in and did the trick.

Rehab was my last formal interview on my voyage of discovery around the former Ottoman Empire, and as I settled myself in my seat as the plane took off, I looked at Cairo sprawling below. I'd had some memorable adventures, met some unforgettable people, and learned an enormous amount about the places and societies I had visited. My original impression, on my first trip to Libya a year earlier, that Muslims in these countries were just people who worried about the futures of their kids, who loved their families, who went to work and came home again just like most of us in the West, had been confirmed.

There was also a politely expressed desire among the people I had met to be left to manage their own affairs, without foreign governments riding roughshod over them. People I talked to might have thought their governments were incompetent at best (a feeling not confined to Islamic countries), but at least they were their own, home-grown incompetents.

As for Islam, I came away with the clear understanding that, like the other monotheistic religions, it is not a monolithic structure, that there are many ways to be a Muslim, and many paths that are followed – but they all lead to the same place.

Then there was the subject of the veil. I had listened and tried to learn, but variations between countries meant that I couldn't even establish what the requirement for veiling was, apart from the direction to dress modestly. The answer to that depended, as so much else did, on the country you were in.

From what I had seen of Islam in action, it was a peaceful and loving religion, far from the violence and terror reported every night on the news. The people I had encountered (with a couple of exceptions, admittedly) were kind and hospitable to a fault.

I had made some good friends, and some friends in unexpected places. It was a delight to be greeted warmly in the deepest desert by someone you haven't seen for a year; it was a privilege to be welcomed as an honoured guest in the houses of people from the Gulf to the edge of North Africa. When I think about how I was sure I wouldn't get out of Libya alive on that first trip in 2003, I cringe . . . I have learned to love Arab music, my wardrobe is full of caftans and leather slippers, and my fondness of perfumes and incense has turned into a blazing passion.

It wasn't all plain sailing there, of course. I learned a little patience in the chaos of Sebha airport, and that things always seem to work out in the end. I discovered that I could rely on the gallant nature of Arab men.

And I learned a couple of sharp lessons. One was that travelling light was better than hauling around sixty kilos of luggage, unless you have your own bearers. The second was that the more I discovered about Islam, the surer I was that I knew nothing.

The plane banked and I could see Zemalek and the palace built for Eugénie, and the Nile, and then the city, before everything was swallowed by the night.

Notes

Prologue

1 Antoine de Saint-Exupéry, *Le Petit Prince*, p. 72.

Chapter 1: Bag Lady

1 Andreas Pflitsch, 'Lugging a Piano to Khartoum'.
2 ibid.
3 Jane Robinson, *Wayward Women*, p. 81.
4 Janet Wallach, *Desert Queen*, p. 99.
5 ibid.

Chapter 2: First Stop, Orientalism

1 Unless noted otherwise, throughout this book, quotations from the Qur'an are taken from the Penguin Classics edition – *The Koran: With Parallel Arabic Text* – translated with notes by NJ Dawood.
2 Mary Wortley Montagu, *Selected Prose and Poetry of Lady Mary Wortley Montagu*.
3 ibid.
4 ibid.
5 Isabel Burton, *The Romance of Isabel, Lady Burton*, p. 385.

Chapter 3: Dancing in the Desert

1 Armen Ohanian, *The Dancer of Shamahka* (translated from the French by Rose Wilder Lane, Dotton, 1923), cited in Wendy Buonaventura, *Serpent of the Nile*, pp 115–16. (See also Karol Henderson Harding, *The World's Oldest Dance*.)
2 ibid., p. 67.
3 Wendy Buonaventura, *Serpent of the Nile*, p. 68.

Chapter 4: Thank God, it's a Dry Day

1 This translation is taken from 'Koran 33: Confederates of the Madina', *The Holy Koran*, on the Encyclopaedia of the Orient website.

2 Physicians for Human Rights, *The Taliban's War on Women.*
3 ibid.

Chapter 5: Sunday School

1 Sheikh Mohammed Centre for Cultural Understanding, 'Open Doors, Open Minds'.
2 Mary Wortley Montagu, *Letters*, p. 108.

Chapter 6: Women of Islam

1 Arab Women's Solidarity Association, 'Arab Women's Contributions to Society, History and Culture'.
2 Ibn Ishaq, *The Life of Muhammad, Apostle of Allah*, p. 26.
3 These teachings can be found in the Qur'an: the murder of infant girls, at 81:8–9 and 16:58–59; property rights for women, at 4:7; and polygamy, at 4:3. See also Dr Jamal A Badawi, 'The Status of Women in Islam'.
4 Cited in Peter F Wiener, *Martin Luther: Hitler's Spiritual Ancestor.*
5 Arab Women's Solidarity Association, 'Arab Women's Contributions to Society, History and Culture'.
6 ibid.
7 ibid.
8 ibid.
9 Jannah.org, 'Rumaysa Bint Milhan'.
10 ibid.
11 *The Infancy Gospel of the Apostle James* is one of the Apocrypha – accounts widely read by early Christians but not admitted to the New Testament.
12 This *hadith* transmitted by Abu Abdulah Muhammad Bin Zaid Ibn-e-Maja.

Chapter 9: Ladies of Letters

1 Elizabeth Robins, 'A Modern Woman Born 1689', p. 44.
2 Mary Wortley Montagu, 'Letter to the Countess of . . ., Spring, 1717', *Letters*, p. 170.
3 ibid.
4 ibid.
5 ibid.

6 ibid., p. 171.
7 ibid.
8 Mary Wortley Montagu, 'Letter to the Countess of . . ., April/ May 1718', *Letters*, p. 168.
9 ibid., p. 167.
10 ibid., p 168.
11 Isabel Burton, *The Romance of Isabel, Lady Burton*, p. 385.
12 ibid., p. 386.
13 Ibn Battuta, *Travels in Asia and Africa 1325–1354.*
14 John Knox, *The First Blast of the Trumpet Against the Monstrous Regiment of Women.*
15 Lucienne Thys-Şenocak, *Ottoman Women Builders.*
16 Lucienne Thys-Şenocak, email to the author, February 2006.

Chapter 11: Sufis Unto the Day

1 Dr Celaleddin B Çelebi, 'Sema: Human Being in the Universal Movement'.
2 Cited in Philip Mansel, *Constantinople: City of the World's Desire, 1453–1924*, p. 184.

Chapter 12: At Home with the Amazons

1 Chris Morris, *The New Turkey*, p. 144.
2 www.gwu.edu/-elliott.
3 Economist, 'Turkish Women: Thou Shalt Not Kill', p. 50.
4 Tezer Taşkiran, *Women in Turkey*, p. 7.
5 Quoted in ibid., p. 11.
6 Mariana Ornelas, 'Women Activists and Politicians'.
7 Ustun Reinart, 'Ambition for All Seasons: Tansu Ciller'.

Chapter 13: Nebi Storms the Barracks

1 Cecil Woodham-Smith, *Florence Nightingale.*
2 *Morning Herald* War Correspondant, 'The Bloodiest Engagement of the Eastern War: Detailed Description of the Fight'.
3 ibid.
4 Deborah Pulliam, 'Florence Nightingale, the Lady with the Lamp'.

Chapter 14: The Road to Petra

1 Cited in Richard Usborne, 'Carving Their Names on the Walls of Time'.
2 Maccabees 2:4-8: 'The prophet, having received an oracle, ordered that the tent and the ark should follow with him, and that he went out to the mountain where Moses had gone up and had seen the inheritance of God.' For more on Egeria, the Spanish pilgrim nun, go to www.umilta.net/egeria.html#Egeria.
3 Andrew Humphreys et al, *Lonely Planet Guides: Middle East*, p. 388.

Chapter 15: A Question of Honour

1 From the transcript of a story on American PBS's *Frontline* to commemorate the twenty-fifth anniversary of the showing of Anthony Thomas's film: www.pbs.org/wgbh/pages/frontline/shows/princess/etc/script.html.
2 Cited in Committee on Equal Opportunities for Women and Men, *So-called 'Honour' Crimes*.
3 Committee to Defend Women's Rights in the Middle East, 'Jordan: Two Recent Cases of Honour Killings'.
4 ibid.
5 Malcolm Knox, 'Her Life as a Fake'.

Chapter 16: Lady and the Dame

1 Isabel Burton, *The Romance of Isabel, Lady Burton*, p. 90.
2 ibid., p. 21. See also http://etext.library.adelaide.edu.au/b/burton/richard/b97zw/b97zw.html.
4 Isabel Burton, *The Romance*, p. 21.
5 ibid., p. 38.
6 ibid., p. 39.
7 ibid., p. 54.
8 ibid., p. 53.
9 ibid., p. 54.
10 ibid., p. 55.
11 ibid., p. 91.
12 Thomas Wright, *The Life of Sir Richard Burton*, chap. X.

13 ibid.
14 Isabel Burton, *The Romance*, p. 404.
15 Freya Stark, *Letters from Syria*, cited in Dea Birkett, *Off the Beaten Track: Three Centuries of Women Travellers*, p. 38.
16 Freya Stark, *Valley of the Assassins*, cited at www.iras.ucalgary.ca/~volk/sylvia/LegendsAsia.htm.

Chapter 17: My First Gigolo

1 Cited at http://en.wikipedia.org/wiki/Death_toll.
2 CNN, 14 February 2005 (http://transcripts.cnn.com/TRANSCRIPTS/0502/14/lol.05.html).
3 Rick Gore, 'Who Were the Phoenicians?'.

Chapter 18: Belles of the Desert

1 St Egeria's travels were transcribed by the monk Valerius in *The Pilgrimage of St Sylvia of Aquitania to the Holy Places*.
2 Cited in Francesco Gabrielli, *Arab Historians of the Crusades*, pp 206–7. (See also Karen Larsdatter, 'Women of Peace and War: The Roles of European Women at the Siege of Acre'.)
3 ibid., p. 207.
4 ibid., p. 204.
5 ibid.
6 For this section discussing Hester's life post-London, I am greatly indebted to Daniel Da Cruz's splendid article 'Queen of the Desert: Lady Hester Stanhope', which appeared in the September–October 1970 issue of *Saudi Aramco World* and on which my research was heavily based.
7 Daniel Da Cruz, 'Queen of the Desert: Lady Hester Stanhope'.
8 ibid.
9 cited in ibid.
10 ibid.
11 Letter from Lady Hester Stanhope to Mary Rich, July 1813 (extract), held in the British Library (MSS Eur C 740), cited in Dea Birkett, *Off the Beaten Track*, p. 17.
12 Gertrude Bell, *The Desert and the Sown* (1907), cited in Janet Wallach, *Desert Queen*.
13 Joel R Siebring, 'Gertrude Margaret Lowthian Bell 1868–1926'.

14 Cited in Dea Birkett, *Off the Beaten Track*, p. 34.
15 Gertrude Bell & Arnold Talbot Wilson, 'Review of the Civil Administration of Mesopotamia, 1914–1920'.
16 Cited in Janet Wallach, *Desert Queen*, p. 100.

Chapter 19: Night Flight from Beirut

1 Samuel Pepys, *Pepys: The Later Diaries*, p. 52.
2 John Hopkins, *The Tangier Diaries, 1962–1979*.
3 Edith Wharton, *In Morocco*, p. 103.
4 ibid., p. 36.
5 ibid., p. 9.
6 ibid., p. 105.

Chapter 20: The Magic Kingdom

1 Cited in David Druckman, 'Churchill's World: Hotel La Mamounia, Marrakech, Morocco'.

Chapter 21: A Brief Life

1 Copies of this and other studio portraits of Isabelle can be found in Annette Kobak, *Isabelle: The Life of Isabelle Eberhardt*.
2 Quoted in Lesley Blanch, *The Wilder Shores of Love*, p. 280.
3 ibid.

Chapter 22: Impossible Queens

1 Reuters, 'Moroccan Monarch Plans Wedding Celebration'.
2 Philip Jacobsen, 'Moroccan Playboy King's Wedding Marks a New Era'.
3 Quoted in AFP, 'Moroccan King to Wed Computer Engineer'.
4 Reuters, 'King Mohammed to Wed This Month'.
5 Fatima Mernissi, *The Forgotten Queens of Islam*, p. 3.
6 ibid., p 1. Politicians in Pakistan quoted tradition when opposing Benazir Bhutto's ultimately successful campaign to become prime minister; it was against nature, they said.

Chapter 23: Industrial Tourism

1 Gustave Flaubert, *Salammbô*, p. 19 (author's translation from the French).

2 ibid.
3 Zayn Bilkadi, 'Heaven's Gate'.

Chapter 24: Toasts of the Coast

1 Virgil, *The Aeneid*, 1.627.
2 ibid., 4.265. (Dryden's language is exquisite: 'Then thus, with winged words, the god began, Resuming his own shape: "Degenerate man, Thou woman's property, what mak'st thou here, These foreign walls and Tyrian tow'rs to rear, Forgetful of thy own? All-pow'rful Jove, Who sways the world below and heav'n above, Has sent me down with this severe command: What means thy ling'ring in the Libyan land?')
3 ibid., 4.345.
4 ibid., 4.360.
5 ibid., 4.315.
6 ibid., 4.324.
7 Ovid, *Heroides*, lines 191–96.
8 Charles-André Julien, *A History of North Africa*, cited in Michael Klossner, 'The Kahina, Queen of the Berbers'.
9 Tunisia Online, 'Women and Civil Rights'. (The Code of Personal Status, adopted in 1956, was amended in 1993.)
10 ibid.
11 ibid. (Law 93-65 was enacted in July 1993.)
12 ibid. (The Child's Protection Code was issued in November 1995.)
13 Tunisia Online, 'Tunisian Women in Figures'.
14 Reuters, 'Tunis: Radhia Nasraoui Ready to Die for Human Rights'.
14 ibid.
15 AFP, 'Morocco Hijab Ban Criticized'.

Chapter 25: Salah Redux

1 Anthony Ham, *Lonely Planet Country Guides: Libya*, p. 78.

Chapter 26: A Passage to Libya

1 Anthony Ham, *Lonely Planet Country Guides: Libya*, p. 78.

Chapter 28: Undercover, Under Fire

1 Cited in Cassandra Vivian, 'The Journey is its Own Reward'.
2 Barbara Hodgson, *Dreaming of East.*
3 ibid.
4 Cited in Cassandra Vivian, 'The Journey is its Own Reward'.
5 ibid.
6 ibid.
7 Susan Travers, *Tomorrow to be Brave*, p. 179.
8 ibid.
9 ibid.
10 ibid., p. 180.
11 ibid.
12 ibid., p. 223.

Chapter 30: Tripoli Treats

1 PB Shelley, *The Complete Works of Percy Bysshe Shelley.*

Chapter 32: Lessons on Islam in the City Victorious

1 Andrew Humphreys et al, *Lonely Planet Guides: Middle East*, p. 138.
2 Student Department, Irshad and Islah Muslim Charity Organisation, *What Does She Expect Better?*, p. 11.
3 ibid., p. 13.
4 Sakar Datoo, 'Fatimid Princess: Sitt Al-Mulk'.
5 ibid.
6 Mamluks were Turkish and Caucasian slaves imported into Egypt to provide a loyal army. The Mamluks eventually overthrew the government and ruled in their own right, until they were massacred by the orders of Muhammad Ali in 1811.
7 Ismail Abaza, 'Shajarat (Shaggar, Shagar, Shagarat) al-Durr and Her Mausoleum in Cairo'.

Chapter 33: Rehab in Cairo

1 Cited in Pat Shipman, *The Stolen Woman*, pp 88, 90.
2 ibid., p. 91.
3 ibid.
4 ibid., p. 92.

5 ibid.
6 ibid.
7 E Herieka & J Dhar, 'Female Genital Mutilation in the Sudan'. See also Office of the Senior Coordinator for International Women's Issues, 'Sudan: Report on Female Genital Mutilation (FGM) or Female Genital Cutting (FGC)', which cites the Sudan National Committee on Traditional Practices (SNCTP) and Save the Children Sweden as saying that 87 per cent of urban women and 91 per cent of rural women practise it.
8 Herieka and Dhar, ibid.: 'Type 1 represents the excision of a part of the clitoris or the whole organ (clitoridectomy). This is commonly known as *sunna* circumcision.'

Bibliography

Abaza, Ismail, 'Shajarat (Shaggar, Shagar, Shagarat) al-Durr and Her Mausoleum in Cairo', Tour Egypt, 2003 (www.touregypt.net/featurestories/shajarat.htm).

Abbott, Nabia, *Two Queens of Baghdad*, Al Saqi Books, London, 1986.

Abbott, Nabia, *Aishah, the Beloved of Mohammed*, Saqi Books, London, 1998.

Adkins, Lesley, *Empires of the Plain: Henry Rawlinson and the Lost Languages of Babylon*, Harper Perennial, London, 2004.

AFP, 'Moroccan King to Wed Computer Engineer', *Khaleej Times* online, 21 March 2002 (www.khaleejtimes.co.ae/ktarchive/210302/theworld.htm).

AFP, 'Morocco Hijab Ban Criticized', Aljazeera.net, 16 June 2004 (http://english.aljazeera.net/NR/exeres/8768AB46-DA03-43DA-80E9-13EC5A074EEE.htm).

Al-Qahtani, Sa'eed Ibn Ali Ibn Wahf, *Fortification of the Muslim*, trans. Khalifa Ezzat Abu Zeid, Dar Al-Salam, Cairo, 2004.

An Nawawi, Imam, *The Meadows of the Righteous*, vols 1 & 2 (abridged), trans. Ibrahim Ma'rouf, Dar Al-Manarah, El Mansoura, Egypt, 2003.

Arab Women's Solidarity Association, 'Arab Women's Contributions to Society, History and Culture', AWSA, visited April 2006 (www.awsa.net/arabwomen.htm).

Armstrong, Karen, *A History of Jerusalem One City: Three Faiths*, HarperCollins, London, 1997.

Armstrong, Karen, *Islam: A Short History*, Phoenix, London, 2001.

Armstrong, Karen, *The Battle for God: Fundamentalism in Judaism, Christianity and Islam*, HarperCollins, London, 2001.

Badawi, Dr Jamal A, 'The Status of Women in Islam', *Al-Ittihad*, vol. 8, no. 2, September 1971 (http://members.tripod.com/iaislam/TSOWII.htm).

Baker, Sir Samuel, *The Nile Tributaries of Abyssinia and the Sword Hunters of the Hamran Arabs*, Macmillan, London, 1867.

Battuta, Ibn, *Travels in Asia and Africa 1325–1354*, trans. & select. HAR Gibb; ed. Sir E Denison Ross & Eileen Power, Kegan Paul, London, 1929 (e-text version: www.fordham.edu/Halsall/source/batuta.html).

Bell, Gertrude, *Persian Pictures: A Book of Travel*, Anthem Travel Classics, London, 2005.

Bell, Gertrude & Talbot Wilson, Arnold, 'Review of the Civil Administration of Mesopotamia, 1914–1920', HMSO, London, 1920.

Bellaigue, Christopher de, *In the Rose Garden of the Martyrs: A Memoir of Iran*, HarperCollins, London, 2004.

Bilkadi, Zayn, 'Heaven's Gate', *Saudi Aramco World*, vol. 43, no. 5, September–October 1992, pp 2–7 (www.saudiaramcoworld.com/issue/199205).

Birkett, Dea, *Off the Beaten Track: Three Centuries of Women Travellers*, Hardie Grant, South Yarra, VIC, 2004.

Blanch, Lesley, *The Wilder Shores of Love*, Phoenix, London, 1993.

Bonney, Richard, *Jihad: From Qur'an to Bin Laden*, Palgrave Macmillan, Basingstoke, UK, 2004.

Brockman, David, 'Death of a Princess', *Electromusications*, April 2006 (www.transdiffusion.org/emc/behindthescreens/princess.php).

Brooks, Geraldine, *Nine Parts of Desire: The Hidden World of Islamic Women*, Anchor, Milsons Point, NSW, 2003.

Buonaventura, Wendy, *Serpent of the Nile: Women and Dance in the Arab World*, Saqi Books, London, 1994.

Buonaventura, Wendy, *Beauty and the East: A Book of Oriental Body Care*, Interlink Books, Brooklyn, NY, 2001.

Burton, Isabel, *The Inner Life of Syria, Palestine, and the Holy Land*, Kegan Paul, London, 1884.

Burton, Isabel, *The Life of Captain Sir Richard F. Burton*, Chapman & Hall, London, 1892.

Burton, Isabel, *The Romance of Isabel, Lady Burton*, vols 1 & 2, ed. WH Wilkins, Dodd Mead, New York, 1897 (http://digital.library.upenn.edu/women/burton/romance/romance.html).

Burton, Richard F, *A Secret Pilgrimage to Mecca and Medina*, Folio Society, London, 2004.

Burton, Richard F, *The Arabian Nights: Tales from a Thousand and One Nights*, Modern Library, New York, 2001.

Carr, Virginia Spencer, *Paul Bowles: A Life*, Scribner, New York, 2004.

Çelebi, Dr Celaleddin B, 'Sema: Human Being in the Universal Movement', Mevlana.net (www.mevlana.net/sema.htm).

City Guide 2003: European Cities VIII – Vienna, Prague, Cracow, Istanbul, Athens, Louis Vuitton, Paris, 2003.

Committee on Equal Opportunities for Women and Men, *So-called 'Honour' Crimes*, Parliamentary Assembly, Council of Europe, doc. 9720.

Committee to Defend Women's Rights in the Middle East, 'Jordan: Two Recent Cases of Honour Killings', *Women in the Middle East*, no. 10, February 2003 (e-text: www.middleastwomen.org)

Crone, Patricia & Hinds, Martin, *God's Caliph: Religious Authority in the First Centuries of Islam*, Cambridge University Press, Cambridge, UK, 1986.

Croutier, Alev Lytle, *Harem: The World Beyond the Veil*, Abbeville Press, New York, 1989.

Croutier, Alev Lytle, *Taking the Waters: Spirit, Art, Sensuality*, Abbeville Press, New York, 1992.

Crowther, Geoff, Mayhew, Bradley & Dodd, Jan, *Lonely Planet Country Guides: Morocco*, Lonely Planet, Footscray, VIC, 2003.

Da Cruz, Daniel, 'Queen of the Desert: Lady Hester Stanhope', *Saudi Aramco World*, vol. 21, no. 5, September–October 1970, pp 8–13 (e-text: www.saudiaramcoworld.com/issue/197005).

Datoo, Sakar, 'Fatimid Princess: Sitt Al-Mulk', Ismaili Web, 2001 (www.amaana.org/current/sittul.htm).

Dirie, Waris, *Desert Flower and Desert Dawn Omnibus*, Virago, London, 2004.

Doughty, Charles M, *Travels in Arabia Deserta*, introduction by TE Lawrence, Dover Publications, New York, 1979.

Druckman, David, 'Churchill's World: Hotel La Mamounia, Marrakech, Morocco', *Finest Hour*, no. 108, autumn 2000 (e-text: www.winstonchurchill.org/i4a/pages/index.cfm?pageid=357).

Economist, 'Turkish Women: Thou Shalt Not Kill', *The Economist*, 21 February 2004, p. 50.

Encyclopaedia of the Orient, *The Holy Koran*, ed. Tore Kjeilen, 2006 (http://lexicorient.com/e.o).

Erdogan, Sema Nilgun, *Sexual Life in Ottoman Society*, Donence Basim ve Yayin Hizmetleri, Istanbul, 2000.

Eyewitness Travel Guide: Istanbul, Dorling Kindersley, London, 2004.

Fewster, Kevin, Barşarin, Vecihi & Barşarin, Hatice Hürmüz, *Gallipoli: The Turkish Story*, Allen & Unwin, Sydney, 2003.

Finucane, Ronald C, *Soldiers of the Faith: Crusaders and Moslems at War*, Phoenix, London, 2004.

Fisk, Robert, *The Great War for Civilisation: The Conquest of the Middle East*, HarperCollins, London, 2005.

Flaubert, Gustave, *Salammbô*, Garnier-Flammarion, Paris, 1992.

Fletcher, Richard, *The Cross and the Crescent: The Dramatic Story of the Earliest Encounters Between Christians and Muslims*, Penguin, London, 2003.

Forbes, Rosita, *The Secret of the Sahara: Kufara*, George H Doran, New York, 1921.

Freely, John, *Inside the Seraglio: Private Lives of the Sultans of Istanbul*, Viking, London, 1999.

Friedman, Thomas, *Longitudes and Attitudes: Exploring the World Before and After September 11*, Penguin, London, 2003.

Gabrielli, Francesco, *Arab Historians of the Crusades*, trans. EJ Costello, University of California Press, Los Angeles, 1984.

Gibb, Lorna, *Lady Hester: Queen of the East*, Faber & Faber, London, 2005.

Goodwin, Jason, *Lords of the Horizons: A History of the Ottoman Empire*, Vintage, London, 1999.

Rick Gore, 'Who Were the Phoenicians?', *National Geographic*, October 2004 (e-text: http://magma.nationalgeographic.com/ngm/0410/feature2/index.html?fs=www7.nationalgeographic.com).

Grosrichard, Alain, *The Sultan's Court: European Fantasies of the East*, trans. Liz Heron, Verso, London, 1998.

Ham, Anthony, *Lonely Planet Country Guides: Libya*, Lonely Planet, Footscray, VIC, 2002.

Hamlin, Catherine, *The Hospital by the River: A Story of Hope*, Pan Macmillan, Sydney, 2003.

Hazlewood, Nick, *The Queen's Slave Trader: John Hawkyns, Elizabeth I, and the Trafficking in Human Souls*, Morrow, New York, 2004.

Henderson Harding, Karol, *The World's Oldest Dance: The Origins of Oriental Dance*, Belly Dance Home Page, 1998 (www.bdancer.com/history/BDhist1.html).

Herieka, E & Dhar, J, 'Female Genital Mutilation in the Sudan: Survey of the Attitude of Khartoum University Students Towards This Practice', *British Medical Journal*, vol. 79, January 2003, pp 220–23 (e-text: http://sti.bmjjournals.com/cgi/content/full/79/3/220).

Hindley, Geoffrey, *The Crusades: Islam and Christianity in the Struggle for World Supremacy*, Constable & Robinson, London, 2004.

Hodgson, Barbara, *Dreaming of East: Western Women and the Exotic Allure of the Orient*, Greystone Books, Toronto, 2005.

Hopkins, John, *The Tangier Diaries, 1962–1979*, Cadmus Press, Los Angeles, 1998.

Horowitz, Tony, *Baghdad Without a Map and Other Misadventures in Arabia*, Plume, New York, 1991.

Humphreys, Andrew et al, *Lonely Planet Guides: Middle East*, Lonely Planet, Footscray, VIC, 2003.

Irwin, Robert, *The Alhambra*, Profile Books, London, 2005.

Ishaq, Ibn, *The Life of Muhammad, Apostle of Allah*, ed. Michael Edwardes, Folio Society, London, 2003.

Jacobsen, Philip, 'Moroccan Playboy King's Wedding Marks a New Era', *Daily Telegraph* (London), 24 March 2002.

Jannah.org, 'Rumaysa Bint Milhan', 2006 (www.jannah.org/sisters/rumaysa.html).

Julien, Charles-André, *A History of North Africa: Tunisia, Algeria, Morocco, from the Arab Conquest to 1830*, Praeger, New York, 1970.

Keay, John, *Sowing the Wind: The Mismanagement of the Middle East 1900–1960*, John Murray, London, 2004.

Kennedy, Hugh, *The Court of the Caliphs: The Rise and Fall of Islam's Greatest Dynasty*, Weidenfeld & Nicolson, London, 2004.

Khayyam, Omar, *The Rubaiyat*, trans. Edward Fitzgerald, Folio Society, London, 1970.

Kinross, Patrick, *The Ottoman Empire*, Folio Society, London, 2003.

Kinross, Patrick, *Atatürk: The Rebirth of a Nation*, Phoenix, London, 2003.

Klossner, Michael, 'The Kahina, Queen of the Berbers', *Whoosh!*, issue 85, January 2004 (e-text: www.whoosh.org/issue85/klossner6.html).

Knox, John, *The First Blast of the Trumpet Against the Monstrous Regiment of Women*, Geneva, 1558 (e-text: www.swrb.com/newslett/actualNL/firblast.htm).

Knox, Malcolm, 'Her Life as a Fake', *Sydney Morning Herald*, 24 July 2004, p. 1.

Kobak, Annette, *Isabelle: The Life of Isabelle Eberhardt*, Chatto & Windus, London, 1988.

Kolmees, Jill, *My Desert Kingdom: Finding a Life in Saudi Arabia*, Bantam, Sydney, 2004.

Koran: With Parallel Arabic Text, The, ed. & trans. NJ Dawood, Penguin Classics, London, 1998.

Lamb, Christina, *The Sewing Circles of Herat: My Afghan Years*, HarperCollins, London, 2002.

Larsdatter, Karen, 'Women of Peace and War: The Roles of European Women at the Siege of Acre', *The Oak*, no. 13, 1999 (http://moas.atlantia.sca.org/oak/13/acre.htm).

Lawrence, TE, *Seven Pillars of Wisdom*, Folio Society, London, 2000.

Lewis, Bernard, *The Arabs in History*, Oxford University Press, Oxford, UK, 1993.

Lewis, Bernard, *The Middle East: 2000 Years of History from the Rise of Christianity to the Present Day*, Phoenix, London, 1996.

Lewis, Bernard, *The Assassins: A Radical Sect in Islam*, Basic Books, New York, 2003.

Lewis, Bernard, *The Muslim Discovery of Europe*, Phoenix, London, 2003.

Lewis, Bernard, *The Crisis of Islam: Holy War and Unholy Terror*, Phoenix, London, 2004.

Lewis, Bernard, *From Babel to Dragomans: Interpreting the Middle East*, Weidenfeld & Nicolson, London, 2004.

Lovell, Mary S, *A Rage to Live: A Biography of Richard and Isabel Burton*, Little, Brown, London, 1998.

Manji, Irshad, *The Trouble with Islam: A Muslim's Call for Reform in her Faith*, Random House, Sydney, 2003.

Mansel, Philip, *Constantinople: City of the World's Desire, 1453–1924*, Penguin, London, 1997.

Mansfield, Peter, *The Arabs*, Penguin, London, 1992.

Maxwell, Gavin, *Lords of the Atlas: The Rise and Fall of the House of Glaoua 1893–1956*, Century, London, 1983.

Mernissi, Fatima, *Doing Daily Battle: Interviews with Moroccan Women*, Rutgers University Press, New Brunswick, NJ, 1989.

Mernissi, Fatima, *Scheherazade Goes West: Different Cultures, Different Harems*, Washington Square Press, New York, 2001.

Mernissi, Fatima, *The Forgotten Queens of Islam*, University of Minnesota Press, Minneapolis, MN, 2003.

Mernissi, Fatima, *The Harem Within: Tales of a Moroccan Girlhood*, Doubleday, London, 1994.

Mernissi, Fatima, *The Veil and the Male Elite: A Feminist Interpretation of Women's Rights in Islam*, Perseus Books, New York, 1991.

Milton, Giles, *White Gold: The Extraordinary Story of Thomas Pellow and North Africa's One Million European Slaves*, Hodder & Stoughton, London, 2004.

Monocal, Maria Rosa, *The Ornament of the World: How Muslims, Jews and Christians Created a Culture of Tolerance in Medieval Spain*, Back Bay Books, New York, 2002.

Montagu, Mary Wortley, *Letters*, Everyman Library, New York, 1992.

Montagu, Mary Wortley, *Selected Prose and Poetry of Lady Mary Wortley Montagu*, ed. RS Bear, Renascence Editions, University of Oregon, Eugene, OR, 1996 (www.shu.ac.uk/emls/iemls/resour/mirrors/rbear/montagu.html).

Morris, Chris, *The New Turkey*, Granta, London, 2005.

Mufassir, Sulaiman, *Jesus in the Qur'an*, American Trust Publications, Indianapolis, IN, 1989.

Mushen, Zana, *Sold: One Woman's True Account of Modern Slavery*, Time Warner, London, 2003.

Nafisi, Azar, *Reading Lolita in Tehran: A Memoir in Books*, Hodder, Sydney, 2004.

Negus, George, *The World from Islam: A Journey of Discovery Through the Muslim Heartland*, HarperCollins, Sydney, 2003.

Neighbour, Sally, *In the Shadow of Swords: On the Trail of Terrorism from Afghanistan to Australia*, HarperCollins, Sydney, 2004.

Norwich, John Julius, *Byzantium: The Decline and Fall*, Viking, London, 1995.

Nydell, Margaret K, *Understanding Arabs: A Guide for Westerners*, Intercultural Press, Yarmouth, ME, 1987.

Office of the Senior Coordinator for International Women's Issues, 'Sudan: Report on Female Genital Mutilation (FGM) or Female Genital Cutting (FGC)', US Department of State, Washington DC, June 2001 (www.state.gov/g/wi/rls/rep/crfgm/10110.htm).

Ornelas, Mariana, 'Women Activists and Politicians', 1999 (www.accd.edu/pac/humaniti/1301_tc/xornelas/projja.html).

Oufkir, Malika, *La Prisonnière: Twenty Years in a Desert Gaol*, Bantam, London, 2001.

Ovid, *Heroides* (e-text: www.etext.org/Libellus/texts/ovid).

Ozalp, Mehmet, *101 Questions You Asked About Islam*, Brandl & Schlesinger, Blackheath, NSW, 2004.

Palin, Michael, *Sahara*, Phoenix, London, 2003.

Pepys, Samuel, *Pepys: The Later Diaries*, Alan Sutton, Stroud, UK, 2004.

Physicians for Human Rights, *The Taliban's War on Women: A Health and Human Rights Crisis in Afghanistan*, Physicians for Human Rights, Boston, MA, 1998 (www.phrusa.org/research/health_effects/exec.html).

Pflitsch, Andreas, 'Lugging a Piano to Khartoum', Qantara.de, 2005 (www.qantara.de/webcom/show_article.php/_c-591/_nr-6/_p-1/i.html?PHPSESSID=586932399788bbaf8).

Pulliam, Deborah, 'Florence Nightingale, the Lady with the Lamp', *British Heritage*, January 1998 (e-text: www.historynet.com/bh/bl-florence-nightingale).

Qathafi, Muammar Al, *The Green Book*, World Centre for the Study and Research of The Green Book, Triploi, 1999.

Queen Noor, *Leap of Faith: Memoirs of an Unexpected Life*, Phoenix, London, 2004.

Randal, Jonathan C, *After Such Knowledge, What Forgiveness? My Encounters with Kurdistan*, Farrar, Straus & Giroux, New York, 1997.

Rasheed Al-Uwayyed, Muhammad, *Women Finally on the Shores of Islam*, trans. Noha Kamal Ed Din, Dar Al-Manarah, El Mansoura, Egypt, 2001.

Rasool, Kay, *My Journey Behind the Veil: Conversations with Muslim Women*, Lothian, South Melbourne, 2002.

Reinart, Ustun, 'Ambition for All Seasons: Tansu Ciller', *Middle East Review of International Affairs Journal*, vol. 3, no. 1, March 1999 (http://meria.biu.ac.il/journal/1999/issue1/jv3n1a6.html).

Reston, James Jr, *Warriors of God: Richard the Lionheart and Saladin in the Third Crusade*, Faber & Faber, London, 2001.

Reuters, 'King Mohammed to Wed This Month', *Morocco Week in Review*, 16 March 2002 (www.friendsofmorocco.org/2002News/Mar02/0316news.htm).

Reuters, 'Moroccan Monarch Plans Wedding Celebration', *Morocco Week in Review*, 3 November 2001 (www.friendsofmorocco.org/2001News/Nov01/1103news.htm).

Reuters, 'Tunis: Radhia Nasraoui Ready to Die for Human Rights', Arab Press Freedom Watch, 11 March 2003 (www.apfw.org/indexenglish.asp?fname=news%5Cenglish%5C2004%5C12141.htm).

Robins, Elizabeth, 'A Modern Woman Born 1689', *Anglo-Saxon Review*, vol. I, June 1899, pp 39–65 (e-text ed. Joanne E Gates, www.jsu.edu/depart/english/robins/docshort/modrnwom.htm).

Robinson, Jane, *Wayward Women: A Guide to Women Travellers*, Oxford University Press, Oxford, UK, 1991.

Rodenbeck, Max, *Cairo: The City Victorious*, Picador, London, 1998.

Rogerson, Barnaby & Baring, Rose (eds), *Meetings with Remarkable Muslims: A Collection of Travel Writing*, Eland, London, 2005.

Russell, William, *William Russell: Special Correspondent of The Times*, ed. Roger Hudson, Folio Society, London, 1995.

Said, Edward W, *Orientalism: Western Conceptions of the Orient*, Penguin, London, 1995.

Saint-Exupéry, Antoine de, *Le Petit Prince*, Gallimard Folio Junior, Paris, 2001.

Saoud, *Burned Alive: The Shocking True Story of One Woman's Escape from an 'Honour' Killing*, Bantam, London, 2004.

Sardar, Ziauddin, *Desperately Seeking Paradise: Journeys of a Sceptical Muslim*, Granta Books, London, 2004.

Sasson, Jean, *Princess: The True Story of Life Inside Saudi Arabia's Royal Family*, Bantam, London, 2004.

Sasson, Jean, *Mayada, Daughter of Iraq: One Woman's Survival in Saddam Hussein's Torture Jail*, Doubleday, London, 2003.

Schuon, Frithjof, *Understanding Islam*, Allen & Unwin, London, 1981.

Sheikh Mohammed Centre for Cultural Understanding, 'Open Doors, Open Minds', Sheikh Mohammed Centre for Cultural Understanding, Dubai, 2003 (http://dwc.hct.ac.ae/expatinfo/sheikhmohammedcentre.htm).

Shelley, PB, *The Complete Works of Percy Bysshe Shelley*, eds Roger Ingpen & Walter E Peck, Gordian Press, New York, 1965 (e-text: www.bartleby.com/106/246.html).

Shipman, Pat, *The Stolen Woman: Florence Baker's Extraordinary Life from the Harem to the Heart of Africa*, Bantam, London, 2004.

Siebring, Joel R, 'Gertrude Margaret Lowthian Bell 1868–1926', Minnesota State University, Mankato, MN, 2001 (www.mnsu.edu/emuseum/information/biography).

Stark, Freya, *A Winter in Arabia*, Overlook Press, New York, 2002.

Stark, Freya, *Baghdad Sketches*, Marlboro Press, Chicago, 1996.

Stark, Freya, *Ionia: A Quest*, Century, London, 1988.

Stark, Freya, *Southern Gates of Arabia*, Modern Library, New York, 2001.

Stark, Freya, *The Lycian Shore*, John Murray, London, 1956.

Stark, Freya, *The Valleys of the Assassins*, Modern Library, New York, 2001.

Storm, Rachel (ed.), *Myths and Legends of the Ancient Near East*, Folio Society, London, 2003.

Student Department, Irshad and Islah Muslim Charity Organisation, *What Does She Expect Better?*, International Islamic Publishing House, Riyadh, 2000.

Taşkiran, Tezer, *Women in Turkey*, Redhouse Press, Istanbul, 1976.

Teixeira da Silva, Jaime A, 'Mining the Essential Oils of the Anthemideae', *African Journal of Biotechnology*, vol. 3, no. 12, December 2004, pp 706–20.

Thesiger, Wifred, *Arabian Sands*, Penguin, London, 1991.

Thesiger, Wifred, *The Life of My Choice*, Flamingo, London, 1992.

Thys-Şenocak, Lucienne, *Ottoman Women Builders: The Architectural Patronage of Hadice Turhan Sultan*, Ashgate Press, Aldershot, UK, forthcoming.

Trad, Keysar, *Islam: For Your Information*, Keysar Trad, Sydney, 2003 (www.speednet.com.au/~keysar/basics3).

Travers, Susan, *Tomorrow to be Brave: The Remarkable True Story of Love and Heroism by the Only Woman to Join the Foreign Legion*, Corgi, London, 2001.

Tuchman, Barbara, *The March of Folly: From Troy to Vietnam*, Abacus, London, 1985.

Tunisia Online, 'Women and Civil Rights' and 'Tunisian Women in Figures', April 2006 (www.tunisiaonline.com/women/index.html).

Ure, John, *In Search of Nomads: An Anglo-American Obsession from Hester Stanhope to Bruce Chatwin*, Carroll & Graf, New York, 2003.

Usborne, Richard, 'Carving Their Names on the Walls of Time', *Saudi Aramco World*, vol. 27, no. 2, March–April 1976, pp 30–33 (e-text: www.saudiaramcoworld.com/issue/197602).

Vassiliev, Alexei, *The History of Saudi Arabia*, Saqi Books, London, 2000.

Virgil, *The Aeneid*, trans. John Dryden, eBooks@Adelaide, ed. Stephen G Thomas, 2004 (http://etext.library.adelaide.edu.au/v/v5a).

Vivian, Cassandra, 'The Journey is its Own Reward', *Al-Ahram Weekly*, no. 486, 15–21 June 2000 (http://weekly.ahram.org.eg/2000/486/tr2.htm).

Wallach, Janet, *Desert Queen: The Extraordinary Life of Gertrude Bell, Adventurer, Adviser to Kings, Ally of Lawrence of Arabia*, Phoenix, London, 2003.

Wharton, Edith, *In Morocco*, Century, London, 1984.

Wheatcroft, Andrew, *Infidels: A History of the Conflict Between Christendom and Islam*, Penguin, London, 2004.

Wiener, Peter F, *Martin Luther: Hitler's Spiritual Ancestor*, Hutchinson, London, 1945 (www.tentmaker.org/books/MartinLuther-HitlersSpiritualAncestor.html).

Woodham-Smith, Cecil, *Florence Nightingale*, Constable, London, 1950.

Wright, Thomas, *The Life of Sir Richard Burton*, Everett, London, 1906 (http://etext.library.adelaide.edu.au/b/burton/richard).

Yalom, Marilyn, *Birth of the Chess Queen: A History*, Pandora Press, London, 2004.

Acknowledgements

There are many people to thank in conjunction with the research and execution of this book. Primarily, they include: William Suganda, Sue Woolfe, Jill Mullens, Dr Brian Brennan, photographer Gilles Vancoillie, and Nevine Phillip.

In Libya, I would like to thank Béchir Trabelsi, his partner Ali M Ettounsi, and Mohammed Nagazi Mes of Sand Ruins Tours, and Salah Amura and his family. In the desert, thanks to the 2003 Touareg team of Milad, Omar, Abu Bakr and Masoud; and Mustapha in Tripoli; and the 2004 Sahara expedition team of Masood, Ali, Yusuf, three (new and different) Abu Bakrs, Mohammed, Shabbani, Ibrahim, Abd-Salaam, Hamid, Abdul Ghadda, Tariq, and Abdul-Hakim Al-Tayaf Abd-Salaam and his family.

As always, I am grateful to my manager, Harry M Miller, and to Linda McClelland, the former general manager of his company, for their continued support and patience. Tom Gilliatt at Pan Macmillan saw what I hoped to achieve from the very start and supported the journey, for which I am very appreciative. Thanks too to Karen Penning, my first editor at Pan Macmillan, and Jon Gibbs, my (long-suffering) second, and also to Penny Mansley; they are all both patient and kind.

Many diplomats were extremely helpful, first among them a dear friend, Bashir MM Abudher, chargé d'affaires of the Libyan People's Bureau in Canberra. My thanks, too, to Nıhat Erşen, the consul-general from the Turkish Consulate-General in Sydney, and his deputy, Recep Peker, and secretary, Şerife Arslan; Amar Amari, consul-general of the Consulate-General of the Republic of Tunisia in Sydney; and Baher Helmy, consul of the Arab Republic of Egypt in Sydney. My thanks also to Terence Mullane, the honorary consul-general for the Kingdom of Morocco, and to the Embassy of Lebanon in Canberra.

Help and encouragement also came from Eddy and Bob Cadry; Cass Jennings from Arabian Treasures Tours; Peter Gisborne from

Dubai Tourism and Commerce Marketing in Sydney; and Michelle Sabti, Sarah Shaw and Mohammad Ghaffari from DTCM in Dubai.

Thanks to Stephanie Rogers-Julian and Claudia Rossi Hudson at Mary Rossi Travel, and Mandy Lovell from Leading Hotels of the World in Sydney, who went 'above and beyond' when trying to find addresses for me.

Michelle Wan, public relations director of the Portman Ritz-Carlton in Shanghai, was always kind and helpful, as were her colleagues Sedef Baran, Lara Otru and chef Geoff Bone at the Ritz-Carlton in Istanbul, and Lorey Heynike of the Ritz-Carlton in Dubai. Also invaluable were the general managers and public relations teams at some of the Middle East and North Africa's most beautiful hotels, including Soléna Le Sann, public relations manager at the One&Only Royal Mirage, Dubai; Sharon Garrett, director of communications at the Shangri-La Hotel, Dubai; general manager Richard Bayard, PR manager Evren Kaya Susmus and the staff at the Çirağan Palace Kempinski Hotel in Istanbul, particularly the concierge's desk; general manager Thomas D Crowley and the staff of Le Royal Hotel in Amman, Jordan, and Le Royal Hotel, Jounieh, Lebanon; Robert Bergé, general manager, and Imane Raissouni, guest relations manager, of La Mamounia in Marrakesh; general manager Paolo Fetz and the staff at La Résidence, Côtes de Carthage, in Tunisia; and Kamel Chakroun and the staff of Le Royal Azur in Hammamet, Tunisia.

Thanks to my guides – Mustafa El Farissi in Morocco, and Lamjed Zahrouni in Tunisia.

In Cairo, thanks to Mary at the concierge's desk of the Cairo Marriott Hotel and Casino, Rehab Farouk El Mezeini at the Association for the Development and Enhancement of Women, and Mone Ahmed Fouad.

In Turkey, I am grateful to Nebi Yaşa Tan, Ayhan Demir, İlgĭay Altuntaş and Egemen Moral from the Turkish Department of Tourism in Ankara; TJ (aka İlhami Gezĭcĭ) of TJs Tours and Hostels at Eceabat on the Gallipoli Pensinsula; Mustafa Kayhan, foreign trade manager of ICI International Carpet Investment Industry; and Vuslat Dogan Sabançi and Felekşan Onar in Istanbul.

In Jordan, thanks to Allen Pakendam, Dr Amal Al-Sabbagh, the head of the Jordanian National Women's Council, and Hana Mitri Shahin of the Noor Al Hussein Foundation.

Craig Brough, the enquiries librarian in the Library and Archives of the Royal Botanic Gardens at Kew, and Jan Turner, deputy librarian in the Information Services and Resources Division of the Royal Geographic Society, helped with my research.

Thanks also to Risa Stephanie Bear of the University of Oregon for permission to quote from her e-text *Selected Prose and Poetry of Lady Mary Wortley Montagu (1861).*

I am grateful too for the friendship of my fellow Sahara travellers from the University of Sydney, particularly, in 2004, Pauline, Joe and Andrée, Marianne, Margaret, Collette, Marie, Robyn and Bruce, Veronica, Gaye and Bill; and, in 2005, Estelle, Anne and Max.

If you've read the bibliography for this book, you will have seen the names of the writers who guided and inspired me. Three of them deserve special mention: Bernard Lewis, Karen Armstrong and the extraordinary Fatima Mernissi.

To all these people, and countless others I met along the way, I will always be grateful. They showed me not only that the world is an amazing place, but also that it is sublime to meet, as Dame Freya Stark described them in *Ionia: A Quest*, 'the giants of the soul who actually feel that the human race is their family circle'.

Christine Hogan
Sydney, May 2006